The Päri in the Luo Community

Migrations, Traditions, Culture and Power

Ukal Kawang Julu Mutho

A Note from the Publisher

The publisher wishes to acknowledge and thank Dr Douglas H. Johnson for his invaluable help and support for Africa World Books and its mission of preserving and promoting African cultural and literary traditions and history. Dr Johnson and fellow historians have been instrumental in ensuring that African people remain connected to their past and their identity. Africa World Books is proud to carry on this mission.

ISBN 978-0-6486541-2-4
© Ukal Kawang Julu Mutho, 2020

Published by Africa World Books Pty. Ltd.
(www.africaworldbooks.com)

All rights reserved. No part of this publication may be reproduced, stored in a retrieval system, or transmitted, in any form, or by any means, electronic, mechanical, photocopying, recording or otherwise, without the prior permission of the publishers.

This book is sold subject to the conditions that it shall not, by way of trade or otherwise, be lent, re-sold, hired out or otherwise circulated without the publisher's prior consent in any form of binding or cover other than in which it is published and without a similar condition including the condition being imposed on the subsequent purchaser.

Design and typesetting: Africa World Books

Dedication

This book is dedicated to my beloved mother
Marta Nyikidi Mutho

List of Contents

Foreword — xiii
Preface — xv
Acknowledgements — xix

CHAPTER ONE Geography and the People — 1
People's economy, 4
Hunting, 8
Types of Hunting, 10
Dwan laange, 13
Basis of Trade, 15
Traditional Mode of Dressing and Decoration, 16
Body Decoration, 17
Importance of Stars to the Päri, 18
Meal Sharing, 19
Cultural Diffusion, 19
Relationships between Päri and their neighbors, 21

CHAPTER TWO Cradle Land and Migrations — 28
The Split of Jur Col from Dimo Group, 37
Giilo and Nyikaango Separated, 40
The Death of Giilo, 42
Luo Settlement at Wipäri, 43
Luo Deserted Wipäri, 44
The arrival of Luo and non-Luo people in Lafon, 45
The First Settlers at Lafon, 46
Dimo Final Destination, 47
Dispute over Lipul Ownership, 48
The Name Pugäri, 49
Lipul Ownership Reverted, 50
The Jage group, 52
Pukwari clan, 52

Rwäth Coogo, 53
The Bɔɔi clan, 54
Geri clan group, 44
Nyuunga the Ancestor of Pucwaa, 55
Pucwaa village, 55
The capture of the Adimac people, 57
The battle between Uyät and Giilo forces, 59
The split of Bɔɔi leadership, 61
Bupi (Dupi) people, 62
Emigration of Kɔɔr people to Parajɔk, 63
Aluur Clan, 65
Thuri, 65
Balanda Boor, 67
Discovering the kinsfolk, 68
Päri People among the Dinke Bor, 70

CHAPTER THREE **Päri clans** 73

Splintering in clan organization, 74
Clan Groupings, 75
Enthronement (Roony), 78
Distribution of bull meat among the Päri, 80

CHAPTER FOUR **Päri Contacts with Outside World** 82

Amukuta (Dervishes) Raids, 83
Anglo Egyptian invasion of the land, 87
The arrival of Missionaries in Lafon, 91
Missionary activities in Lafon, 93
Benefits of Western Education, 98
Other Christian Congregations, 99
Introduction of Islam in Päri Country, 100
Chief Suleiman Uciel, 102
Attack on Lafon by Sudan Armed Forces, 104
Attack on Lafon by SPLA Forces, 107

CHAPTER FIVE **Formation of Age group (Laange)** 110
Classification of members of an age group, 113
Privileges of Social Status, 115
Initiation Rites, 117
Women Age Grades, 120
Age set names, 120
Historical Notes, 124

CHAPTER SIX **Political Institutions and Authority** 126
The Monarchy, 126
Päri Kings, 127
Power struggle among the princes, 129
King Alikoori Uwitti Nyilang, 130
Weegipaac (ruling age set), 133
  a) The plot to takeover power, 139
  b) The Worship of Mt. Lipul, 144
  c) The Process on the transfer of Power, 148
  d) Making of fire, 153

CHAPTER SEVEN **Institutions of Power, Relational Linkages and Justice** 162
Assembly House (Kaboora), 162
Relationship between the Ruling age set and the king, 164
Relationship between the ruling age set
  and the bird controller, 165
Social Sanctions, 166
Renewal Group, 168
Distribution of meat of slaughtered bull, 169
Chieftaincy, 169
Juridical settlements of disputes (Likwɛɛri), 173

CHAPTER EIGHT **Marriage** 178
    Betrothal, 178
    Premarital sex, 179
    Marriage Talks, 180
    Exchange of visits, 182
    Bride Wealth Payments, 183
    Extra Wealth Payments, 184
    End of Bride Wealth Payments, 184
    Married Couple Work Test, 184
    Daily Meals, 186
    Building of a family home, 188
    Early life in a new house, 189
    Types of marriages, 191
    Marrying a distant sister, 191
    Marrying a close sister, 192
    Co-wives, 193
    Forced marriage (rwɛɛc), 194
    Elopement of a girl, 196
    Isolated wife (ajäära), 196
    Divorce, 197
    Widow, 198
    Purification rite for married couple (Awuɔr), 199
    Adultery, 200
    Impotent man, 200
    Naming of a child, 201

CHAPTER NINE   **Beliefs and customs**   **204**
   Sorcery, 206
   Kuuk Blessing, 207
   Lam (invocation), 208
   Gwieth, 209
   Cien (curse), 210
   Wizardry (Jwɔk), 211
   Aliga, 212
   Muna disease, 213
   Bii, 213
   Calamity during birth, 214
   Winyo, 214
   Women Annual Gathering, 215
   Cultivation period, 219
   The role of bird controller, 219
   The making of fire, 221
   Sacred Places, 223
   Blessings of food (Libangga), 223
   Beer blessing, 225
   Feast of Harvest (Nyalam), 226
   Amoyo blessing, 229
   Blessing of domestic animals, 230

CHAPTER TEN   **Traditional burial customs**   **232**
Cala Rituals, 238
Funeral Dances, 239
Death rites of a king, 240
Changing attitudes towards death, 241
Totem, 244

Epilogue   247
About the author   251
Bibliography   254

List of Tables

Table 1.1	Päri villages and their honorific titles (paak)	4
Table 1.2	Types of animals hunted	8
Table 1.3	Päri villages and their camps	12
Table 2.1	Dimo migratory route expressed in a song	39
Table 3.1	Päri clans	73
Table 4.1	Trained teachers and catechists	98
Table 5.1	Päri Age sets names of Bari origin	121
Table 5.2	Päri age set names and their meanings	122
Table 5.3	Names of generation sets and their order of correspondence	123
Table 6.1	Päri Kings	128
Table 6.2	The generations of the Wic system of governance	137
Table 7.1	Names of the chiefs who ruled the country from 1909-2018	172

List of Photographs

The scene of Bura village before it was burnt down in 1993	4
Fishermen building keek on the Atoondi River to catch fish	8
A hunter carrying a head of roan antelope (Umɔr)	10
Hunters dividing Thomson gazelle (Adɛɛl)	12
Traditional leather skirts and apron used during dances	16
The ruling age set and their wives	159
Ipuura dance	160
Girls age at the start of love affairs	179
Photo showing fresh grains not yet harvested	221
Workers building sorghum's comb	222
Sorghum's shelter	222
High yield crops	224
Women threshing sorghum	224
The high priest and elders blessing the youth's spears	228
Cattle at thwɔrɔ of Wiatuo village	230
Women mourners of King Peter Upwoyo	243
The tomb of King Peter Upwoyo	244
The mourners of King Peter Upwoyo	244
Käruma dance	249

Lists of Maps

The flow of Atoondi and Cɔl rivers	7
Migratory routes of the Luo in Sudan	252

Foreword

I felt profoundly humbled and honoured by the request of the author that I read, possibly make necessary corrections or additions, and write a foreword to the manuscript. To me, it was also a rare opportunity to peep into the Päri legends and mythology, and compare them to my knowledge of the Chollo (Shilluk) historical records.

I must say that, from the point of view of a non-humanities student like myself, Ukal Kawang Julu has done a great job for the Päri. The idea and act of putting on paper this knowledge about the Päri people must be commended and glorified. This is a welcomed departure from the classical practice that foreign scholars come to study and write books about our people. The last ten years has witnessed a proliferation of South Sudanese authors proving that our people can write and publish their stories, lack of in-depth theoretical investigation notwithstanding.

The Päri people, I may say from the legend, is a mix made up of nearly all the Luo clans. Their location, in Lafon, is a magnet that attracted, and became a resting point of all those Luo people in their southward's migration. This migration, which came in waves of clans, originated from different directions. Most of these movements have been triggered by perennial internal conflicts, recorded also in the oral legends. This is an area for intense investigation and further research. The sooner this was undertaken, the better. Most of the elderly custodians of oral history are dying and it will be very difficult in the next ten years to get people knowledgeable in customs and traditions perpetually under attack by modernization occasioned by socioeconomic and political development of South Sudan.

Mr. Ukal may need to investigate further and compare the written literature on the other Luo groups, and thus emit light on those ones with little known history. It has been said that the Thuri (Shaat) in Awiel and Raga are or were the proto-Luo. This needs to be investigated as well as the *Jur Manaŋer* living among the Dinka in Gogrial. There is much to learn from the relations between the Thuru (Bahr el Ghazal), *Jur Manaŋer*, Thuru (northern Shilluk in the area of Akorwaa), and the Ethur in Karamoja in Uganda.

Prof. Peter Adwok Nyaba
Juba, November 2019

Preface

My interest to learn the Päri way of life dates back to early nineteen seventies. Since then, not only did I observed but participated in the traditional customary practices of my people, the Päri. From time to time I asked elders about those traits of culture which are unfamiliar. Given our home was placed close to the main camp where elders reside during the day, I had the opportunity to meet them (at times sitting around the hearth), and learnt different stories they narrated. In 1987, I decided to have these traditions and culture documented.

Works of the seventeen and eighteen centuries on Nilotic traditions was mainly done by European explorers, travelers, missionaries, colonial authority and anthropologists. But looking at the results of fieldworks available in the ethnographers' published works we find very little has been done on the Päri. There are still gaps, errors, omissions, wrong place names and contradictory statements in the literature readily available. The works by Crazzolara on the Lwoo migrations and traditions (1950, 1951) has a historic credit. Nevertheless, historical changes in social organizations and traits of culture are less documented. Crazzolara didn't even track changes in the political institutions and understand the casual links. His report on Luo migratory routes from the cradle land to Wipäri runs parallel to the information given so far by the natives.

It is understandable that the collection of oral traditions posts a real challenge especially for non-native speakers: language barrier, lack of good interpreters and unfamiliarity with local environment apparently limited their abilities to conduct comprehensive informational searches. Consequently, some researchers were left with no option but to make guesses and eventually draw a rash conclusion. Admitting to the difficulties faced by researchers in collecting and interpreting the data, for example, Crazzolara (1950:11) notes,

> '...a particular traditional narrative may often represent events in such a complicated way that it may be difficult to pick out the tiny kernel of truth which it perhaps contains or to form an appropriately correct idea of the actual events.

Since 1950s, no major studies on Päri culture were produced until in 1980s when Eisei Kurimoto (an anthropologist) and Torben Andersen (a linguist) appeared and published a number of articles. Globalization undermines traditional cultures or displaces indigenous institutions. Its winds blow across class, ethnic and national boundaries without being easily stopped. This causes disorder in the already established systems. Today, all societies are experiencing its effect in one way or another. In Africa, for instance, we find changes taking place at an alarming rate, a fact which raises surprisingly little public concern.

Taking a social developments evaluation of the processes taking place in Päri society we may say that globalization has brought real disturbance to social order within Päri society: it has created a change of attitude of the youth to the fulfillment of the societal moral standards; caused changes in institutional rules, language discourse, etc. Much of these changes have occurred within the present generation, although it had begun thirty years ago. What is striking about this community is the lack of awareness shown by their leaders to protect societal cultural values. The fact that the community continually falls into the trap of modernity, nothing is being done to counter it. The question is, 'who should take the responsibility?' At the community level, intellectuals must develop strategic responses aligned to the changing social imperatives that affect the community and launch real campaign designed to protect society's basic values.

This is because culture is a lens through which we see the world and acquire knowledge and skills necessary for one to interact in a given society. Thus, protection of shared values- the standards and principles that the community deem important in their lives must be taken a serious concern by its members lest it should vanish in consequence of the influence of other major cultures that tend to invade it while in its underdeveloped form. For this reason, I have undertaken a study of the rich Päri culture, traditions and customs with the purpose of saving them from disappearance. I have also recorded cultural forms which have been either overtaken by challenges or currently threatened with extinction. Much of what I've absorbed from elders in seventies are included in this book as a memorial to the present generation and to those who may want to learn what the Päri people know and say about their own past and present. I have also written down oral traditions on Luo migrations as the Päri people know and say it. I think it is useful to reconcile the various versions about the Luo migrations as different scholars report it.

The present works is an expanded and revised version of the first edition. This is to take full account of new changes in the past years. The rudimentary aim of our efforts is to help readers understand historical traditions and culture of this society. We intend to keep intact the traditions not to lose the heritage of the past, and keep it alive now and in the future. Although we have tried to document the traditions and even the characteristics which make this society what it is, interested scholars are to know there are still potential for progress in this area. Hence, researchers have ample time to study and compare. We belief this study will enable social scientists gain important new insights about Nilotic history.

Ukal Kawang Julu Mutho
Juba, October 2019

Acknowledgements

I am grateful to those who reviewed the first edition and all those who have given me comments in various ways, not least among them, Fr. Vittorino Dellagiacoma, Prof. Samson Samuel Wassara, Prof. Simon Monoja Lubang, Victor Keri Wani and Jackson Ukello Akur.

This second printing has given me the opportunity to correct some misprints as well as to improve on some unclear interpretations. I am grateful for the corrections, comments and suggestions from Prof. Peter Adwok Nyaba and Prof. Samson Samuel Wassara both of whom read the whole manuscript and whose critical comments and suggestions I included in the final stage of writing. I am greatly indebted to Professor Eisei Kurimoto, not only for some of the photographs included in this book were produced by him, but for sending the relevant books and archival records from Japan and London which greatly helped me with regards to referencing. I greatly thank my father Celestino Uyo, not only for having shown me the road to education but for he worked mightily to instill in me such values: honesty, respect, discipline and hard work. I would like also to express my deep gratitude and thanks to Dr. John Gai Yoh for his role in connecting me with the management of this famous Publishing House. Similar thanks go to Dr. Benjamin Gabriel Apai, Dr. Thabo Nyibong, Dr. Lampton Erinayo Lomeja, and all those friends whose names I have not included here. I thank them for having given me much of the needed encouragement to publish this works. Particular appreciation is given to my wife Rose Anyango and my beloved children; Utong, Rebecca, Amin, Grace, Uwili, Akor, Irene, and Joel. Never did they complain about the long time I spent on this book.

Chapter One

Geography and the People

THE PÄRI ARE A LUO ETHNIC GROUP RELATED TO THE FOLLOWING communities of South Sudan: Anywaa, Luo (Jur col[1]), Cɔllɔ (Shilluk), Acholi, Balanda Boor and Shaat. They fall under a racial division classified as 'Nilotes. The word Nilotes or Nilotic was created by Tucker and Bryan. In their survey of the non-Bantu languages of North-Eastern Africa, Tucker and Bryan (1956:94-105), group 18 languages and dialect clusters as one family calling them 'Nilotic'. Later, following a suggestion of Köhler, Nilotic group was divided into three main branches namely; Western, Eastern and Southern Nilotic language family, (cf. Greenburg, 1966:85). Anne Storch and others have further classified 'Western Nilotic' branch into four larger groups[2].

1 Burun   a) Northern (Mayak)
           b) Southern (Mabaan and Jumjum)
2 Dinka (Jääng)
3 Nuer (Nuäär/Naath)
4 Luo   a) Northern (Shilluk, Anywaa, Päri, Luo (Jur col), Acholi, Balanda Boor and Shaat
           b) Southern (Jo Padhola, Alur, Acholi, Kumam, Lango, Labwor, Luo of Kenya)

---

1   Jur chol is Dinka word for foreigner or non-Dinka
2   Compare this with Anne Storch's paper 'Aspect and evidentiality in the Luwo (Jur) Verbal System' presented on the 9th Nilo Saharan Linguistic Conference, Khartoum, 2004.

The Päri is one of the two Luo speaking communities in Equatoria region the other being the Acholi. Both communities are found in Eastern Equatoria state, the Päri being in the northern part of the state while the Acholi are in the southern part. Their land is geographically situated on the northern borderlands of the Utuho community. In the west, the Päri are bordered by the Bari; in the east by the Toposa; in the north by Murle and Dinka Bor. The Lopit live to their south east while the Lokoya to their south west. The Mundari of Gemmeiza is found to their north west. The uninhabited land bordered by Gemmeiza area has been demarcated by the regional government in Juba in 1975 as a game reserve called '*Bande gilo* which is actually a mispronunciation by outsiders. The Päri name for the place is *Buur Giilo*; Giilo being the name of the person who was a Luo leader during Luo migration. He died and was buried in the area. Buur in Päri language means 'grave'. Buur Giilo then refers to the grave of Giilo. Today the place is considered a holy site. In the village of Wiatuo, a priest from the clan of Nyikeeu to which Giilo belonged performs rituals and cures people affected by various illnesses by invoking the spirit of their dead leader.

The Päri country is divided into six villages: Bura, Pucwaa, Pugäri, Kɔɔr, Angulumɛɛrɛ and Wiatuo. These villages are clustered around mount Lipul. The name Lipul is derived from the color of a bull known as Upul (ugɔr). But due to misspelling and mispronunciation by outsiders, the mountain came to be known as Lafon.

Generally, the villages are built compact in structure. The huts are mud-walled with conical shaped grass thatch roofs. They are built very close to one another making it difficult for a stranger to locate the borderline between one village from another. You can hardly differentiate for example, the borderline between Pucwaa and Bura villages or Bura and Wiatuo villages. The villages have several homesteads. And every homestead is fenced with wood (kallɔ) a traditional practice adopted in the past when villages

Geography and the People

have to be fenced to protect the inhabitants from wild animals and enemies.

According to the 1983 national population census, Päri population was put at 11,017. The low figure is due to the reluctance and fear of the people being counted. Moreover the population of Päri has not been reported in the population census of 1993 because the area fell in the SPLA controlled zone. However, the Lafon population census of 2008 is 36,521. These people call themselves Päri a word originating from the verb päär which means to jump as they had to jump or past through many places before reaching Lafon hill. Other tribes call them other names: For example, the Bari people call them 'Bäri/bori Lɔkɔɔrɔ or Berri' which is certainly a mispronunciation of the name Päri. The Toposa and Murle call the Päri 'nyurru/ nyur/nyor' a name which the Päri do not understand. Their kinsmen the Anywaa call them Jɔ pu-nywaa or Jɔ-Bɔɔi.[3] Nevertheless, the Lotuko their neighbor in the south, rightly call them 'Päri'. On solemn occasions, one hears Lotuko people uttering words such as jɔk illo Päri meaning, let diseases/misfortunes go to the Pari people. The Acholi call them many names: Lɔkɔɔrɔ, Ocam bɛɛl gi-rio which means those who harvest their grain crops twice in a year. They too called them Gäälä macɔl meaning black government. Päri legends say, their warriors fought many wars against their neighbors and tribes beyond their borders. They did that with the purpose of increasing their population. The name Gäälä macɔl probably came as a result of Päri brutal action against the Acholi and other tribes. Nevertheless, the name Lɔkɔɔrɔ given by the Acholi a long time ago has overshadowed the name Päri. But, the Päri regard this as misleading because it is not their real name. They insist they be called Päri their original name.

---

3   Note: the name Bɔɔi belongs to one clan. It should not be used to identify the whole community

Table 1.1 Päri villages and their honorific titles (paak)

Village name	Honorific title
1. Wiatuo	Jo Bɔɔi, Aula, Karnyakithɔk
2. Kɔɔr	Jo Giilo, Cicɔɔr, Poodho, Cwoodho
3. Bura	Buracɔɔr, Nyirwotho, Nywɔlɔ
4. Pugäri	Mindatum, Päcca, Riemujɔɔrɛ, Rim
5. Pucwaa	Bilwarɔ, Akwaru, Karmaac
6. Angulumɛɛrɛ	Nyibwooro, Kɔthɔrɔ

The scene of Bura village before it was burnt in 1993.
Photo by Kurimoto:

People's Economy

Economically the Päri people depend largely on subsistence agriculture. Their land is very fertile with sufficient rainfall. Yearly they cultivate a variety of food crops such as sorghum (nyithiinh) beans, sesame, pumpkins, okra, ugodi. Other vegetables includes;

Geography and the People

kwarubile, thakuri, acwɔbɔ, ukuro, akɛɛyɔ, atharu, udhingo/anginyja (dried mulɔɔthɔ). Besides, the land is rich with valuable resources such as petroleum, wild life, gum Arabic, forestry and other resources.

Earlier, the Pӓri did not grow root crops such as cassava and potatoes. In 1970s, the Norwegian Church Aid (NCA) agriculture section successfully introduced these crops to the area. In the same period, two farms were established in Pӓri land, one owned and managed by the NCA and the other one by the Sudan Prison service. The two farms which grew only sorghum proved very economical for they produced a large quantity of sorghum annually. Most of the produce was transported to the market in Torit for sale and consumption. Moreover, the Pӓri land was proved good for the production of cotton. During the Anglo Egyptian rule around 1950s, a cotton farm was established in Pӓri country right at a place called *Nyitɔtti*. At that time the land was found productive in this cash crop. The Nzara Ginning Factory used to receive some of its cotton from the Pӓri country. Unfortunately, Lafon mechanized scheme closed down in March 1956.[4] That is, after the independence of the country the subsequent regimes never bothered to continue the project.

Besides cultivation, the Pӓri also practiced pastoralism by keeping a good number of cattle, goats and sheep. These animals are mainly kept for milk and marriages. Some families rear chickens for food as well.

Geographically, the Pӓri land is flat with mount Lipul (Lafon hill) rising to several hundred feet from ground level. The country is drained by only two rivers named Atoondi and Cɔl. Both rivers flow from south originating at the foot of the Imatong Mountain. Atoondi which passes very close to the foot of the mountain in the east, is the one from which the people fetch their drinking water. During its flow the people catch fish from it. But later during the dry period, it dries up leaving people depend on dug wells. In 1945 Fr. Negrini dug three wells for the people: Two in front of the mission compound

---

4 See JD/57.C.3. 'Annual Report, Torit District 1955/56)

and one along the main road. Later Br. Tognon dug two wells at the river bank: one was for the general public and the other was for watering the garden for the missionaries. After Comprehensive Peace Agreement (CPA) was signed in 2005, many organizations came to Lafon and drilled many boreholes in all the settlements. Today, the community drinks clean underground waters provided by humanitarian agencies.

River Cɔl flows a bit of a distant from the people settlement in the west of the mountain. It is the continuation of river kineiti that passes through Torit town. During floods its waters spread out over the Päri territory due to the flatness of the land. When the floods subside the river follows its course again leaving pools (baadi) in series along its bed. Along the banks of this river grow green vegetation and especially a kind of a grass called 'abow' which is eaten by cattle.

River Cɔl is the main supplier of fish to the Päri people who are famous for this commodity in Torit, Katire, Magwi, Kudo, Juba and other trading centers in Eastern Equatoria state. The Päri carry out fishing activity on individual and group basis. That is, the individual fisherman does not need to ask any landowner to fish in any part of river Cɔl or Atoondi. He simply picks his hooks and fish where he chooses. But group or community fishing is done on approval from the landowner who usually checks the depth of the pools during winter when the water level is low. If he finds a lot of fish in the territorial waters, he invites the community to fish in the area. Traditionally, before people start fishing, the owner offer prayers to God wishing the people to have a good catch while at the same time cursing dangerous animals and reptiles that might be found in the river to cause no harm to the fishermen. Just as he finishes the prayers, people begin fishing. In this type of fishing men use spears (bidhi pl.bithe) and hook (gɔɔlɔ pl.goolee.) while women use baskets (urwathu pl.urwathi) and udhuulu which is a bundle of grass tied together for trapping and catching fish. Another traditional

Geography and the People

THE FLOW OF ATOONDI AND COL RIVERS

method by which Päri obtain large quantity of fish is by means of what is called *'twier* and *keek* respectively. *Keek* type of fishing is constructed mainly across river Atoondi while twier is constructed on the river Cɔl. For keek there is a specially plaited wood called *rwook* which is usually placed beneath a waterbed to trap fish. Once the fish are inside it, they cannot come out until removed by the fisherman. On the other hand, twier is designed in such a way a hole is dug on both banks of the river such that the fish are forced to fall in the pit and later removed by fishermen.

Fishermen building keek on the Atoondi River to catch fish.
Photo by Kurimoto.

Hunting (dwaar)

The territory in which the Päri live has a great number of wild animals of various kinds. Varieties of big game are run down in winter (ooro) and summer (cwiir) seasons. Among the animals targeted a few are listed below;

Table 1.2 Types of animals commonly hunted

Name of animal	Päri name
Antelope	Anger
Aardvark	Mua
African wild cat	Kwɔru
Bush pig	Kul
Buffalo	Joobi
Bohor reed buck	Aburi

Bush buck	Roonna
Common genet	Anyaarɔ
Civet	Aywiel
Common duiker	Muur
Cheetah	Ucii
Eland	Ajäägi
Elephant	Liɛc
Giraffe	Rii
Hyena	Udiek
Hunting dog	Urut
Jackal	Uthoo
Lion	Nguu
Leopard	Kwac
Mongoose	Ugɔr
Otter	Ulwiny
Oribi(grant's gazelle)	Tiɛdu
Porcupine	Theewi
Roan Antelope	Umɔr
Rhino	Umua
Ratel	Cir
Stripped pole cat	Nyinaam
Seral	Gwang
Tiang	Tääng
Thomson's gazelle	Adɛɛl
Temminck's ground pangolin	Kɔng
Warthog	Kul/ beela
Water buck	Buba
Zebra	Mugwar

Types of hunting

Traditionally, the Päri practice four types of hunting.

Dwan nyicwieny: this hunting is carried out by teenagers usually directed at small animals, such as squirrels (aidhe/aidha), monkeys (ayoomo), jackal (uthoo), Ulwiny, Common genet known as anyaarɔ and others. This type of hunting is carried out in the bushes close to homes. The animals killed are roasted and eaten right there without bringing any meat home. This is because women do not eat such kinds of animals.

Dwan abɔɔya: This kind of hunting is carried out by the villagers during afternoon hours. Usually, people go to the woodland Savanah just close to the village in the afternoon to get some fresh meat for the meals. This kind of hunting is directed at animals with hoofs (litiendi uboongi) like oribi and gazelle, bush buck etc. If big animals like buffalo or elephants found they could be killed for meat as well.

A hunter carrying head of roan antelope (Umɔr)

Dwan akuuyya: This kind of hunting is carried out by the whole society in far off distant areas. In other words, it is a public hunting involving the entire Päri people. It is to be noted that unless the owner of a particular hunting ground allows the entire people to hunt animals in his hunting area, people will not decide on their own to hunt animals in such a zone. It is always after the owner has surveyed the site, usually with the help of spies (liewwe), who assures that a lot of animals live in such territorial hunting ground, does he inform the wegipaac about hunting. After such assurances, the wegipaac then announces to the public to go hunting in that particular area. Normally, after the announcement, people walk to the site close to the hunting ground in the evening hours and spend the night there. While waiting for the dawn to come, the people pray to God to enable them kill many animals for meat. They also curse beasts like lions to be killed without harming anybody. At dawn they encircle the area targeted. In order that the people are aware that both men at the end of the curves have met, these men must yell (kuuy) indicating a signal that a complete circle has been made. Such a sound is repeated by all people. This assures everyone that all animals have been encircled. For this reason this kind of hunting was named akuuyya a word derived from the verb kuuy (i.e to yell). At sun rise, the hunters move in to attack the animals. When animals come, the people spear them. The first animals killed (usually ten or more) are set aside for elders and the diviner who could not go for hunting. The youth carry this meat and hand it to elders in Kaboore. Any animal killed after that is divided by the hunters accordingly.

The meat brought to Kaboore will always be distributed to old people who could not afford going for hunting, poor people and the diviner (ajwaa).

Before the SPLA/SPLM war, the people used spears to kill animals. These days, they use guns to kill animals. Consequently, so many animals get killed in Lafon area every year.

Hunters dividing Thomson Gazzelle (Adɛɛl). Photo by Kurimoto.

Table 1.3 Päri villages and their camps (Baali)

Village	Camps			
Wiatuo	Geri	Dyɛr	Mɔlnyang	Nyikwanya
	Buppi	Kaboore (*Assembly house*)		
Kɔɔr	Atuo	Lijäälo	Ajiba	Liboongi
	Pukaal	Kaboore (*formerly at Lokidomok*)		
Pucwaa	Padieri	Licorothom Wiira		Kaboore
Bura	Pukurjo	Paraau	Adimac	
	Kaboore (formerly at Liluuro)			
Pugäri	Libaalu	Laali	Jwɔm	Pukwari
Kaboore				
Angulumɛɛrɛ	Adɛɛba	Pukwänyi	Adula	
	Kaboore (*formerly at Likwothulo*)			

Note: the above camps have been re-established in the new settlements after the villages were burnt by the SPLA in 1993.

Dwan laange

This type of hunting is performed by an age group. Unlike public hunting in which animals are killed for meat, this type of hunting is mostly aimed at big and wild animals to show bravery of individuals or group as a whole during the killing of such animals with spears. In this game, members compete among themselves to know who has killed more animals or not. Those who killed many animals are regarded as brave men. The animals targeted include elephants Rhinos, leopards, lions, buffalos, etc. When the group finds herds of elephants or buffalos, they can kill as many as they can and take home some meat and leave many animals to rot or be eaten by carnivores or birds. What matters to them is the number they have killed to compete with other opponents.

Elephants and leopards are considered valuable to this society. If a group kill an elephant, the person who speared the animal first, takes the trunk (cingi liec) and its tusk (laki liec). The trunk is usually taken home to be consumed by the clan elders. It will always be divided equally between the maternal and paternal uncles of the man who first speared the elephant. However, the tusks exclusively belong to the man who speared the elephant first. He will sell it and use the money for his needs. Similarly, the one who speared the leopard takes the skin and leaves the meat to be divided by the people. Traditionally, the one who kills a leopard does not keep the skin for himself but gives it to his step-brother to wear during dance parties and celebrations.

Note, Päri traditional weapon is spear. To them, the bravery of a man is measured by the use of a spear in the event of fighting. Fighting with a gun is not considered bravery. The Päri argue that a fight with spears truly shows who among the group is brave or coward. This is because the enemy or wild beast is speard at close range. Where as a person who uses a gun can shoot the enemy or wild beast at safe distance not allowing the enemy to make counterattack.

Usually when members of an age group arrive in the bush, they camp under a tree. In the evening they perform *lam* (invocation) asking God to let them find and kill such animals; elephants, buffalos or rhinos, leopards and the like. During lam a bat may come to the place where the group is camping. The mammal usually sings. The song of the bat is always construed or understood by experts as messages of success or warning of imminent danger to come. For that matter, the period of lam is called '*cwɔndi winyo*' literally meaning the calling of the bird[5]. Actually, it is the bat which is being called to foretell the success or failure to find the animals targeted.

After lam, comes the time for making an oath (ayiɛmɛ). What happens is that, two individuals with equal measure of bravery come forward and promise before the hunters that they would not fear wild animals that the group may encounter. In pairs, members from the lower group (thare) start making the oath. They will be followed by the middle group (koore) and concluded by the senior group members (wie). The bravest man of the group, who holds the black flag (alullu), swears alone. And so does the greatest runner. After swearing, the group sleeps. In the morning, they go hunting. When they find the animals they are looking for, they attack. During the fight, if a member is found to have feared the animal, that person would automatically lose the badge given him by the group. From that time, no one regards him as brave man but a coward.

Brave or coward individuals can also be identified during stick fights. Usually, after harvest of crops, youngsters engage in stick fight. That is, one age group fights with another age group. The Päri regard sticks fight as a sport mainly done to train the youth to be brave ready to face outside aggression. At times, a fight between the youth of one village and another may lead to adult from both villages getting involved in the fight.

---

[5] Note: the Päri classify a bat as a bird

Basis of Trade

The Päri engage in commerce and trade with the neighbours. The main items the Päri obtain for sale is fish and sorghum. They catch fish in large quantities from river cɔl and Atoondi. The fish is bisected in a format known as adanga/adangɛ; its internal organs removed, cleaned and are smoked into adunga or adungɛ. Adanga is normally bisected and dried in the sun. Pari also dry some fish in a whole some form known to them as akuuda in singular (pl.akuude). This type is usually consumed locally.

The Päri sell their sorghum surpluses from their annual yields which are intended mainly for consumption. They take this commodity to Torit, Juba and other trading centers in Torit distict. Because of the popularity of Päri sorghum, buyers from Lopit, Lotuko, Lokoya villages used to come to Lafon to buy sorghum. Some of these buyers bring cattle, goats, sheep, pots, groundnuts to be bartered with dura. Others use money to buy the products. The money got from this commodity is used for buying manufactured goods such as salt, soap, clothes, shoes, beads, stockings for dancing and many other items of importance.

Although the Päri do not rear cattle, goat and sheep for commercial purposes, sometimes the need arises to sell them for obtaining dura at times of starvation or to buy such items as mentioned above. The major challenge faced by this community is poor road infrastructure. The country has no good roads linking major towns to Lafon commercial center. The settlement is linked by only one road, the one joining it to Torit town. This road which is sixty four miles from Torit town was upgraded by the Norwegian Church Aid Sudan Programme in 1977. Since then there has never been an attempt to repair and improve its condition. During the raining season, one can hardly reach Lafon using this road.

In the past, there was a road linking Mangala town to Päri

settlement. That road was constructed by the British colonial government when Mangala was the capital of Equatoria Province in 1920. The road was no longer passable after the colonialist left. However, pedestrians used it for walking to the town of Juba. In 2015, mini buses started taking passengers from Juba via Mugiri to Lafon using this road. Nevertheless, the road is passable during dry season and closes during raining season.

Traditional mode of dressing and decorations

Before western clothing was adopted, the Päri women wore leather skirts made of goat's skin and apron also called *päri* made of calfskin or goat's skin. In 1950s, skirts made of clothe known as *thanuura* and a garment called *abaanda (known to Shilluk as laau)*

Traditional leather skirts and apron used during dances.
The author is second to the right.

was introduced to Päri women. Despite this, women remained traditionally bare-breasted and men continued to be naked. After the Addis Ababa peace agreement of 1972, which ended the civil strife in the Southern Sudan, Albano Urua was appointed by the inspector of local governemt in Torit following his selection by the Päri as their paramount chief. He enforced the law which stipulated that all men must wear clothes, and any one found naked was lashed and warned of more punishment if found naked again. Today, all Päri people wear clothes.

Body decorations

The generations that lived before 1970s could be identified by the following distinct marks: the lower lips of both men and women were pierced and in them, men wore *nyabibac* while women put on *aliiwa (pl. aliiwe)*. The ears were pierced and rings called *gwil* and *acuth* were worn by both sexes. On their fingers, men dressed copper rings and round their arms, they wore copper bangles *ariwwe* bracelets made out of aluminium of old pots melted down; while women wore *gooke* heavy bracelets on their wrists and above their ankles. Girls' bodies (arms, waists and stomachs), were printed with decorative marks 'scarcification'. Experts used a hook and a razor blade to cut those tiny dots formed into some structure of animals or other natural objects on the body. Boys do not have a uniform style of decoration printed on their bodies. Each age group chooses a picture and was printed on their bodies as a symbol of the group. For example, the Akeyo age group has a car tyre picture printed on their shoulders whereas their junior partner, the Maridi age group, printed the picture of giraffe on their stomachs.

At the age of ten, the four lower incisors of both boys and girls are removed. An expert use a tool called *balima* to do that. After the teeth were removed, each one takes them and throws them up on the roof of the hut. Individual members who fail to remove their teeth are insulted as *mugiili* and often isolated from the group. At times, they are beaten to force them adopt the culture. Although boys have now abandoned teeth removal and body decorations, girls continue to wear beads round their necks, waists and ears and continue printing marks on their bodies.

Importance of stars to the Päri

The Päri base their interpretation of occurrence of events on positions of certain stars to which they have given names; *dääk (*Orion), *liɛc* (great bear), ceci lio (morning star), ceci nyalam, yöö*nni* etc. Every year in the mid-November after harvest of food crops, the Päri stage a celebration of the feast called 'nyalam'. Nyalam refers to a community holiday celebrated at the end of the harvest season. Normally, before this feast is conducted, some men take it upon themselves to wake up very early morning to locate the star in the east known as 'ceci-nyalam'. On spotting the star, the priest of mount Lipul who lives in Pugäri village sends his messenger to the village of Wiatuo. There in the assembly house, he meets a man from the clan of Pukwari and informs him about the appearance of the star and the need for them to help in organizing the ceremony. For more information on 'nyalam' occasion, see page 225.

Päri also regulate their daily activities according to the position of certain stars. For example, the morning star is used as time teller for going to the crop fields to work and for setting off on journeys. *Dääk, liɛc* and *yöönni* stars are used to determine the seasons of the year. The word liec refers to elephant. According to the Päri, certain stars are position in such a way that they form an elephant shape. There are two such elephants in the sky. The one which lives in the north is for the Päri. The other one that lives in southern sky and is lame is for the Lopit their neighbor in the south east.

Meal sharing

The Päri people eat in groups called 'nywaak' and which means sharing. That is, a group of persons walk together and share their meals as they move from one home to the next. A person who consumes his ration alone is considered greedy an insult derogatory to one's reputation. Earlier, people used spoons (pät, sing. paalo) to eat with. In the middle of 1970s however, this custom started fading away. Many people started using their bare hands when eating food. This is a foreingn culture adopted after the Pari made contacts with outsiders.

Cultural diffusion

The dissemination and borrowing of culture is an integral and vital part of the history of culture. Generally, the inhabitants of the six Päri villages are made up predominantly of Luo clans and an insignificant number of non- Luo elements who were assimilated into the society a long time ago. Päri oral history noted that when the first Luo arrived at Lafon from wipaac (Wipäri), they encountered the Pugäri people who spoke different languages and used bows and arrows as weapons which was not the traditional weapon of the former who carried spears. The Päri named them *'mind-atum'* meaning in their Luo language a curved wooden weapon (bow) to which was tied a plaited string (atum). Other sub-groups include Laali who originated from Dinka, Pukwari group believed to have come from Bari and the

Jagɛ who are believed to have originated from the Lolubo tribe. The fact that these sub-groups can still trace their origins, they have lost their languages and are now full members of the society enjoying all privileges as others. The whole community is identified as Luo people.

Although the Päri have maintained some of the old Luo cultures, their emigration and settlement in Lafon for many decades had exposed them to alien cultures. The Otuho (Lotuko) culture had some significant influence on the Päri culture. This is seen in social institutions. A type of dance called Kathar by the Päri is known by the Lotuko as *nahathar* which has actually originated from them. The Lopit a sub group of the Lotuko speaking people also brought their culture to bear on the Päri especially in the administrative system for the ruling authority called wic. What is in reference here is the *mojomiji (monyomoji) s*ystem of the Lopit known to Päri 'weegipaac'. Even the drums for the Päri 'buul' dance were borrowed from the Lopit. Initially, the Pari had two small drums. These drums were beaten only if something bad had happened or about to happened. For example, these drums could be beaten to call people to conduct an immediate function such as defence of the community against attackers 'uduuru'. It could also be beaten to inform the public about the sudden death of a prominent person in the community. The cultural impact of the Bari on the Päri can be seen in the common drink known as koongo (white stuff) brewed from the grain dura which the Bari called 'yawa'. The Päri simply refer to it as 'bari' because it was got from them. The traditional beer of the Päri is called *p*äri and is similar to the Shilluk drink called *tharbub* and which the Acholi called 'lacwi'. While lacwi is sucked using a wooden tube, the 'päri' and *tharbub* is drank using a calabash.

Relationships between Päri and their Neighbors

The inhabitants of Southern Sudan, the Päri among them, during most of the nineteenth century had experienced a lot of devastating tribal wars among themselves and these wars have affected them so much. In the course of these wars, captives were taken by Jɔ Päri from the tribes they attacked and brought to Lipul to swell their number because they were few being a small group of Luo who decided to settle in Lipul as the other Luo groups pressed southwards in their migration. For example, there are a number of individuals who were brought by Päri warriors as far as Moli the northern part of Madiland, from Lotuko, Bari, and Dinka and Acholi tribes.

The Päri raided Moli during the rule of Alangurre age sets and brought a lot of boys, girls and some women and animals from there. The main clan whose members were captured and brought to Lipul was the Mogili. There are several songs which preserve these historical events. Even the descendants of the Madi captives can still trace their roots back to their clans in Moli. A Madi researcher, Victor Keri Wani who comes from Moli confirms that several children from northern part of Moli according to tribal legends have been abducted by the Lɔkɔrɔ (Päri) and Lokoya warriors. The event occurred in 1929. According to Keri, the Päri attackers got his uncle and some other men sitting in the hut. The attackers were wearing ostrich feathers on their heads and bells under their armpits. Before they attacked the area, they closed the bells with grass to avoid any noise. After they attacked the area, they opened the bells to make noise to scare the people. In that attack, the Päri warriors burnt the houses killing several people and taking several children and women. And according to Keri, the men who were found in the hut managed to kill one Päri warrior and escaped.

Similarly, after Jɔ Kɔɔr had returned to Lipul from Parajɔk, the Päri fighters led by Alikoori made an expedition to the Acholi country and carried out what can be called a revenge attacked to the villagers of Obɔɔ. The reason why the Päri attacked their kinsmen was based on the accusation made by the inhabitants of Kɔɔr to the people in Lafon that the people of Obɔɔ had killed some of its pedestriants who came to visit their relatives in Lafon while they were still in Parajɔk. So, the warriors led by Alikoori went to the Acholi village of Obɔɔ and attacked the village. In that fight, the Päri defeated Obɔɔ fighters and took several children and women and added them to the group. Among the captives were boys named Okumu and Kaang. Both of whom were captured by the man called Mothodaan the head clan of Adimac. Mothodaan himself was a cousin brother of king Ulum of Kɔɔr village. Ulum has no son except daughters. Thus, he was worried as to who would inherit his throne after his death. When he learnt that his cousin brother Mothodaan had brought young men from Acholi land, he approached him immediately and asked him to give him one captive to adopt as a son. Mothodaan accepted the request willingly and so Okumu was given to him to adopt as a son. Ulum who wanted to keep kingship in his family line entrusted the leadership of Kɔɔr people to his adopted son. Aware of what might happen after his death, he told the adopted son to keep this in secret to avoid his brothers not to know lest they would kill the boy. Then, he gave Okumu a club (*uluk*) to keep. This uluk symbolizes power and authority. Again, Ulum strictly warned *Okum* not to tell anyone about this move. However, he told this secret to his daughter called Ayiɛɛdhɛ but with the warning not to tell anyone until after his death. Ayiɛɛdhɛ who was married to a man from Laali clan of Pugäri village, kept this secret in her heart as per instruction.

Some times later, King Ulum became sick and died. The king had a number of brothers who rivaled over the kingship. When they learned about the death of king Ulum, they rushed to the king's palace to know the successor. But nobody appeared. This created confusion. And for a period of time, the people live in a state of dilemma until, one day, during the processesion (*ipuura*), Ayiɛthɛ emerged carrying the blessed club (uluk), handed it to Okumu who raised it and placed himself infront of the people in procession. It was from there; the people came to know him as the successor of the king.

The step brothers of king Ulum notably Alimo Ubala, Mutho Ukal, and others became very jealous of Okumo. They argued that a foreigner should not have taken over the throne of their ancestor. The move created bad relations between Okumu and the princes. Attempts by elders to make peace did not succeed. Thus, the king and his opponents resorted to the use of curses *(cien)* which are conventional methods for dealing with potential rivals. It is said, the wife of Ubala and that of Mutho died after this dispute. The people associated such deaths with curses maliciously carried out by Okumu. Similarly, when the wife of Okumu died, the event was also linked to the action of cien caused by his opponents. The relations went badly for a period of time. But at the end, the princes gave up their struggle and made peace with Okumu. As a stranger, the people never expected Okumu to become the king and so they nicknamed him '*Liyiime*'. In other words, his appearance was seen like the shade coming down over the people.

During the reign of Akeem age sets around 1860s, the Päri warriors went several times to plunder the Bari people. They brought cattle, goats, many young boys, girls and some women which really increased their number. The Päri would have continued plundering the Bari people had it not been for the intervention of the British colonial government statationed in Mangala. The prevention of inter-tribal warfare deprived the Pari of their means of gaining new prestige, territory and wealth. Today, descendants of these people can still identify themselves with the Bari roots.

The relationship of the Päri and the Lokoya their neighbor in the south west has been cordial until a section of the Päri living on 'Opone' mountain (in the present day Lirya village) came under attack from Lokoya warriors. In the first fight, the Päri were defeated because, the Lokoya had used bows and arrows that could shoot a person at safe distance while the Päri were using spears that fly short distances. After this defeat, the Päri changed their tactics. They ordered the rainmaker to cause heavy rainfall during the fight with the Lokoya such that, their bows would become wet and could not shoot properly. Using this tactic, the legend says, the Lokoya were defeated. After the fight the majority of the warriors returned to Lafon but left behind a few people who later became known as 'Opwolang clan' which comprises of: Ongole, Ohwaa, Ohalla and Ongorway. Since then, the two tribes have maintained peace among themselves. They traded with each other normally. Moreover, during the Sudan People's Liberation Movement war of 1983, many of this people took refuge in Lafon and joined their kinsmen. When the war was over, they returned to Liria, their settlement.

The Päri are continuously at war with the Lopit their neighbor in southeast. Several times the Päri attacked, killed people and seized cattle, goats and sheep of the Lopit people. At times, the Lopit attacked and killed the inhabitants of the Päri. In 1986 several Päri people who went looking for grain dura in the Lopit land (because they had poor harvest that year) were massacared in Lacaruk, Haba and other villages of Ngaboli. The funny thing is, while the Lopit and the Päri do fight each other, they also maintain their trade relationships. At times of starvation, the Lopit would bring their cattle, goats, sheep, pots, groundnuts and other trading items to Lafon in exchange for dura. Alternatively, when the Päri people have a poor harvest in a given year, they too take their trade goods to the Lopit country to obtain food items.

During the reign of Bongcuot, the Päri led by Alikoori attacked the village of Lokiri a Lotuko tribe. Because of the curse by the man called Alappa who comes from *Angulumεεrε* village, the Päri were utterly defeated. Later, when Nyimangore blessed the community, the Päri counter attacked and destroyed the entire area after slaughtering its inhabitants. The few survivors sought refuge in Loronyo village and Torit town. A few years later, the survivors of that attack came back to Lokiri and resettled in the area without obstruction from the Päri.

While it would seem the Päri warriors were always the attackers of other tribes to capture young people to swell their population, their area too had once been attacked by a band of Toposa warriors around 1940s. The Toposa warriors clashed with the Päri defenders at a place called 'Dithoorri' a few meters away from the foot of Lipul hill close to Bura village. The Toposa were almost annihilated and only a few individuals managed to escape. Following this fight, the Päri and the Toposa made an agreement never to raid each other again. So, the blade of the spear was unsharpened (*tong ki guuro*) *against* the stone as an oath to avoid another violent conflict. But the Päri people violated the agreement made several decades ago. In 1964, a group of fourteen warriors from Bura village (believed to have been cursed) went stealthily to Riwoto village of the Toposa in order to raid it and wrestle its cattle. This group on arrival in Riwoto village was attacked and all got killed except one man called Kolle Nyakonoidhi who managed to escape and reached Lafon via Lopit to relate their ordeal.

In March 1977 the villagers of Lokiri came to fish in river 'thithir', a river that belongs to Päri territory. There, they found Päri fishermen namely; Ariega Ubala, Fidele Utong Mutho, Upala and Arukka fishing. The people of Lokiri arrested and took these fishermen to Torit as prisoners. However, one man escaped and reported the incident to the ruling age set of Kɔɔr village. When the people heard the news, the warriors of Kɔɔr village rushed to the site. And it is a Päri agreement that an attack of one village means attack of all villages. Immediately warriors from all the Päri villages followed and joined the people of Kɔɔr but only to find that the people of Lokiri had long evacuated their settlement and ran to Torit and Lorony village in search for safety. A few elders and disable that were found in Lokiri village were left without being harm or harrassed. The next day, the commissioner of Eastern Equatoria, Hon. Henry Bago, the district commisiioner of Torit stepano Jambo together with Lotuko chiefs, elders and the captives came to thithir to meet Päri people in order to resolve the issue. They met King Fidele Ungang, Matia Urec and his brother Udiega Urec of Kɔɔr village, Timon Arugo the paramount chief of Lafon and a number of Päri elders. First lieutenant Justine Yac, the Prisoner Wardern (a Dinka) stationed in Lafon also attended the meeting. The meeting resolved that the Lokiri people should not fish in river thithir but only with permission from Päri people the owners of the land.

Tennet is a community related to Didinga, Boya and the Murle tribes. They belong to a linguistic group classified as Surmic. The Päri called them 'Ajiba' while the Lopit know them as 'Irenge'. They have three villages: Lodohore, Ohitojo and Omohoto (Tarri, Ngatimedu, and Lofi). These people are said to have parted from Didinga and after a long journey, they settled in northern Lopit Mountain. Their land is situated south east of Lafon. In 1993, war erupted between the Päri and the Tennet tribe. This war was provoked by some Tenet criminals that came at night and shot dead (in his hut) a Päri man called Umirri and escaped. When the people followed their foot marks, they saw the foot marks entered the village of Tennet. Immediately, the Madaan who were the ruling age set by then declared war with the Tennet. In no time, Päri warriors were mobilized and went to attack the Tennet villages. In that fight, people died on both sides. But in the end, the Päri burnt the area and drove off with the cattle to Lafon. After this fight, the relationships between the two tribes worsen. However, in 2009, the two communities made peace mediated by a group of Päri and Tenet intellectuals in Juba.

The author of this book was the organizer and chairman of the peace conference held between the two communities. The meeting was successful and the peace attained holds to this day.

Chapter Two

Cradle Land and Migrations

IN LITERATURE, WE LEARNED THAT AS EARLY AS 1826 ANDRIEN BALBI, FOR purposes of ethnic and linguistic classification, had divided Africa into five geographical regions, within each of which he recognized various families of languages. His theory finds adherents among the horde of social scientists as the best way to study different societies. Among scholars who adopted this theory are Tucker and Bryan. In their survey of the non-Bantu languages of North-Eastern Africa, Tucker and Bryan (1956:94-105), group 18 languages and dialect clusters as one family calling them 'Nilotic'. However, following a suggestion of Köhler, Nilotic group was divided into three main branches namely; Western, Eastern and Southern Nilotic language family, (cf. Greenburg, 1966:85). But what is this Nilotes in Tucker's view? What is its origin? Etymologically, the term Nilotic and Nilote derive from the 'Nile valley'. This term was used to classify Nilotic peoples based on ethnicity and linguistics. And from Wikipedia, the free encyclopedia, the Nilotic peoples are peoples indigenous to the Nile valley, who speak Nilotic languages, which constitute a large sub-group of Nilo-Saharan languages spoken in South Sudan, Uganda, Kenya and northern Tanzania.

If classification of African peoples was based on ethnic and linguistics, then it would be inappropriate to associate the Nilotic proper with the so called 'Eastern and Southern Nilotic (Nilo-Hamites) groups. For this group namely; Bari, Lotuko, Fajulu, Kakwa,

Mundari, Kuku, Lopit, Lokoya, Toposa, Karimojong, Kitebo, Teso, Maasai, Kalenjin, Nandi, and others, are a different race altogether from the Nilotic proper. They have an identity that makes members of their community recognizable the same, small and short unlike the Nilotes (Dinka, Nuer, Shilluk, Anywaa and others) who are tall legged and darker skinned people. Yes. The people of Mundari and Bari of Gondokoro bordering the Dinka have many tall people among them. But those individuals acquired these genes from the Dinka through intermarriages. Otherwise the majority of this people appear short.

Languages are assumed to have a common origin when it indicates genetic relationships. But, attempt by Greenburg (1966:86-89) to prove the genetic relationship of the Nilotic and the so called Nilo Hamitic languages did not yield a satisfactory evidence. We noticed that many areas have not been tested. For instance, no attention was paid to 'phonology (tone). Core vocabularies like sun, tree, head, nose, hand, and toe (in fact, all human body parts), kinship terms, names of animals or plants have not been compared to ascertain their relationships, establish sound correspondences, know the similarities, disimilarities and hence, reconstruct proto language from which they descended. Again, a fricative is not a feature in Luo languages. But in his comparision of Nilotic and Nilo Hamitic vocabulary, Greenburg (1966:86-88) sought to strengthen his argument by the citation of Shilluk words which he wrongly spelled: fik 'water', ča: k 'milk', falo/fal 'knife'. The correct word for water is 'pii', milk is caak, and knife is 'paal or *paalo*'. The /c/ in caak is not a fricative for the middle tongue articulates at the palatal. The similarities of pronouns cited by Greenburg might have happened as a result of Areal affiliation and historical accidents. It is not enough to conclude for genetical relation. These are two groups of languages and not a family. For a 'group' signifies that the languages were geographically contiguous or had certain features in common, but there was no clear evidence of common origin.

Moreover, there is a widely held view among members of this group (Bari, Lotuko, Lopit, and others) that their ancestors at time immemorial, emigrated from Ethiopia and after a brief stopover at the shore of Lake Rudolf (now called Turkana), the group divided into two. The Kalenjin, Nandi, Maasai, Datoga, and others, moved southwards some of whom reached northern Tanzania. The larger group migrated westward, moving towards South Sudan. Upon reaching the place called *Lotuke,* they settled. Some years later, the group abandoned the settlement due to conflicts caused by scarcity of water. The people started disintegrating, all at different times moving further inland region towards the Nile valley. The Kakwa, Fajulu, Kuku, Nyangwara, Mundari and Bari people parted first from the group. They were followed by the Lokoya, Lopit and Lotuko. The Toposa, Karamojong and the Ketebo who remained behind for some time also left the area. The Toposa moved a short distant north east of Lotuke and settled. After all have deserted the Lotuke settlement, the Didinga people (Surmic group) came in and occupied it remaining there up to this day.

The Ketebo people live approximately 60 miles west of Lotuke. In their new settlement, the Ketebo people were joined by Luo emigrants of Acholi who came from Uganda. The two groups met at a particular place called 'Lorum'. During that gathering, the two groups ate together the roasted meat with ugali/asida: and hence the place and people are called 'Lorwama'. This name derives from the word 'rwama' meaning eating roasted meat with ugali/asida. The integration of these two racial communities created a language known as *Okolyei*. This word derives from a place called *Okol* in Kitgum district of northern Uganda.

If Eastern Nilotic peoples migrated from the east to their present homelands as maintained in the tradition, then it would be misleading to classify them as Nilotes. I think the term *plateau* or *highlanders* would be appropriate. This is because, if not all, most of

Cradle Land and Migrations

these peoples live either under, by the side or on top of hills whereas, most of the Nilotes live in the swampy areas.

Some historians maintain the view that the Nile basin was, in ancient times, the cradle of the one homogenous, African civilization, which in turn gave birth to a universal human culture. George Bureng Nyombe favours this view. According to him,

> The original home of the Nilotes, and by extension the Bari people, was further north, from the alleged Bahr el Ghazal area, but probably further north than the present northern Sudan, Nyombe (2007:3)

It is noticeable in Nyombe's statement that 'Egypt' is the cradle land of the Nilotes, because Egypt is the country that lies north of Sudan. But this raises some questions. If the Nilotes originated from Egypt, then where in Egypt is the original home situated? Was it in the upper or Lower Egypt? Were the ancient Egyptians black or white?

In another statement he writes,

> ...the home of the Nilotes was in the Nile Basin, **or** in the Sahara east of the Nile Basin before the Sahara dried up around 7000BC (Nyombe 2007:47).

But such a vague statement (indicated by the word 'or') gives an impression to the reader that Nyombe himself is not certain about the original homeland of the Nilotic he is proposing. And this makes us cautious about accepting his theory about Nilotic origin.

He further said that the Nilotes deserted the Nile valley due to ecological change casued by the drying up of the Sahara and the pressures from all manners of invading hordes of whites from the earliest times: Canaanites, Hebrews, Phoenicians, Mongols, Arabsm Berbers, Greeks, Romans and so on. Nyombe continued,

> In this general atmosphere of uncertainty and extreme inhospitality the Nilotes left their ancestral home in all directions. They

fled to the west, following the edges of the Sahara to the Atlantic Ocean, to southwest into the Congo tropical forests, south into the sudds of southern Sudan, and east along the Red Sea and along the coast of the Indian Ocean and into the Ethiopian highlands. (Nyombe, 2007:47-48).

It is clear from the above statements Nyombe alleges Egypt cradle to homogenous African civilization, which later got replaced by invaders's culture. The questions remain, what triggered the conflict between the Nilotes on one hand and the attackers (Asians, Arabs and Europeans) on the other resulting to mass migration? Which race first attacked the Africans and when? Who were their political leaders through whom history can be traced? All these and much more need answers to tell us about the origin and heritage of the Nilotes.

Greenberg (whose thesis is widely accepted), classifies African languages into four units, known as phyla: Nilo-Saharan, Niger-Congo, Afro-Asiatic and Khoisan. And Nilotic is a subgroup of Nilo-Saharan language family. But in the above statement we find Nyombe calling Black Africans Nilotes. But, the term 'Nilotic' as we have seen earlier, refers to people indigenous to the Nile valley, who speak Nilotic languages. It is also one of the Negro races along side with Bantu, Sudanic, and others. In this context, to call Black Africans 'Nilotes', causes nothing other than creating historical confusion.

Further, if the ancient Egyptians were of one race as Nyombe asserts, then their physical, cultural and linguistic certainly must be the same or closely related. But in reality, the Bantus, Nubians (Kunus, Mahas, Dongolese, etc), have languages and cultures of their own different from that of the Nilotic. Physically, they have light or brown skins compared to the Nilotes who are tall with darker skins.

The King of Anywaa by name Agada gives similar story about Egypt being the center of African civilization. In quest for information as to where the cradle land of the Nilotes was, he said,

The Nilotes originated from Egypt. Led by Juma, the group migrated southward (following the White Nile) and eventually settled in various areas of the present day South Sudan [6].

Again the evidence provided here is incomplete. First, the king has not revealed the cause of civilization collapse leading to the dispersion of the people from the assumed cradle land. And in this research, we found neither the Dinka nor the Nuer remember such a leader (Juma) in their traditions. And when members of the Anywaa ethnic group were consulted to reinforce the view, no reliable information was found in support of this opinion.

Some scholars like (Crazollara 1950; Simeon 1978; etc) have postulated the Nilotic cradleland is somewhere east of Rumbek in 'Bahr el Ghazal' region. This proposal contradicts the claim by those who said Egypt was the cradle land of the Nilotes. How can these two parallel viewpoints be addressed? Perhaps the best way is to study the languages of these groups. This is because, the links with our past can be known through a language. For, a 'language is the archive of history, said Emerson, quoted in Crystal (2000:41).' It does this by expressing through the grammar and lexicon of its texts, the events which forms its past', explains Crystal. In other words, these critical claims need more evidence. And we suggest a study of philology of Nilotic languages has to be undertaken to give light that will show the dim past about Nilotic origin and eventually reach conclusive evidence. Nevertheless, this task does not concern us here. That is, a sufficient linguistic analysis cannot be given here for all these groups, as our interest is limited to traditional-historical narratives of the community understudy.

I have talked at length trying to analyse the views presented by other scholars regarding the cradle land of the Nilotes. We now turn to the community understudy to know what their traditions say about the cradle land.

---

6   The author interviewed king Agada in Gereif West, Khartoum, on 22nd February 1994.

Generally, the Päri do not precisely know where the cradle land is located. But in their minds, they see their original home located somewhere west of river Nile (Kiir). Crazzolara (1950) cited the cradle land of the Luo people to be in the region of Atuot country east of Rumbek town. Given Lafon town is about forty five miles east of Mangalla (a town situated at the bank of river Nile), makes the proposal by Fr. Crazzolara a good basis for establishing its position. In this place, the Päri legends say, the Luo, Dinka and Nuer people (at a certain era), lived together as a group. They spoke the same language and had one leader. The Päri refer to this territory as *Wi- paac* or *Wi- pan dwong* which means deserted homeland or the largest deserted homeland. In the beginning, life was said to be good. But as the number of their domestic animals increased coupled with population rise, problems started among the inhabitants. The competition over the grazing lands caused misunderstanding among the Dinka, Nuer and Luo cattle keepers. The situation developed to the extent that the Dinka and the Nuer began raiding cattle of the Luo especially those living at the periphery. Several raids intensified until one day the affected people complained to the Luo king to help solve the problem. But the king ignored their complaints by saying '*yio baa wo ngeedo ki tɛɛngi pienni?*' meaning doesn't a rat eat the brink of the bed? The king used this idiomatic expression to minimize the gravity of the complaint from the sufferers. With this attitude, the condition of the Luo neighboring the Dinka and the Nuer deteriorated badly. However, the king reacted after more aggressions were committed by the hostile neighbors upon his subjects. Eventually he ordered his men to take revenge. The Luo warriors carried out the orders and consequently fighting spread all over the region. In the course of these terrible tribal wars, a man called 'Gicaak' and his followers evacuated the land. It is not known which group this leader and his section belonged and which direction he led his followers. Could it be the Gajaak 'the section of the Nuer people currently living at the border with Ethiopia?' It does'nt seems so either because Nuer migration to the east started in 1860s.

Equally the same, the Päri legends do not mention the name of the king nor talk about the reign of the Luo king at the cradle land. All they remember is his children; Dimo, Nyikango, Giilo, Uthienho and their sister called Acol. Dimo is said to be the eldest son and according to Luo tradition, he has to inherit the kingship of his father. His brother Nyikaango was known for being violent and ambitious. He was eyeing for the leadership position of the people. But after his father's death, Dimo assumed the responsibility and was handed all the insignia of a Luo king which included a sacred spear called 'Tɔng Laau', the blessed spear. This special spear was used to bless the people whenever they went for war against their enemy.

At Wipaac, people practiced hunting. One day, people organized themselves to go hunting. According to the story, the son of Nyikaango (whose name is not remembered in the Päri legends) went to his uncle Dimo to lend him a spear to go hunting. Dimo gave him one. But after the hunter had gone to the bush, Dimo realized that the spear he had lent to his nephew was the sacred spear which belonged to the entire community. He became worried afraid of losing the spear. Indeed, the spear was lost. The son of Nyikaango did spear the elephant that escaped with it in its body. On returning home, the boy informed his father Nyikaango about the loss of the spear. When Nyikaango heard this, he immediately went to Dimo and told him the story. Dimo became furious. He then told Nyikaango to let his son follow the elephant to recover the lost spear because the spear was sacred used for the protection of the whole community. Although Nyikaango begged his brother to have the spear replaced with another one, Dimo insisted that he wanted that particular spear back. As there was no alternative, Nyikaango told his son to look for the spear, bring and give it back to his uncle Dimo. So, the son of Nyikaango left the following morning for the bush to look for the spear. He followed the elephant guided by the blood droplets sprinkled on the ground. Luckily, after wandering for some times, he came upon it lying dead with the spear still in its body. He pulled out the weapon and returned home. When he arrived, he handed the spear to his father who took it to king Dimo. When Dimo got the spear, he became relieved but Nyikaango was not happy. Yet the two brothers continued to live together in one place.

One day, as the children were playing, a child of Dimo swallowed the bead (tio) belonging to the child of Nyikaango. The child went home and reported the incident to his father Nyikaango. When Nyikaango heard this, he immediately went to king Dimo and demanded that the bead of his child be produced. Dimo told Nyikaango that he would give another bead of the same kind to replace the lost one. But Nyikaango insisted that he needed the one swallowed by the child. So, for a number of days, whenever the child defecated, the feces was scattered in the hope of recovering the bead. But all these searches were in vain. At last, Nyikaango told Dimo to let the belly of the child be cut open so that the bead could be recovered. This was done and indeed the bead was found and handed to Nyikaango who took it home. There, Dimo went to his house and buried the dead child. After this action, the relation between the two brothers got strained. The situation worsened until one day, Dimo together with his followers deserted the land moving southwards and leaving the larger section of Luo at Wipaac.

The Split of Jur Col from Dimo Group

Dimo is a well-known leader at wipaac. According to Cɔllɔ (Shilluk) tradition, Dimo's group separated and made off in a southern direction (Cf. Crazzolara (1950:38). The Päri tradition says, Dimo and his group came to Lafon from the west. He left the cradle land due to the differences he had with his brother Nyikaango the ancestor of Cɔllɔ (Shilluk). Children caused the dispute. He therefore led his followers along Kiir River. Having moved a short distance from the cradleland, Dimo's sister named Acol parted from the group and moved with her followers towards Wau region passing through Tonj. The reason for the split of Acol and her group from the main group under Dimo is not mentioned or known. It is most likely Acol and her followers broke off from the main group under Dimo due to some disagreement or disputes. This is because after separation the Päri called this splinter group 'Jur-o' meaning our strangers. The word 'Jur' means stranger. The /o/ attached to the word 'Jur' is a suffix indicating a possession 'our'.

Although Acol and Dimo separated, the Päri still know them as their kinsmen originating from the same ancestor. My respondent Arikwiy Acheri refers to the Luo of Wau as, '*tuungo mu adɔɔ piny*' meaning 'members of our clan groups that returned down there'. He said this while pointing to the west, in the direction of Bahr el Ghazal region.

After this event, Acol and the group moved towards the direction of the west. Shortly after crossing river Tonj, they stopped and built a village. The Dinka who inhabited the area saw the Luo people as strangers and called them 'Jur col'. Sometimes later, the Dinka fought these occupiers and chased them. The Luo then left their settlement heading towards Wau from where they fought, overpowered and displaced the Bongo tribes from their lands and occupied it. The village they abandoned near Tonj river was later called Ongäc, Crazzolara (1950:38). As the group advanced, they found a river (now called Jur River), stopped and settled at the river bank. This place was later called 'Abul' situated at the shore east of Jur River. For some years, the Luo stayed peacefully in this new settlement but later, owing to some disputes, the group separated. One group led by Ngor went back to the east in the direction where they had once come. They advanced, while displacing the Bongo from their lands. When they arrived at a place called 'Alur' they stopped and settled. Today, 'Agur', which means *peg down*, is the last Luo village under Alur area bordering the Zande in the south, Bongo in the east and Dinka of Tonj to its northeast. The second group crossed the river and moved northwest of river Jur conquering and occupying the lands of the Bongo people. Today, the Luo people living northwest of Wau are called 'Ya Amac' or Ya Akwac'. Those living east of Wau and the river Jur up to Tonj are called 'Ya Abat' referring to fore leg of an animal.

It is to be recalled that, after Acol departure, Dimo and his son Alɛɛl continued leading the remaining group towards river Kiir and crossed to the eastern bank of the Nile. As they moved further south, they found a group of Dinka called jääng koth living south of Bor. It is said Dimo men took this people together with their leader called Ayak with him. However, it is not stated explicitly whether real fighting took place between the Dinka and the Luo groups before they were subdued. When we look from the point of view of the characteristic of the Nilotic people, particularly their habits of resisting outside intrusion, we can assume that some kind of resistance was made by the jääng koth. Probably because the forces of Dimo might be stronger than those of jääng koth, the later gave up and hence the group and their leader was taken as prisoners of war. In Lafon, the captives formed a clan and called it 'Laali' which has become a sub clan of Pugäri. Although they are fully assimilated into Luo culture, they still identify themselves with Jääng koth.

After Jääng koth were added to the group, Dimo continued to lead his group southwards following the Nile. When the group came closed to the present day Mangala area, they turned to the east in the direction of Lafon. As they went further, the group eventually arrived at the foot of mount Lipul. Here is a famous song alluding to the route taken by Dimo during migration from the cradle land to Lafon written below.

Table 2.1: Dimo's migratory route expressed in a song.

Agaak monda ywɔk kwigi Dimo
   A craw sang very early over Dimo.

Kic a-oo käända ligoodul.
   Bees came, bringing epidemic diseases.

Amana Nguuda ba de neenno ki wangɛ.
   Should Nguuda come to see with his own eye

Linguungi akwalɛ na dɛ mudhɛɛ kwɔbɔ.
   He snatched Linguungi without having said a word.

Wanga nyi ukɛɛdi na dɛ mukwäre lɔɔyyɔ.
   Should my grandmother, the daughter of Ukɛɛdi narrate the history of our grandfathers.

Kwara Alɛɛl oi ka bari kiir, u-rɔɔmbo kɛ ka aywɔm.
   My grandfather Alɛɛl (son of Dimo) came through kiir of Bari. He has no connection with a monkey

Thaping ka arwooni gira thi duol.
   Thaping ka rwooni is the last to die.

Lithir arɔmɔ kɔkɔ a-athiki kaal.
   That strong man died for the people.

*Thɔmbɛɛk ywongi cwɔnda Apilikwäänga wärlingo.
Bɛ luube ki jɔgi adaandi mau acoot.*
   Thombɛɛk cried calling Apilikwäänga the quiet man, and told Jogi that the gourd for the oil has broken.

As mentioned in the above song, Dimo and his followers passed through the present-day Bari country (in the north), and later, turned to the east and eventually arrived at Lafon. The question is' why did Dimo and his followers take the route eastwards far away from the fertile valley of the river Nile? It appears the Bari might have already inhabited the land and that Dimo and his group did not want to be disturbed by the settlers in their migration to search for a better place.

Giilo and Nyikaango Separated

Giilo and Nyikaango who remained behind after king Dimo departed also separated. The Päri legends explained that it was the sudden departure of king Dimo that had frustrated his subjects and created division among the Luo. When Nyikaango felt that many people hated him for the flight of Dimo he decided to abandon the settlement and with a few followers moved northwards towards Kiir River. He passed through Dinka and Nuer villages and these people joined and swelled the group. As he moved further, following river kiir, his group encountered the Funj people at Malakal region. The two groups clashed and the Shilluk warriors defeated the Funj conquering their lands and forcing them to move further northeast. After the fight, a sizable number of Funj people surrendered and became part of the Cɔllɔ. So, the Shilluk then tookover a strip of land, mainly on the left bank of river Kiir (White Nile) which begins from Papwojo in the south to Kaka in the north. While the Shilluk own the land west of Kiir, the eastern part belongs to the Dinka of Padang. The Dinka villages however were built far from the river. This enabled the Shilluk people crossed over to the eastern side of the Nile and in an empty area, they settled. Crazzolara (1950:42) adds;

> The Cɔllɔ have also occupied, since old times, the lower Athulpi or Sobat River. Shilluk villages are to be found also in the right bank of the Kiir River, nearly the whole length of the phodhi Cɔllɔ. In some parts, especially around Malakal and the mouth of the Atar, large villages are well esatablished, while elsewhere villages are built or again abandoned according to the political atmosphere, i.e according to the friendly or unfriendly relations holding at the time between the Cɔllɔ on the one side and the Naath (in the S.) or the Jääŋ (E. and N.) on the other, who are the masters of the country but, generally, only at a certain distance from the Nile. Such more less temporary settlements are established by individuals who are out in search of new lands or cultivation, and are generally named after the original villages on the opposite or left bank.

In other words, Shilluk settlements south of Malakal town such as, Tonga (Tunja), Ogod, Pakwar, Nyilwal including Anakdier in the east, were additional lands taken from other tribes.

It should be noted that the Shilluk warriors did not stop their march after occupying these lands. They continued their March northwards building and leaving villages along the Nile. The towns of Kosti, Rabak, Kawa, Gezira Aba, and Ed-Duiem now belonging to Sudan, were once Shilluk villages.

The death of Giilo

After the departure of Nyikaango, Giilo and the bulk of Luo who remained behind abandoned the cradleland. Before he migrated, Giilo told his people that the kind of bead which was removed from the belly of Dimo's child and which caused Luo dispersion would be called '**dimuy**'. Today, this bead is used by the Anywaa people as wealth in settling marriages. The group then moved southward following the track of Dimo. But after they had crossed to the eastern bank of river Nile (around the present day Gemmeiza town), they lost the way. Instead, of moving to south, the goup followed the watercoure (tributary) in the easterly direction and after a short distant, they stopped near a big water pool and settled. It must be noted that this tributary is the continuation of river kineiti that passes through Torit town. Its waters pass through Päri territory and joins river Nile at Gemmeiza area.

In this new place, the followers of Giilo organized the' Nyikiro dance' which was done occasionally for pleasure. Giilo is said to be a good looking man with a set of white teeth. Not only that, he was a good singer and composed good songs. Often during nyikiro dances people admired him and love his songs. His brother called Uthienho was said to be an ugly man. During dancing, people did not admire him nor love his songs. Because of this, Uthienho became so jealous of his brother Giilo and planned to kill him. He thought deeply about this thing until one day during hunting, Uthienho carried out his plan by spearing Giilo to death. The people buried and mourned for him in this place. After mourning for the death of Giilo, the followers abandoned the area and moved eastwards direction following the watercourse known as 'nyingabieyyi'. The group moved eastward till they came to the place now called Wipaac or Wipäri and settled. The deserted settlement was later named 'buur Giilo' which means the grave of Giilo but misspelled 'Bande Gilo' by outsiders.

The burial place of Giilo has become holy. In the village of Wiatuo, a clan of Nyikeeu to which Giilo belonged, offer sacrifices by invoking the spirit of their dead leader. To this day this place is taken as sacred. Whoever visits the place must offer to god a bit of whatever he/she carries like tobacco, oil, flour or meat and throws them to the holy site as sacrifice to god to divert misfortune.

Luo settlement at Wipäri

Wipäri is about a hundred miles north of Lafon Mountain. When the Luo people arrived at this vast area, each clan under a clan leader chose and occupied a zone and settled. The settlement was enclosed in a fenced made of woods known to the people as 'gang'. Life was said to be very good in this new place. People had plenty of food for them and had sufficient grazing lands for their cattle, goats and sheep. As a result, the population increased and their animals multiplied tremendously. And it is the custom of the Luo that at the end of every harvest, people meet to pray and thank God for the gifts he has given to them. This type of meeting is known to Päri as Koor. Before the meeting takes place, the king used to send his messengers to clan leaders inviting them to turn up for this important meeting. This message used to take two to three months to reach every person. The long period message rotation showed the population at wipaac was too big and that they covered a wider area. When all the people have come, they assemble under a tamarind tree known as 'cwan Koor'. During those meetings, the Luo reviewed their past lives and thanked God (Jwɔk Atääng) for giving them glories in the previous years. They also ask God in their prayers to send away diseases and curse their enemies and wild beasts as well. The tamarind tree under which the people used to assemble stood there until 1989 when it caught fire and burnt. Its place can be located at wipäri.

Luo deserted Wipäri

The king who ruled the Luo at Wipäri is not remembered. His wife called Nyagau ruled after the death of her husband. At Wipäri, everything went well until the queen was provoked one night by a criminal. The criminal entered her hut and assaulted her. In other words, the man committed a sexual assault on a woman who was unaware because she was deeply asleep. According to Päri legends, the queen tried to catch the man but in vain because the criminal escaped. This action angered the woman so much that she planned to punish the whole population at Wipaac (Wipäri) by the use of curse (cien). So far, the queen kept that in her heart until the moment of her death when she cursed the whole population by inflicting famine on the society. The curse made by queen Nyagau made Luo people spontaneously deserted the settlement. The Anywaa people migrated to the north and settled along river Sobat and in the area between river Baro and Akobo while the bulk of Luo migrated southwards to Uganda, Kenya, Tanzania and Congo leaving behind units of Luo communities all along the way.

In 1860s the Nuer people crossed from the swampy areas (Bentiu) to the east and displaced the Anywaa people who had long settled along the Sobat River. They occupied the villages of Ulang, Gelaciel and 'Nyium'. The Nuer renamed Nyium, 'pan lwal thon' which eventually became known as 'Nasir'. In the same period, Dinka Ngok came and displaced the Anywaa from their village of Adong and then renamed it 'Baliet'. About 1940s, the Nuer encroached into the Akobo settlement the land that belongs to the Anywaa people and occupied it to this day.

Note: Sexual assault (liibo) is still being practiced among the Päri people. It is done at night times when a victim is asleep. A person who commits this immoral act is known as 'lilibi'. Once a raper is caught red handed he would be beaten by the people. After beating, the criminal is sued to face criminal charges in the native court and made to pay one or two cows to the victim.

The Arrival of Luo and Non-Luo people in Lafon

The present Päri people did not come as a single ethnic group from a particular common homeland. Various groups with distinct cultures and traditions came separately from their original homelands in waves of migrations and stopped in what came to be known as Lafon. The year in which the immigrants arrived at Lafon is immemorial. Oral history says the settlers came to Lafon using different routes. In other words, the migrants did not come together as a whole. Each clan group moved alone and eventually joined the rest of the settlers. Throughout these movements, each group made a lot of stopovers. That is, when the group found sufficient water and a fertile land, they would stop and settle. After a brief stay in a place, they would advance again. Usually before the group moved further, they sent spies (liewwe) ahead to survey the path and the next settling site. When the spies get another good place, the group would evacuate the area of occupation and move to the new settlement site. Today one can still be shown deserted homelands (withi-mieri) and rest sites during migration from wipäri all along to Amiru and Witäär in the vicinity of mount Lipul. In these places, one can still see the prehistoric remains such as broken pots, stools made of mud and the like. The previous settlements of the following clans are known: wi pu joobi, wi pu-Bɔɔi, wi pu Jwɔm, wi pu Libaalu wi pu Geri, wi pu ukweere, wi pu peeno, nam Alwɔri, wi pu juma, ligoot, and many more.

The First Settlers at Lafon

The distant of Wipäri from Lafon town is over one hundred miles. It was from there the Luo traveled and eventually settled at Lafon. The first clan that arrived Lafon is said to be the *Libaalu* clan. After their long journey from Wipäri, they halted at various places: wi-pujoobi, nyilori and amiru. Amiru is about five miles northeast of mount Lipul. Although Lafon Mountain is near to the settlement, the migrants could not see the mountain due to a thickness of the forest. Later, some men who went hunting saw this tall object. At the first sight the hunters thought they were seeing anti-hill (liɛl). As they moved closer toward the hill, they discovered it was not an anti-hill but a different object. There, the hunters probably not believing their eyes climbed up the mountain to search for its mouth because the anti-hill has some openings. Indeed, when they searched the hill, they found a fairly large cave (ngang) under a giant rock. Then they stopped apparently having convinced themselves that it was the mouth they were looking for. There, they buried an object called atheero[7] beneath the ground and just near the cave. To avoid other by- passers from suspecting burial of an object in a freshly dug ground, the Libaalu hunters light a fire over it and roasted the animals they had killed and ate them. After this discovery, the hunters returned to amiru and informed the group about the new discovery. On hearing this good news, the group led by Kaaja left their settlement and moved to the new place and settled on mountaintop. Although the group had abandoned their settlement on mountaintop and are settled down on the foot of the mountain, their ancient drums can be still seen at the deserted village. Nevertheless, the skins with which the drums were dressed are worn out by climatic condition leaving the wooden parts only.

---

7   Atheero is a tool made from iron or alliminium and used for killing of animals, rats or birds. It can be the head of an arrow

Dimo final destination

Dimo and his group came to Lafon at the time immemorial. When they arrived at the foot of Mt. Lipul they found nobody except some footprints of people. Then they said to themselves,'some people are living here. Let's find them out'. There, they climbed up the mountain following the footprints of the strangers. The group stopped and settled by the side of the mountain. This area was later named 'Liluuro'. Still in Liluuro, the group continued to look for the strangers. In the course of their search, they found a fireplace near the cave up on mountaintop. As can be recalled, this was the fireplace of the Libaalu hunters where they roasted their animals. Beneath this fireplace was buried the athɛɛrɔ to lay ownership of the land. According to the legends, the group of Dimo dug this fireplace and after a few inches, they got the *athɛɛrɔ* buried down. Instead of throwing away the object, they played a trick. They dug the hole a little bit deeper and placed their atheero first, buried it half way to create a layer of earth, and then put the atheero which they got in the hole on top of the soil layer covering their own atheero and buried it altogether. Like what the Libaalu hunters did, the group collected some firewood and roasted the meat of some animals they had killed. After they had eaten, they went to their settlement in liluuro. The puzzling question which requires satisfactory answer is, why did Dimo's men suspect that something was buried beneath this particular fireplace? Is this kind of attitude peculiar or normal to people of that time who were in the process of massive emigration? Could it be that a man from the group of Libaalu clan was captured by Dimo's men and who because of intimidation supplied the group with information that led to this discovery? These questions remain to be answered.

Dispute over Lipul ownership

Both Libaalu and the Dimo groups lived on the same mountain without knowing each other. It is a common sense that the Dimo followers were living in the state of anxiety especially after discovering the footprints of strangers and finding of atheero. However, one day, the Dimo group saw smoke on top of the mountain and immediately they climbed up towards it and for the first time the two groups met. In the ensuing arguments as to which group arrived first and discovered the mountain, the Libaalu people said they were the first to arrive and therefore, they are the owners of the mountain. The Libaalu people said they had a proof of being the first to reach the area. But Dimo group dismissed the claim and said with confident that they were the first to discover the mountain and they could prove if the Libaalu people insisted. The argument was so bitter that Dimo men demanded a proof from the Libaalu people. The later unaware of the trick played by the followers of Dimo' eagerly took the group to the place they had buried the object. There, the Libaalu men dug the fireplace and removed out their atheero and showed it to the Dimo men. But Dimo's men, who until this time remain patient, finally asked the Libaalu men to dig a little bit further in the same spot to get their own proof. So, the man dug the same place and after a few inches, he got another atheero. With this evidence, the Dimo men claimed the ownership of Lipul Mountain. But Libaalu men rejected the evidence shown. They knew that it was a trick. They then went back to their village with the idea that the mountain belongs to them. However, the two groups continued to live on the same mountain but in different locations. The Dimo's group was settled at Liluuro an area situated by the side of the mountain while the Libaalu people occupied a place on the mountaintop. Sometime later, the Libaalu group apparently angered by this event evacuated their settlement and migrated to the Lopit country and stayed there for two years before returning back to Lafon. Although they returned and joined the Pugäri people, the Libaalu people remained opposed to Dimo's claim of owning the Lipul. To this day, they do not pay allegiance to all religious activities performed by the descendants of Dimo to which other Päri clans do.

The name Pugäri

When king Dimo died, he was buried at Liluuro. His son Alɛɛl succeeded him as leader of the group. Some years later, Alɛɛl himself died and was buried at Liluuro too. Then, Gäri his son succeeded him. It was during the reign of Gäri that the group transferred to the present site where the Pugäri people are found today. The name Pugäri by which the whole group is known derived from the name Gäri. The village was named after Gäri because he was the first rwäth to settle in the present location. The word 'Pu/pa' refers to 'home/village of. And 'Gäri' is a name of a person. So, Pugäri means the home /village of Gäri. The inhabitants of the area are called, 'Jo Pugäri' and which means the people of Gäri. As far as the meaning of the terms are concerned, there appear to be a connection between the names 'Pugäri and Pageri. Linguistically, the phrase *Jo Pugäri* in Luo (Päri) refers to the people of Gäri (pu-people of) which coincidentally carries the same meaning in Madi who say (pa- for children of) Geri. It is not clear whether pageri is a breakway section of the Pugäri people or vice versa. More investigation is needed to discover the truth.

Lipul ownership reverted

Before the group of Witäär thought of resuming their trek further, they came in contact with the people of Pugäri and other groups who had long settled in Lafon. The two groups developed good relationships and from time to time they exchanged visits. Among the individuals who visited the residents of Lipul was Abongo the mother of Libala. The people there welcomed her and lived happily among them. One day, as the children were playing, the grandson of king Dimo hurt the eye of Libala with a stone using an instrument called 'apiet'. The incident angered Abongo so much so that she demanded compensation from the parents of the offender. According to the practice, the offender must compensate the victim by paying a cow or goats for such a crime.

However, before the elders of Pugäri came to solve the problem, some men from Libaalu approached Abongo and instigated her not to accept payment of any kind other than taking the ownership of Lipul Mountain. As can be recalled, the ownership of Lipul was taken from the Libaalu through the trick made by the followers of Dimo. Obviously, the Libaalu people are jealous and wanted the ownership of the Mountain be taken away from the clan of naam to which Dimo belonged. So, the Libaalu men advised Abongo not to disclose what she wanted as compensation except in front of the court which must be held before rwäth Jɔgi in Witäär. Abongo accepted the advice but then kept it in her heart.

When the delegation sent by Gäri came to pay the compensation, Abongo refused to discuss over the issue. She told the delegates that she would disclose her demand before the court which should be held by the council of elders in Witäär and under the chairmanship of rwäth Jɔgi. On hearing this condition, the elders of Pugäri returned and informed the king accordingly. Then, Gäri called and asked the elders of Laali and Geri to accompany him to Witäär to hear the demand of Abongo. Before the day of court hearing, men from Libaalu clan went secretly to Abongo and told her to carry a piece of stone to be presented to the court as her demand for the compensation for Libala's eye. The piece of stone would represent the mountain. Abongo accepted their advice.

On the day of the court hearing, Abongo and the elders from Pugäri, Geri and Laali clans walked to Witäär. When the group came close to the court scene, one elder exclaimed '*Ha!*, *Abongo na oo ki jaaki paan moro ka!*' The council of elders wondered as to why Abongo was leading such a group of elders. When they arrive, Abongo presented her case before the council of elders chaired by Jɔgi. In the proceeding of the court, Abongo showed a piece of stone which she kept in the bag (upir or nyabongkoot) to be given her as compensation for Libala's eye. When the elders of Pugäri heard this, they said, 'Abongo, why did you trouble us by walking all the way to Witäär? Had you told us right there in our village we would have given you the ownership of the mountain'. So then, the elders of Pugäri agreed to transfer the ownership of Lipul Mountain to Abongo. By this declaration, the ownership of Lipul Mountain reverted to Bɔɔi clan to which Abongo herself belonged.

After this event, the whole group at Witäär deserted the settlement and moved to Lafon and joined the other settlers already there. Before the group reach the destination (approximately one kilometer from the foot of Mt.Lafon), king Jɔgi died. The people immediately buried him there and then climbed up the mountain. On reaching Liluuro, the deserted homeland of the Dimo group, they settled. It was in Liluuro the village was named 'Bura' or Burri dhaanho'.

Although the ownership of Lipul has been passed to Bɔɔi clan, all the sacrifices performed at the cave of Lipul are entrusted to the care of Pugäri people. A priest from the clan of Naam has always been in charge of the sundry sacrificial rites to the protecting spirits of the community. For example, when a piece of rock falls or get broken (kidi upɔn), the priest often sends a message informing the king of Bɔɔi in Wiatuo about the incident and the need for them to give a black goat for offerings to appease the spirits whose warnings has been signaled by the fall of the rock. This is always given without delay and the sacrifice is performed at Lipul cave (Ngang Lipul).

The Jagɛ Group

Besides Libaalu and Dimo groups, there lived the people of Jagɛ. A man called Liigi headed this group. They are said to have come from the Lolubo community which are Sudanic people. There are variations in Päri legends concerning the arrival of this group in Lafon. Some said the Jage came after Lbaalu and Dimo group had arrived in the area. Others said the group settled before the Luo groups arrived at the area. However, there is consensus that the Jagɛ group was found after the dispute between Libaalu and Dimo's men has ended. They were found by hunters settling by the side of the mountain which is presently occupied by the *Angulumɛɛrɛ* people. Nobody knows when the group settled there. Whatever the case maybe, the clan of 'naam' to which Dimo is the founder became the owner of the mountain until the bulk of Luo arrived from Wipäri and joined them.

Pukwari clan

The people of Pukwari led by Ajuuk are said to have left Bari country and joined the Pugäri people. At Lafon, some of is clan members left Pugäri village and joined the village of Wiatuo. Although they are fully assimilated into the society, they still vividly remember their Bari origin.

Rwäth Coogo

According to Päri oral history, the Pugäri people were the ones who witnessed the passage of Luo who deserted Wipäri in waves of migrations. The groups that proceeded further south to Uganda, Kenya and Tanzania and other places are said to have passed through Lafon. Of all the groups that passed by the largest one was led by rwäth Coogo. This group settled at Lafon in a place called 'agamalaau' which is located about a kilometer from the foot of the mountain east of Pugäri village. During their brief stay in Lafon, an epidemic disease struck the group killing a lot of people including rwäth Coogo himself. The people buried king Coogo in a place called 'agamalaau'. Thereafter the survivors of the group left the area and moved southwards and settled at Pacidi and Payiira respectively. Some years later, Luo deserted Pacidi and Payiira settlements and moved to Uganda. As they were moving, they left units of people behind who then formed the existing Luo communities namely; the Acholi of Magwi, Panyikwaara, Oboo, Parajok, etc. From Uganda, the Luo divided futher some going to Kenya (Jo Luo) and others proceeded to Congo (Aluur) leaving the bulk of Luo in Uganda viz Jo Padhola, Acholi, Laango, Aluur and others. Today, Jo Payiira has finally settled at Got Goma at Liira in Uganda.

Bɔɔi clan

According to Päri legends, the king of Bɔɔi at Wipäri was called Umeenya. He had a wife called Abongo who had born him a son called Libala. Umeenya has a brother called Ukwiri. He was also married to a woman called Athɔɔ who bored him a son called Jɔgi. Both Umeenya and Ukwiri died at Wipäri. Umeenya died leaving his son a young baby. According to Luo law of succession, Libala was the legal king of Bɔɔi clan. But when the group left Wipäri, Jɔgi had to lead the group on behalf of Libala because he was an infant. The group he led comprised of Jo Bɔɔi, Tɔng, Cuai, Pucwaa and Geri clan groups. They left Wipäri and halted at Witäär at the vicinity of Mount Lafon. After gaining friendship with the settlers at Lafon, Jɔgi and the group deserted their settlement and moved to join the settlers in Lafon. Before the group reach the destination (a few meters from the foot of mount Lipul), Jɔgi died. The people buried him immediately. After the burial, the group climbed up and settled at Liluuro an area situated by the side of the mountain.

Geri clan

During the dispersion of Luo from Wipäri, the clan of Geri also known as Pu-jaal split into two groups. A small group called Buratio left the main group and moved in a different direction toward Lafon. On their march, they passed through buodo, ugwɔri, and halted at a place called ukwänya about eight miles east of Lafon Mountain. After some years, they deserted their selttlement. Instead of moving south towards the Lopit Mountain, the group turmed west and eventually arrived at Lafon. There, the people of Pugäri welcomed them and gave them land to occupy and settled. The main group of Geri later came together with Jɔgi group and settled at Witäär. Today, the place they occupied have grown a lot of acacia trees (alaandɛ) and is now referred to as *alaati nyigeri* which means the acacia trees of Geri. Later, members of Geri that came with Jɔgi divided: one group joined their clan members at Pucwaa village, another group known as *Abuodo* joined the people of Angulumɛɛrɛ village and the main section of Geri remained in Wiatuo village.

Nyuunga the ancestor of Pucwaa Clan

The leader of Pucwaa clan at Wipäri is called Uruo. He had a son called Congoori. When Uruo died, a man from Tong clan inherited his wife and born him a son called 'Nyuunga'. Both Congoori and Nyuunga separated during Luo dispersion from Wipäri. Congoori went to Anywaa country while Nyuunga came to Lafon. Before the group deserted their settlement at Wipäri, Nyuunga asked his brother Congoori to go with him. But the later refused. Instead, he allowed his son Libay to migrate with Nyuunga while he went to Anywaa country. Nuunga and his nephew then joined the group led by Jɔgi and continued their long journey until they halted at a place called 'witäär' about six miles north of Lafon Mountain. During the movement, Nyuunga felt a pity at the condition of Abongo who was carrying Libala on her back and so, he helped her carry the baby. Because the ancestor of Pucwaa helped carry the prince of Bɔɔi clan, it has become a tradition that whenever a new king is enthroned, Pucwaa people have to carry him on their backs during the ceremony. Hence, the people of Pucwaa are referred to as "miethe" which means baby carriers. The area deserted by Pucwaa is known as 'apɛɛti nyipucwaa' located east of a famous tree known as *Adiit* in the land of Wiatuo.

Pucwaa village

King Nyuunga, who came with the group from Witäär, joined the people of Geri clan who had already settled in the area. They settled at a place called Ngunyagwega. After staying for some times, the clan of wiira headed by Diiji came and joined the group. Oral history says Wiira clan group did not reach Witaar. From Wipäri, they passed through buodo, Wi- pu- joobi, nyilori and halted at Amiru before joining the settlers at Lafon. While in Amiru settlement, Dimo sister's son who the people of Pugäri had chased away joined them. According to the story, Dimo sister's son whose name was not mentioned was singled out as different because he originally belonged to Jur col. He came with Dimo during migration leaving his father and mother moved to Bahr el Ghazal. In Lafon, Dimo entrusted him a responsibility of distributing meat of sacrificial animals. He was specifically assigned a religious role to perform rituals at the Lipul shrines that opens at the bottom of the hill in the east. This made some clan members who were eyeing for the post become jealous of him. The enmity reaches to the extent that some members planned to eliminate him. When he noticed that, he deserted the area and went to the bush. And as he wandered about; he met the daughter of Kwäängi called Agɔl looking after the cattle of her father. The man told his story to the girl. The girl had a pity on him, took him home and told the father all about his troubles. Kwäängi then welcomed this stranger and adopted him as a son. This stranger was then made to rear cattle together with Agɔl. Everyday they would take the cattle for grazing and bring them back home in the afternoon. During this activity, the man fell in love with the girl and eventually pregnated her. Although the event was shocking, the father of the girl did not act drastically. Instead of punishing the man for having commited such a crime, Kwäängi allowed him to continue produce children with the woman on the condition that the children they produce belong to him. Today the descendants of this jur fellow have multiplied and are called 'tuung *Lidhir*' which means the clan that was pushed aside. Mr. Bwona Wirik a decendant of deposed Jur man headed this group. Yearly, he conducts sacrifices at the Lipul shrine that opens at the foot of the mountain from the eastern side. The same priest is responsible for controlling winds which causes arson. Traditionally, the first hunting is always carried out in his territorial hunting ground. Others follow it.

The fourth clan that joined Pucwaa, Geri and Wiira clan groups is Alwɔri clan. This clan was founded by the nephew of king Nyuunga who originally belonged to Lɔlɔ/Alɔlɔ clan in Pukurjo. Their clanhead is known as Ugutta. In hierarchy, rwäth Nyuunga placed Alwɔri clan next to kingship clan followed by Wiira and Geri respectively. But the order of clans was later changed during the reign of Awäälämug. My respondent Masimo Acheri Anyotha explains that the king's decision was taken after Alwɔri people had a stick fight with the kingship clan during which the people of Pucwaa were defeated'. So Wiira clan was placed to a second position next to kingship clan because their fighters came in support of the kingship clan, beat and chased out the Alwɔri fighters.

The capture of the Adimac people

Long after Bɔɔi and Pucwaa people had settled in Lafon, a burning fire was seen at a distance. Men from Pucwaa, who lived on the mountain, saw the fire. As he was eager to swell the size of his group, king Nyuunga quickly mobilized his forces and went to attack the strangers. The forces encountered the strangers at the place called Ukwänya. The warriors surrounded and ordered them to submit. On compliance, the strangers were asked to identify themselves and tell where they had come from. They replied that they were people from Lomia coming from Lopit country and that they were emigrating in search for a better place to live. They were also asked as to why they were carrying a piece of rock. They answered that they intended to plant that rock in a new place where they would settle. They said the rock would grow into a mountain and become as big and tall just as the one they had left behind. Seeing no logic in a piece of rock which cannot grow, king Nyuunga ordered the Lopit to drop down the rock. The order was obeyed. Today, this piece of rock can still be seen in Ukwänya forest about eight miles east of Lafon Mountain.

After this, king Nyuunga and his forces took the captives to the village. As they were coming towards the village, they met Uyat with his forces coming for the same purpose. Uyat was a notorious warrior who like killing of strangers whenever he met them. He was greatly disappointed when he found Nyuunga was in full control of the captives. As there was no way out, he joined the king and all came home together. When they reach river Atoondi which is about three miles from the foot of the mountain, Uyat initiated a general inspection be conducted upon the captives to prevent them taking things of evil nature to the village. Nyuunga accepted the idea and the general inspection were carried out in the skin bags known as 'upiri' (singular, upir) of all the captives. During the checking, a piece of stone called 'ugwiɔ' was discovered in the bag of their leader. The stone was immediately thrown into the river and thereafter the group crossed to the other side of the river bank. Nyuunga then took the captives to Pucwaa village and gave them a piece of land which lay between Pucwaa and Pugäri villages. The Lomia people settled there as a sub clan of Pucwaa. The Päri named these captives 'naa dimac' which later shortened to Adimac. This means people who were discovered because of the burning fire.

In this new settlement, the Adimac people met lots of challenges. On several occasions, unknown people used to come at night and speared people to death and escaped. Whenever the elders of the Adimac complained to the leadership of Pucwaa, they got no solution. The situation worsened until the group was eventually relocated to a new place just in the center of Bura village and settled. Since then the Adimac became a sub clan of Bura and never again considered part of Pucwaa whose leader brought them. Today this people have become important clan in Bura village and indeed, in Päri society. For example, when wegipaac organize a periodic ceremony in the place called 'gär', where the stone 'ugwiɔ' of the Adimac leader was thrown in, a priest from the Adimac clan makes fire in his shrine and gives the new fire to the ruling age set who would take and light it to warm up themselves during that night when the group would be assembling in the open. Moreover, the place where the stone was throne became a sacred place. In this place, a priest from Adimac normally offer sacrifices to god to heal people affected by certain diseases. In return, parents of the victims pay him things in kind such as beer, goats and dura.

The battle between Uyät and Giilo forces

The largest group that came and joined other settlers at Lafon was led by rwäth Ajuuri. The people are popularly known as 'Jɔ Giilo'. They migrated from Wipäri and rested at a place called 'kud' about eight miles north of Lafon Mountain. The hunters from Lafon came to know them after the group had spent considerable period of time at Kud. It was the son of Mucuga called Uyät who took it upon himself that he would fight Ajuuri, subdue him and bring him and his forces under the leadership of his father. But rwäth Mucuga, aware of the strength of Ajuuri whose forces outnumbered that of his rejected the scheme of his son. But Uyät insisted he would go and fight the man. He had sworn that he would kill king Ajuuri and use the fats in his intestine to smear the handles of his spears with. He therefore mobilized his forces from the Adimac clan and without the knowledge of his father left for kud. There he launched an attacked on the forces of Giilo. Unfortunately, his forces were destroyed only a few escaped leaving many dead bodies behind. Uyät himself was wounded by a man from Pukwänyi clan. Because king Ajuuri had instructed his forces to bring him alive, Uyät was not killed immediately.

The warriors brought him to the king who told him he would not be spared because he had earlier boasted that he would kill the king and use the fats in his intestine to smear the handles of his spears. After Ajuuri talked to him, he ordered his forces to finish him. And in no time, Uyät was killed.

But instead of leaving his body to be eaten by birds or rot outside like the bodies of his forces, the king ordered his men to bury him. The burial process began with the killing of a black bull. Then the skin of the bull was removed and the body of Uyät wrapped in and buried in the tomb. The actual reason why Uyät was given a special burial was because the king treated him as a prince. Since then it has become a customary for the Päri people to bury the dead king using the skin/hide of a black bull freshly killed for the purpose. The tributary of river kud where the Adimac fighters were killed in large number during their fight with the forces of Giilo was named 'wɛɛnda Adimac.' Since that battle, it has become a tradition for the Adimac people to run to the village before hunters finish hunting. This is done to avoid another hazard from happening again to their members like the one they had experienced with Giilo forces.

Before he was murdered, Uyät cursed Jo Giilo to abandon their settlement at kud and join the rest of Luo at Lafon. And indeed, after the battle, the followers of Ajuuri deserted the area and moved to Lafon. The son of Ajuuri called Ranga Amulenya led the group. On arrival, they occupied the western part of the mountain. Because their number was big they almost encircled the mountain. The settlers named them Jɔ kɔɔr *lwaak* meaning 'the people who came after the majority of people had arrived'. The word kɔɔr means behind or after. Kɔɔr lwaak means the people who came behind others.

The split of Bɔɔi leadership

Jɔgi has three sons namely; Mucuga, Uyuw and Uthienho. After the people had settled at Liluuro, the clan of Tɔng left the village and settled north of Atuo clan a sub section of Kɔɔr village. There, they called their village 'Wiatuo' which literally means 'head of Atuo' but is in fact north of Atuo. As time went by Uthienho the brother of Mucuga left Bura village and joined the clan of Tɔng.

In the order of birth, Uthienho was the youngest but the most favored son of his father. He had two other brothers namely Mucuga the elder son, and Uyuw the second born. Before Jɔgi died he promised Uthienho to succeed him as king. He made this decision to punish Mucuga his elder son for having pregnateed one of his wives. Nevertheless, to avoid any malicious act from his brothers, Jɔgi warned Uthienho never to tell anyone about this thing except after his death. Actually, Jɔgi's decision was regarded contrary to the customary practices of the Päri in which the elder son takes over the kingship after the death of the father. In any case, Jɔgi refused to disclose who among his sons would succeed him as king. And that created a power vacuum after his death.

In those days, there were regular clan feasts. During the feast, a bull was killed and its meat cooked and eaten by elders. The skin of the slaughtered bull was cut into strips known to Päri as *cäri in sing Pl cäcce*. Those strips were distributed to all the attendance to wear above their ankles as ornament. Long after Jɔgi died, the people gathered for this ocassion. So, a bull was killed and its meat cooked. According to the tradition, the king should have the meat of the right hind leg known as *cuoodho*. Customarily, the king is served before other people get their ration. But when the meat was ready for distribution, the servants got stuck. They did not know who should receive the right hind leg since king Jɔgi had not disclosed the one who would succeed him after his death. However, all eyes were put on Mucuga. As the elder son, people expected him to take over in accordance with the traditional law of succession. To the surprise of many, Uthienho got up, went straight and picked out the right hind leg from the cooking pot, removed the meat from it and took the boney part of it. He told the attendants that they could eat the meat and that he was to take the bone because it symbolizes power left to him by his father. Accompanied by his maternal uncles (Jɔ Tɔng) they left Bura and went back to Wiatuo village. After he left, the people of Bura ate the meat. Hence, the people of Bura are referred to as 'dhi-ringo' (piece of meat) a derogatory name given by other Päri people. From that time, Uthienho became the king of Wiatuo.

For his part, having found himself with no absolute power over the people, prince Uyuw left Bura village and joined the clan of Jagɛ who were settling west of mount Lipul. He was welcomed and accommodated by Liigi the head of that clan. After living among the Jage people for a certain period of time, Uyuw who was influential and ambitious founded a clan and called it 'Bura'. Thus, Bura became a royal clan in Angulumeere village with Uyuw as its first king.

Bupi (Dupi) clan

A group of people called Bupi but formerly known as Dupi arrived at Lafon and joined the settlers. The year they arrived at Lafon is not remembered. Upon their arrival, the people of Wiatuo, asked them their identity, and their leader answered *'nan dupi'*. This is a Bari language which means 'we are slaves'. 'Dupi' is the plural and 'dupet' in the singular.

It is said that the Dupi people originated from the Lolubo tribe, a community that borders the Bari tribe in the south. The question is why did they communicate in Bari language? Have they lost their language? If not, then we may suggest that the group did not come directly from the Lolubo country. They must have been held in captivity in Bari land before they escaped. And as it is known, Bari society is divided into classes: freemen, blacksmiths, professional hunters and slaves. The lowest class in the Bari social order is dupi (slaves). According to George Bureng Nyombe, the dupi sole function was to cook for the freemen especially during social occasions. And when a chief or a wealthy noblemen died, he was often buried with his dupet' Nyombe (2007:6). This could possibly be the reason for this people to runaway. They had to escape to find freedom and a better place to live. And according to the story, the people of Wiatuo (their captors and hosts) welcomed them and gave them empty land that lies between nyikwanya and Atuo clans and settled. Since then, the group enjoys freedom like anybody in Päri society.

Emigration of Kɔɔr people to Parajwɔk (Parajɔk)

When king Ulum of Kɔɔr and King Nyilang Alikori of Wiatuo were in power, differences arouse between members of the two villages which led to the fight with sticks. In that fight, the people of Kɔɔr saw other Päri villagers supporting the people of Wiatuo. Because of their love of freedom and independence, the people of Kɔɔr who felt oppressed by people of Wiatuo decided to evacuate the settlement and moved to Parajwɔk (Parajɔk). King Ulum with his group left Lipul about 1880 and migrated to Parajɔk (Crazzolara; 1951:159). The departure of Kɔɔr people to Parajɔk earned them the name '*poodho*' meaning, the people who proceeded ahead. In Parajɔk the Acholi asked them who their name was. And they answered, 'wana Jɔ kɔɔr,' we are the people of Kɔɔr. It is to be noted that Jɔ Giilo were the last group to arrive Lafon from Wipäri. And so, the settlers at

Lafon named them *Jɔ kɔɔr lwaak* or *Jɔ kɔɔrɔ* meaning the people who came behind us. Linguistically, the word *Jɔ* or *Jii* in Luo language refers to people. Kɔɔr means behind or after. So the group became known to the Acooli as the Jɔ-kɔɔrɔ Crazzolara. (1951: 159). Later, the Acholi changed the phrase *Jɔ Kɔɔrɔ* to become Lɔ kɔɔrɔ. But the correct name for this people is Pӓri; a name derives from the verb 'Pӓӓr to jump (referring to people's movements during migration when they have to move from one place to the next).

At Parajɔk, the people of Kɔɔr lived happily. They had a lot of food to eat. Moreover there was no political rivalry like the one they had experienced at Lafon. Meanwhile, in Lafon, the people were facing hardships. Enemies used to come at night using the space created after the people of Kɔɔr left the area and speared people to death and escaped without being caught or revenged. In addition, there was also famine ravaging the country. All these factors frustrated King Alikori very much and regretted for having missed the people of Kɔɔr who could have sealed the empty space that the night raiders used for infiltration and thus defended the country against the enemies. King Alikori Nyilang thought of making reconciliation with king Ulum. But as he envisaged failure in any sort of direct talks with Ulum, he thought of applying curse (cien) on the people of Kɔɔr so that they would hate the Acholi country and return to Lafon. So, he approached a dying person to help him cursed the people of Kɔɔr. The sick man called Kamure told him to bring new pair of shoes **war** and a piece of dry human feces to him. Alikoori brought these items and the sick man spat on the shoes and told Alikoori to send these items to king Ulum in Parajɔk. The pair of shoes was a gift to Ulum such that when he wore them he would feel a great urge of going back to Lafon. Human feces were meant to hate the Acholi land like the bad smell of human feces. These items were sent immediately to king Ulum at Parajɔk.

It is said that, when Ulum received and wore the shoes, he felt excited and developed nostalgia for Lafon and king Alikoori who sent him this gift. Not long after he received the items, king Ulum and his followers suddenly abandoned the Acholi land and returned to Lafon leaving behind food crops like sesame, sorghum, potatoes stored in granaries. During his return to Lafon, Ulum came with some persons from the Acholi community. The descendants of those who came with Jɔ kɔɔr can still trace their origin back to Parajɔk. They spent nine years in Parajok after that they returned home.

Aluur clan

The Aluur migrants did not pass at the foot of Mt. Lipul. After leaving wipaac (Wipäri), they passed through Kud (about eight miles north of Mt. Lipul) and stopped and settled at a place closed to Mugiri (a Bari village) located west of Lafon. After some years, the group abandoned their settlement and moved south wards passing through the Lokoya area, Nimule area and eventually entered Uganda and settled in the West Nile. From Uganda, a contigent of the group proceeded to Congo and settled. The land they abandoned near Mugiri was named 'Pu Aluur' meaning, the village of Aluur. This name later became known as *Pulur* and is about forty five miles west of Lofon town.

Thuri

Thuri or better known as Shaat/Caat is a small community of Luo found in Western Bahr el Ghazal region. This people live in small units dispersed among the Dinka. Some of its units are found west of Ndogo a Bantu tribal group. In my search for information linking this group with the rest of Luo, Mark Nyipwoc who comes from the

Jur (Luo) referred me to a man called Marko Uywom Ubur; age 70, a person of high authority in Thuri society. During the field work, I met a group of elders who advised me to approach the same man (Mark Uywom) who was knowledgeable in Thuri traditions, and this is what he narrated,

The Thuri together with the Jur col parted from the larger group of Luo at Nile Basin. Migration started in 17th century. Misunderstanding between Nyikango and Dimo caused Luo dispersion from their settlement. So, the Thuri and the Jur col group moved westward following river Kiir. When they arrived at the place now called 'abiey' they settled for a period of time. Later, the group advanced further west following the river kiir. And at places called 'abu zebra' and 'maroya', they stopped and settled among the Arab tribes. In the course of time, they adopted Arabic culture. In late 18th century, the Luo people and the Arabs of the Rezigat fought. Unfortunately, the Arabs defeated the Luo and forced them to cross river kiir to the south. When the group arrived at Nyamlela (Nyamlel), they settled. Because the population was huge, the settlements extended to the following areas; Watwil, Akewic, Marial Bai and Lol. It was at a place called khor-chel (chelko) that the group divided into Thuri, bwodho and Luo groups. My informant Marko Uywom claims his grandfather named Duok Nyingkwai was buried at Lol.

In (1930-31) the British colonial government adopted a policy of re-distribution of tribes in Sudan. One of the tribes affected by this policy is the Belanda Bviri which abandoned some of its territories to the Thuri people. These includes, Deim Zubeir, Khor jamus, Khor Hajir, Abul (Ya-Abulo) and Kuru. In 1927, the people of Thuri were told to go to Raja area. But, the group under chief Wad al Mak refused and therefore, remained at Arayo in Aweil district. Another group of Bwodho remained in Pumoro settlement in Aweil district. In 1928, the Thuri led by Cengeny Girjwok arrived at Deim Zubeir and settled.

In spite of this, the district commissioner of Reja complained that Nyamlel and Chelko belong to Raja and not to Aweil. So, the issue was raised to the governor of Wau for solution. But the complaint was turned down. Thus, to this day, the community has not attained tribal unity having one common territory. I think Ubur's account is worth noting, for they throw light on a little known tribal history. Although these people speak Luo language, many of its members speak Dinka, and at times feel ashame to speak its mother tongue among the Dinka people.

Balanda Boor

The name Balanda by which the community of Boor is known today was once pronounced 'Belanda'. The name Belanda' says Santandrea (1964:108) 'is a shortened form of Beer-landa, a Bongo name. The Bongo call all their Luo-speaking neighbors Beer, and to make a distinction between the Jur and the others, call the former Beer- gusi (i.e the Beer of the east) and the latter Beer-landa (i.e the Beer of the hill): Landa means hill or mountain in Bongo. This people trace their origin to the Luo. Their leader called Boor parted from the Luo main group at Nile Basin in time immemorial. The group marched to the west and eventually settled amongst the Bviri tribe, just by side of river sue in the region of Raffili Rapids (cf: Crazzolara, 1950:85). The two tribes co-existed and became one people with hybrid of cultures. Meanwhile, both tribes continue to maintain their differences. The Luo speaking section call themselves 'ka Boor' and the Bviri tribe (a Bantu group) are identified as 'ka Bviri'.

The diffusion of cultural elements gave birth to a new language structure and phonetics. And although there is shared retention of basic vocabulary with the Jur, Päri or Shilluk say, in personal names (Ubur, Ucala, Ukelo, Othoo, etc.), the presence of large number of

Bantu roots in Belanda indicates Bviri greater influence on the Luo speaking tribe. Features such as, gb, ngb, kp, currently used by the Balanda in their speech are Bantu phonemes.

Note the Balanda people do not live in one geographical area but scattered. The group that lives in Nagero (a town situated near Tombura town and south of Wau town) is referred to as 'Balanda Bazia'. This town was named after Vincent H. Bazia, the former chief of the area. The other section mixed up with the Bviri at Deim Zubeir, under Chief Ulau Baggari is referred to as 'Balanda Baggari' (Cf Santandrea 1964:108-109).

According to Shilluk mythology or legend, Bwor (Boor) was the eldest son of Nyikango, whom as the entourage was moving towards the north, Bwor decided to return to his uncles (Bviri). According to the legend, Nyikango ordered Dak's mother, nya-Thuri, Achol to accompany Bwor where he founded the Belanda Bwor.

Discovering the Kinsfolk

The dispersion of Luo from the cradle land is still being remembered by modern Luo people. In December 1979 the king of Shilluk (Cɔllɔ) Reth Ayang visited Lafon the burial place of rwäth Dimo. After he was accorded a warm welcome usually reserved for a Luo king, Reth Ayang met Päri elders especially Muthokori Licinga the descendant of Dimo, king Fidele Ungang, Ligulu, Abula and many prominent elders. He was narrated the history of Dimo as the Päri know it. Reth Ayang in a comment said Dimo was the elder brother of Nyikaango the ancestor of Shilluk and that it was a historic moment for him to be in Lafon. Reth Ayang was the first Shilluk king to visit Lafon and to see the historical realities of Luo traditional history concerning king Dimo.

The Luo migrations are recounted in legends by various Luo

communities sometimes with similarities and sometimes with differences. These are reflected in writings of various researchers on Luo history. For example Fr. Crazzolara who has investigated Luo traditions very intensively has concluded that the migratory routes of Luo people run from the cradle land somewhere east of Rumbek town where Dinka Atuot are found today Crazzolara,(1950). He further stated that the migrating Luo led by Giilo left the Collo (Shilluk) country in the region of Malakal and turned south after crossing river Sobat and eventually arrived in Wipari.

.However, the Päri have a different story regarding this movement. According to them, the migrating Luo led by Giilo moved southward from the cradle land and then turned eastwards after crossing river Nile somewhere in the present day Mundari land. As the group moved further in eastern direction while following the water course, they halted at no great distance from Gemmeiza. There, king Giilo was murdered by his brother Uthienho. The place where Giilo was buried is named 'buur Giilo' located about 45 miles northwest of Lafon. After Giilo was buried, the people deserted the area and moved to the east following the water course known to Päri as *nyinga bieyyi,* and eventually arrived at Wipäri. It was from Wipäri that the Anywaa people migrated northwards until they reached the present settlements between river Baro and Akobo while the bulk of Luo migrated southwards in waves.

Giilo and Nyikango, according to Shilluk legend, moved together in the same entourage until Pijo (the Nile-Sobat confluence) where they separated because Giilo did not want to travel further north. He turned eastwards following the Sobat River and founded Obango, Abwong, Adong, Gelaciel, Adura, where some clans branched to follow bad-Giilo River towards Akobo, Pochalla, etc., while the others followed Openo (Baro) to Gambella, Buri up to Gore which they found very cold and returned to settle in the plains. There is need to revise this part which in fact resonates with the legend that the Päri are a branch of the Anywwa. King Ulum after whom the Ilemi triangle is named was an Anywwa King who ruled over that area before the coming of the Taposa.

Päri people among the Dinka Bor

A large population of Dinka Bor bordering Lafon traces their origin to the Päri. According to the legends, a section of Päri known as Abii left Lafon under the leadership of Thodoh Gorbek. The group led by Thodoh's eldest son, Anuet Thodoh, eventually settled in the land situated south of Bor. The area that was deserted by this group is called 'thim Abii/Abie' meaning the forest of Abii. It is located 10 kilometres north of Lafon Mountain. In 2014, the Wild Life Conservation Society built an office in the area to monitor the migration of wildlife from Jebel Boma to Burgilo (Bandegilo) Animal Park. In his new settlement, Anuet acquired a lot of cows and was living a happy life with his four sons: Ajak Anuet, Kuot Anuet, Chol Anuet and Bol Anuet. One day, the story says, the sons of a man whom Anuet had entrusted to help him keep his cattle began to steal some cows. But the youngest son, Mach Luol (nick-named Mach-ayiel), told Anuet where his cattle were hidden. So Anuet went to the man's kraal and picked out his cows. This angered the young men who had stolen the cows but their father intervened and rebuked those who wanted to harm the young man. After their father died, other family quarrels emerged between them and the fight broke out. The descendants of the young man who had reported the case to Anuet were chased away. They ran to Abii and were rescued by the descendant of Anuet. Before this incident, Yar Geu Mach, one of the grand-daughters of Mach-ayiel, was married to Anuet's grandson, Chol Ngong Ajak. The new arrivals were there welcomed as in-laws. After this incident, the two groups made peace and life returned to normal.

Anuet's sons are presently represented by three communities in Bor and one community in Lake State. The Abii clan (also known as Nyara) is from Ajak Anuet lineage, Anuet clan descends from Chol Anuet lineage, and Adol clan is from Kuot Anuet lineage. Unlike other descendants of Anuet, Adol clan was named after their great-grandmother called Adol Bior-baŋkɛr from Gol clan. Today, these communities occupy three big villages with a sizeable population in Bor. Bol Anuet and his followers crossed to the western bank of Nile in an attempt to return to Wipaac near Rumbek. They eventually settle in Awerial in the modern-day Lake State. They identify themselves as 'Nyarar' or 'Abiei'.

In 2017, however, a conflict occurred between Anuet's and Mach-ayiel descendants over the name of the land which was occupied by Anuet at the time of his arrival from Lafon. This is because the land was renamed during the SPLA era as Panwel (meaning a village of Wel Abiryai, a great-grandson of Mach Luol). The groups who had lived together in harmony for many centuries could not agree on one name for the land and Payam. The group of Abii wanted the land and Payam to be named as 'Anuet' claiming he was the founder of the area, whereas the group of Mach-ayiel (supported by their allies of Biong, Kuot, Padoor, Awan and Nyicak) preferred the land and Payam to be called 'Pan Wel'. Sharp differences occurred. So, the authorities called for arbitration and asked each group to present their arguments. One of Abii's elders and former Civil Administrator of the Payam, Ber Ngong Ajak, and a great-grandson of Ajak Anuet represented his side.

He is said to be well versed with the history and still speaks Päri language and remembers songs as well. Ber (in his opening speech) proudly identified himself as Päri origin and sang Päri songs before the public, a move that surprised many Dinka people. Thereafter he related the history of the area by making strong points that their opponents could not defend. The group that favoured 'Pan Wel' lost the arbitration and became furious and violent erupted in December 2017, which ended with twenty-two persons killed. The second wave of violence broke out again in February 2018 and another twenty persons were killed. The government of Jonglei State finally intervened and made a buffer zone separating the two warring groups. Abii group were relocated southward to Jam and Bangachorot villages, near Mundari border. Mach-ayiel and their allies were moved further north to DDR protection camp north of Pariah town. The disputed area was left empty but guarded by the soldiers. The case was later taken to the court for a solution. As I write, the case remains unresolved.

Chapter Three

Päri Clans

Päri community comprises of many clans some of which have disappeared. On the facing page is the list of existing clans as they are found in each village:

Table 3.1 Päri Clans

Wiatuo	Kɔɔr	Bura	Pugäri	Pucwaa	Angulumɛɛrɛ
Gumar ((kingship)	Liding (kingship)	Laandi (kingship)	Jɔ Naam (kingship)	Pucwaa (kingship)	Bura (kingship)
Ukɔth	Karamini	Lidu 1	Among	Wiira	Akaya/Lirra
Ungang	Kirkik	Lidu 2	Ukwiri	Alwɔri	Adula
Jaal	Pukaal/Ciro	Aluum	Dierpire	Geri (Nhaadhi)	Pukwänyi
Lidu	Peenɔ	Ligoot	Pukwari		Adɛɛba
Lingorokol	Payweeri	Pumɔɔl	Laali		Abuodo
Ading	Lijäälo	Pukaal/Ciro	Jwɔm		Jagɛ
Ucala	Ajiba	Paraau	Libaalu		
Uyät[1]	Thwɔrabaac	Ukwɛɛrɛ			
Tɔng	Nyikɛɛu	Pukurjo/Lɔlɔ			
Pukwari	Atuo	Adimac			
Pukaal /ciro	Ukwɛɛrɛ				
Punywaagi/ Cwääi	Pacuth				
Nyikɛɛu	Puywaa				
Geri (nhaadhi)	Bulär				
Mɔlnyaang (määr)	Abɛɛk				
Dyer clan subdivided: into (Cilriew & Acäng)	Lɔlɔ (Wändi)				

Nyikwanya (Peeno)	Liboongi
Bupi	Ligoot
	Ajige
	Pukändi
	Nyangkwat
	Kuruki
	Tuung diɛl

Splintering in clan organization

As can be seen from the six villages that make up the Päri society, members of one clan are found in more than one village. Circumstances that cause this split is mainly linked to disputes among clan members forcing individuals to abandon their clan altogether and join another clan. Often, members who have decided to detach themselves from the main clan and joined another clan in another village, their decendants may thereafter, in time, become an independent or different clan. For example, Pukaal clan (originally from Giilo group), and who were hosted by Wiatuo and Bura villagers formed an independent clans in these villages. The Pukwari clan members (that left their main clan in Pugäri village) have formed an independent clan in Wiatuo village where they migrated to. The founder of Nyikeeu (in Wiatuo) is said to have come from Kɔɔr village on account of problems he had there with his clan members. He joined his maternal uncle known as Ading in Wiatuo. In 1977, however, his decendants detached themselves from the clan of Ading and formed a clan of their own. Lɔlɔ (snake clan) is divided into units: some of its members are found in Kɔɔr; other units like Pukurjo are settled in Bura village and Alwɔri in Pucwaa. Uyät was said to be a strong man from Paraau clan. He was seized by the servants of king Udiek who attached him to kingship clan of Wiatuo. King Udiek married him a wife who bored him children. After Udiek's death the descendants of *Uyät* detached itself from the kingship clan and formed a new clan now called *tuung Uyät*.

Three clan groups namely; Uwitti clan, Liriathiigo clan and Ngolormeeri clan still remain attached to Gumar clan. Ngolormeeri originally came from the clan of Ungang. King Alikoori attached him to kingship clan as a reward for having saved him (Alikoori) from being killed by the fighters of Lokiri during that terrible war in which the Pari lost several warriors. Technically, these clans have become far from the center of power and are expected to exit from Gumar clan in the future.

Clan groupings

There are groupings of clans within Päri society. That is to say, two or more clans are grouped together to form a larger number of people. A combination of two or more clans is termed *Phratry*. Lowie (1948:240) describes the Phratry as 'evidently nothing but a convenient term for a 'kin linkage'. Precisely, two types of groupings exist in Päri society. The first type of groupings is exemplified by *Pukaal* and *Lijäälo* clan group. The two clans (found in Kɔɔr village) are united by the recognition of mutual obligations; the group merges in mutual alliance against an outside group; they have joint responsibility in blood compensation; attend to communal service; and on solemn occasions, they share food or meat together. However, each clanhead maintains authority over its subjects, Relationships between clan heads are seen as a balance of power. In the early 1970s however, relations which at one time were competitive between the two groups ended. The head clan of Pukaal eventually assumed the overall power of the group. And although each clan still maintains its name, the power is now centered in the hands of one man who comes from Pukaal clan.

Social institutions like lineage or clan becomes non-existent when its members have all died. In principle, even if one member or two are left, a clan viewed as a social insititution is already dead because it does not perform any function. Under this circumstance, it is not surprising that remaining individuals develop tendency to willingly attach themselves to larger clan. They form a clangroup in which the exact genealogical relationship is not reckoned. In many cases, when you make other people come to you, you suddenly become the one controlling the situation. And the one who has control has power. He determines individual's occupation, role, prestige etc. This is the position of Pukändi clan. It has been joined by Nyankwat and Kuruki clans. As a host, Pukändi clan head assumed the headership role for the whole clan group. Other clans' heads are of subordinate statures. Often, when group members meet, they identify themselves by the name Pukändi. Other names are not used but only in certain circumstances. It is a common sense, when all members of a particular clan die; the name of that clan disappears forever. For example, *Aying clan* in Kɔɔr village is extinct. Below are clan groups with a mythical ancestor.

Bɔɔi clangroup (with Jɔgi as their ancestor)
Kidi Gumar (Wiatuo village)
Ukɔth Nyangiro
Ungang
Jaal
Lidu
Lingorokol Awaran
Ading
Landi (in Bura village)
Lidu 1 (in Bura village)
Lidu 2 (in Bura village)
Alum (in Bura village)

Bura, a kingship clan (in Angulumɛɛrɛ village)
Akaya also called Lirra (in Angulumɛɛrɛ village)

Paraau clans comprise:
Lipidia (head clan)
Ucäng
Uthienho
Pukaal (Lima)
Ukwɛɛrɛ

Adimaac clans comprise the following:
Wɛɛri (muur clan) Originally from Lopit of Omia clan (head clan)
Licinga (muur clan) Originally from Lopit of Omia clan
Adiijo (muur clan) Originally from Lopit of Omia clan
Wang-ki-daau, originally from Giilo group (Luo).

Pukändi clangroup comprise of:
Pukändi clan
Nyangkwat clan
Kuruki clan

Jo dhi ngang (people of the cave) with Dimo as their ancestor
Jɔ - Naam (headclan)
Among clan
Ukwiri clan
Dierpire clan

Jo Liding with Giilo as their ancestor
Liding (headclan)
Karamini
Kirkik

Enthronement (Roony)

There are two villages in Päri society that practice enthronement namely; Wiatuo and Kɔɔr. Other villages do not. To them when a king dies, the son automatically takesover. But for Wiatuo, when a king passes away, the prince is installed as king. During the occasion, people from all Päri villages gather in Wiatuo village to participate in the ceremony. Initially the people assemble at the dance court yard (thwɔrɔ) while some elders enter the drum house (duondi buul) where the prince is kept. There, they dress him in leopard skin. On top of the leopard skin, fresh leaves are put so as to cover the whole body. After this they make him lie on the flat wooden bed (peem) and carry him out to the people who are waiting eagerly at the dance court yard. There, the people pray to God to bless the new king to live longer and rule well. After prayers, Jo Pucwiy (the people from Pucwaa and Pugäri) come forward and some strong men begin carrying the king placed on the wooden bed. Four men start raising the king and later replaced by another four. The people follow them in procession all moving to the king's common ancestral tomb. There, they move round the tomb three times and then take the king to his palace and put him in the throne placed in the veranda (*dooro*). Once the king has been placed in his throne, the people who carried him return to the dance courtyard and join the celebration. Because the people of Pucwaa carry the king during enthronement, they are being refered to as 'miethe' meaning baby carriers.

During this occasion, the people stay segregated according to clan groups. Members of each clan drink and enjoy food distributed to group. Clan members who had detached themselves from the main group and formed a sub clan in another village come and unite with the main group. For example, the Mɔlnyaang, Nyikɛɛu, Nyikwanya, Pukaal, Pukwänyi, Pumɔɔl, Ligoot, Diɛl clans are united with their main clans in Kɔɔr village. They are called Jo Giilo group. Pukwari join their main clan at Pugäri. The Geri in Pucwaa and Abuodo in Angulumɛɛrɛ joined with the Geri of Wiatuo. Alwɔri clan joins their main body in Pukurjo. Similarly, members of Booi clan group in Wiatuo and Angulumɛɛrɛ unite with their clan members at Bura their original village. Individual members who were adopted or attached and integrated into the clan group were singled out as different. Consequently, they join the group of their biological fathers.

Like Wiatuo, the people of Kɔɔr celebrate when they install their prince a king.

On this day, the following clans come and participate in the ceremony.

Liding or Loding
Karamini
Kirkik
Pukaal (ciro)
Peenɔ
Payweeri
Ajiba (note; Ajiba is a given name. The original name is peeno)
Thwɔr abaac
Nyikɛɛu
Atuo
Ukwɛɛrɛ
Pacuth
Puywaa (Jɔ- ywaaya)
Bulär
Abɛɛk
Lɔlɔ (Pu-wändi)
Liboongi
Ligoot
Ajige
Pukändi

Kuruki
Tung diɛl
Pukwänyi
Mɔlnyaang (note: Määr is the clan name. Mɔlnyaang is a given name).

The above clans also known as Jɔ Giilo gather in the assembly house of Kɔɔr village in the morning and conduct the ceremony. According to Angole Madas, members from the clans of; Ligoot, Nyikɛɛu, Bulär and Nyangkwat carry the king during the procession. Nowadays, this custom is not being practiced. It ended after enthroning king Kidi Gumar of Wiatuo and King Ulum of Kɔɔr villages. Kidi descauraged the continuation of this practice because it made individuals trace their origins back to their biological fathers and hence, created disorder in the society.

Distribution of bull meat to the six Päri villages

There are certain occasions in which people of the six Pari villagers meet together as one community. During such occasions, a bull is killed and its meat divided among the six villages as follows: Wiatuo and Bura villagers called (Jɔ-Bɔɔi) receive the right back leg (waadhi *cwiic*). In their division Bura king would be given some meat from the thigh leaving the Wiatuo king the bony part of it. The Kɔɔr villagers (Jɔ-Giilo) receive the left back leg (waadhi *caam*). This group doesn't share with any other villagers. They are considered to be an independent group and hence their epithet name is Jɔ-cuodho. The Päri called the femur *cuodho* because when it is boiled or roasted the content of its hollow part resembles the colour of mud. The king of Kɔɔr takes the bony part and leaves the meat to his brothers. Angulumɛɛrɛ people get the right front leg (badi *cwiic*).

Ademac clan would receive the neck. Pucwaa and Pugäri villagers are combined as one group known as 'Jɔ pucwiy'. They are given the left- front- leg *(badi caam)* and divide/share it as follows: Pucwaa king takes the upper shoulder *baac* and cuoodho while the Pugäri villagers are given the lower part of the leg known as *lidang*.

Chapter Four

Päri Contacts with the Outside World

Like many other tribes of southern Sudan, the Päri people were untouched by outside influences until in mid-nineteen century when their area was first reached by Fr. Angelo Vinco an Italian of the Verona fathers' congregation. Father Vinco ventured to Päri country in 1851 from his base in Gondokoro among the Bari people.[8] The priest probably unaccompanied by any porter in his journey to mount Lafon passed through Bilinyang and later Liria in Lokoya country. Not far away from the Pari villages, Vinco encountered a lion and he climbed up a tree before the beast could attack him. The next day, some Päri hunters were on their way to hunt animals and they came upon a lion lying under the tree and a white man was sitting in it. The hunters scared the lion which ran away. Then Vinco was rescued and climbed down the tree. Without doing any harm to him, the hunters took Father Vinco to the village apparently to let the villagers see him. On the arrival, the hunters took the priest to the slope of the mountain where the villagers lived. The Päri people were amazed by his white color and became the center of curiosity.

The Päri legend about the arrival and reception of Father Vinco indicates that there were no hostility shown to him despite the fact that this was their first time and experience to see a white man.

---

8 Crazzolara, J.P., The Iwoo, Part II, Verona 1954, p. 168.

Moreover, at that time, the Päri were on guard against enemies and their villages were enclosed in a large fence called 'gang' with small doors watched by defenders every night. Any stranger who approached the fence was dealt with accordingly. Father Vinco himself was on an exploratory visit for fresh territories and people to be included in his program of evangelization to Christianity. He spent fifteen days among Jo Päri who treated him as a guest.

Here is his opinion about the evangelization of the Pari people[9]

> They are very fierce and wild, but all more or less disposed to be civilized and to receive the light of the Gospel, whenever missionaries of great virtue and experience, despising all dangers and even their life, resolve to remain among them with apostolic zeal, in order to instruct and regenerate them in the salutary waters of Baptism.

During his stay in Lafon, he saw from the top of mount Lipul (Lafon) the following mountains; Lopit mountain, Imatong mountain ranges, Lokoya hills and parts of eastern bank of the Nile and there he drew a sketch map of this region. [10] This map became a guide for other missionaries who came to the region.

Amukuta (Dervishes) Raids

After the departure of Father Vinco from Lafon in 1851, it took many years before other strangers arrived in the area. The Päri legends say that the second contact with the outsiders was marked with hostilities because these people came as an organized armed band that used their arms against the Päri. The Päri called them 'Amukuta'. These armed strangers who moved with women as porters were spotted

---

9   See Comboni Missionery Lafon, 1963 ,St. Paul Major Seminary, Khartoum
10 Interview with Fr. Tito Giuntoli, at Khartoum, 6th Oct. 1994.

by the vigilantes of the Päri from their mountain. Immediately the warriors were mobilized and descended the mountain and marched to face the approaching enemies a distance from the villages, apparently to prevent their women folk, children and their cattle, goats and sheep getting engulfed in the fighting. In the ensuing fierce fight, the Päri in their clash with the enemy lost a good number of men. The enemies were shooting at them with muzzle loading guns which the Päri named 'arooka' while the Päri were using spears. From there, the Päri retreated to their mountain. After assembling in a place called Laali a place situated by the side of the mountain, the attackers followed them and another fierce fighting erupted.

On realizing the difficulty the gunners faced in loading their weapons in order to shoot and the long time they spent to fix the bullet, the Päri after experiencing a salvo of fire attacked with their spears. Very soon, they overpowered the enemy and the few who survived fled leaving their dead and wounded colleagues behind. The Päri chased them up to a place called 'pulolo' and beyond. A number of the gunmen were captured and brought home as prisoners of war. And it was the Päri tradition the captives were not killed but adopted as sons and daughters of those who captured them. The adopted sons were given girls in marriages as their wives and the women were married to Päri men as daughters of those who captured them. The descendants of those captured can still be traced up to today.This event was confirmed by El Amin Rabeh (employed as Bari interpreter at Mangala) when he says,

> I went with the Dervish force to smash Alikori at Jebel Lafon. We tried to get up their mountain; we had rifles, but the Berri (Päri) let us get up a track among rocks, and then threw big rocks and stones on us and spreared us from behind rocks; they killed at least 30 that time alone, and captured 16 rifles; they were armed with spears and shields; they have no bows and arrows[11]

---

11 INTEL. 6/5/16. NRO, Khartoum. Note iv: Historical RE: The Berri and Jebel Lafon

Generally, most southern tribal communities came into face to face confrontation with foreign aggressors in the middle of nineteen century. These people who were composed of government and private traders were drawn into the southern Sudanese soil by their greed to obtain huge economic gains for themselves and their governments. Initially, it was Mohamed Ali the viceroy of Egypt who invaded the Sudan in 1820. His main objectives were to obtain gold and to supply slaves for the Egyptian army. During the 1820's, the Egyptian control was extended over Kordofan to the southwest of Khartoum. Egyptian forces raided for slaves to east and west particularly into the Nuba Mountains to the south Kordofan[12]. Having made Khartoum as the new capital, the Turkish colonial rule in 1821 imposed a centralized system of government as a means to loot the resources of the Sudan[13]

It was not until 1840 that the Turko-Egyptian forces overcame the fierce front lines tribes; Shilluk and Dinka and penetrated deep inside southern Sudan. At first, their activities were confined to those tribes living along the Nile valley. Later, the hunting for slaves and elephants (ivory trade), made them reach inland regions.

To understand the reasons for the Amukuta to enter the Päri country, historical facts about the establishment of the Turco-Egyptian authority in the southern Sudan must be mentioned briefly. The pressure imposed in 1838 by the European governments on Mohamed Ali to allow foreign traders especially Europeans to go further south, led to the opening of the hinterlands in the south. From gold mining which has proved a failure, Mohamed Ali shifted to ivory trade.[14] Thus the areas like the Päriland which teems with elephants, rhinoceros, leopards, lions and several other animals became a fertile spot for such trade. And so hither went a band of the armed men the 'Amukuta' to seek their fortunes. These private armies, mostly

---

12 (see Shillington, K., *History of Africa*, London 1989, p. 281)
13 Daly, M. W., *Modernization in the Sudan,* New York 1985, p. 51
14 (Shillington, op.cit. p. 283)

alien merchants plundered the southern Sudanese in their search for ivory and slaves. This economic activity, however, put those armed adventurers into direct confrontation with the oppressed southerners who were to defend their cultures, values, customs and resources. Eventually, the raids resulted in bloodshed and chaos spread over the previously well-established peoples of southern Sudan.

The cause of this barbarism is further explained by Sandersons who states;

> The destruction of government's monopoly had removed all the prospect of financial gains; meanwhile the private traders used violence as short-cut to profit; the market for trade goods among the self-sufficient peoples of the southern Sudan was soon saturated; they then saw no further reason to exert themselves by hunting elephants. The only goods they valued were cattle and cattle could be obtained only by local raiding, or by intervening in and even fomenting local wars.[15]

Now the Amukuta, the Päri are referring to, must have been an expeditionary detachment from the Turco-Egyptian army based at Gondokoro or even merchants; and Lafon falls about sixty miles east of Gondokoro. The Amukuta at that time were probably in search of cattle to feed the soldiers of the Turco-Egyptian army stationed in Gondokoro. If they were merchants, they were in search of cattle to sell to earn them profits. The Päri called them Amukuta. They described them as, red colored people having long noses; large transparent ears and bow legged.

According to the Päri legends, the invading band was led by a man called Al Nur. There is a song in local language which contains information about this historical event. And the song says:

Limojo da loobo ki kɔr Anur. Cuur da yäng pulolo.
Ya Lipɛɛthareŋ na loobo ki kɔrɛ,

---

15 (Sanderson L.P. –Sanderson G. N. *Education, Religion and Politics in Southern Sudan, 1899-1964,* London 1979, p. 10.)

ii aur miyang, aur miyang monyo pɛɛrɛ.

This war song goes further to say that the Päri defenders at the time consisted of Bongcwot and Limojo fighting age groups. It is to be noted that the Bongcwot was the ruling authority and Limojo was the fighting wing of that group.

The defeat of the Dervishes (amukuta) by the Päri warriors has been reported by Jennings-Bramely, who says,

> In 1897 the Dervishes, under Arabi Daffalah, beseized them for thirteen days, but as the Berri (Päri) rushed the water each night at a different place, the Dervishes were unable to subdue them[16].

This first encounter was the beginning of violent raids, which continued in the years that followed.

Anglo-Egyptian invasion of the land

After the defeat of the Amukuta, the Päri remained alert to face any further invasion of their land. But nothing happened. Even the changeover of administration in Equatoria from Amin Pasha in 1889 to the Mahdists, the Päri remained unaware of this change. The Mahdists never reached the interior. When the Anglo-Egyptian defeated the Mahdists in 1898, it took them more than five years to reach all parts of southern Sudan. The two urgent problems which faced the new Anglo-Egyptian administration in the south were establishment of administrative system and the pacification of hostile tribes.[17] Pacification was not an easy task. Some of the tribes looked upon the administration in the same light as the Turco-Egyptian or

---

16 See Uganda Protectorate, (Vide APPENDIX 'D') Intellegence Report, No. 23, July 1904, Uganda National Archives, Entebe

17 (Bashir M.O., The southern Sudan Background to conflict, London 1968, p. 19)

Mahdists administration[18]. It was in April 1904 that colonel Borton Bey of the Anglo-Egyptian forces finally penetrated the Päri land from the Bari country. On return to Mangalla, Borton reported that the Pari were wild, indiscipline and never obey government. With Borton's report, the colonial authority in Mangala organized for punitive patrol against hostile tribes namely, Murle, Päri, Lopit, Toposa and Boya (Larim).

The troops under Captain Arden left Mangalla on 20th December 1912.[19] These forces had gone with preconceived ideas that the Päri people were wild, obstinate and they had to meet them with a show of force. They arrived at Jebel Lafon on 7th February and camped at Akwo, a short distant from the foot of the Mountain. At that time, the villages were on the mountain. When Kidi saw the soldiers, he climbed down and met them at the camp. Owing to lack of food and carriers, they asked Kidi to let the community contribute some grains, cows and porters to help take the supplies to Mangalla. But 'three villages of the Berri (Päri) refused to assist. Only chief Kidi and his section (village) came with a few carriers and some grain"[20]. The Päri saw these strangers, just like the Amukuta and overlooked them with the belief that they would defeat them. The attitudes of southerners towards foreign intruders were always of defiance. For instance, Sandersons has this to say,

> Southerners had since 1840 seen many apparently powerful strangers come to their land: Turco-Egyptian, Khartoumers, Mahadists, Belgiansn and French. But they had seen them go. Even a small people like the Berri (Päri) could as late as 1904 look on the government as equal from the military point of view.[21]

---

18 (op.cite)

19 SIR, No 212 (March 1912), see APPENDIX,' Southern Column Beir Patrol'. (ENTEL 6/7/23. NRO, Khartoum

20 See (INTEL 6/7/23. N.R.O. Khartoum (M.I.R. No. 172)

21 (Sandersons, op.cite. p.15)

It must be noted that the Päri have six villages. And if only Wiatuo villagers had responded to the demand of the soldiers, it means five and not three villages failed to cooperate with the government. Sudan archives conveys this event which deserves to be quoted in full,

> In reply to a request for grain and carriers to take the column into Mangalla Chief Kidi protested that all his efforts were stultified by the action of a truculent section under a chief named *Dwot*[22]. Inspite of giving them a day or two to become reasonable and after a promise of payment in cows, chief Kidi confesed he could do no more and the people would not listen to him. It was then decided to operate against only one section of the jebel, known to be the most truculent and obstinate, with the hope that seeing one section punished the remainder would be reasonable. At 9:30 a.m the two sides fought lasting up to 3 p.m. On that day, several prisoners were taken and a considerable quantity of grain. The enemy (Päri) made a stout resistance, but the operations were carried out with the small loss to the soldiers of two killed and seven wounded. For the most of the night, the, Berris on the Jebel, beating their war drums and blowing horns, defied the "Turks" to come on, saying that on the morrow, they would show the Turks which were the most powerful, etc. At day break, Chief Kidi came into camp, and reported the other sections would come in; so he was sent back to the Jebel to warn them that if the sub chiefs did not come in, further operations would be taken. He returned two hours later saying it was hopeless and that they wished to fight the governemt. He added he was glad and hoped the government would punish them severely, as they would never believe or listen to him. Consequently, the operation was carried out that day against the whole Jebel lasting till 4 p.m. A great

---

22 Note. Dwot is the chief of Pugari village

quantity of grain was found and a large number of prisoners taken, mostly women and children[23].

In this two days fighting between the Päri and the invaders the later triumphed over the former due to their sophisticated weaponry. The Päri lengends further stated that the Anglo Egyptian forces killed several people and that the blood of those killed flowed from up the mountain down to the foot of the mountain. In their records, the colonial authority acknowledged stout resistance been put up by the Päri people, but fell short of mentioning the number of casualties inflicted on the Päri people. They only mentioned two of their soldiers killed and seven wounded.

The colonial forces under Captain Arden defeated the Päri at the time Limojo and Amerkolong age sets were the rulers of the country. He took several men (mainly the Alangurre age group, the fighting wing) as prisoners to Mangala from where they were taken to Khartoum and finally ended up in Port Sudan prison. Earlier, the Päri regarded the British led expeditionary force to be weak like the Turks. But after they were subdued, they called them 'Madir' an Arabic word spelled 'mudir' and meaning administrator.

The assumption by the British jurisdiction and control brought about changes in Päri society. The Mojomiji who have become weak, were then punished with hard labor for their stubbonness. The colonial government made both the youth and Mojomiji build the road with stones from Liria to Kudo. The work was too heavy especially for the elderly. When the youth (Ukweer age group) saw the difficult condition their elders were going through, they told them to go back home and decided to work alone. The mojomiji thanked them and went home. When the work got finished, the Ukweer age group went back home and joined the community at Lafon. Since then, communication with the government was normalized. Chief

---

23 Reports on the finances, Administration and Conditions of the Sudan: Sudan Archives, Durham. (Historical Notes 1912: p.199)

Kidi and his councilors could visit the governor in Mangala and returned with gifts from there. The Päri also ceased to raid the Bari round Mangalla and on the river, as was their custom before the government came. In 1912 Lafon finally was placed under the British colonial administration. In 1930, the Päri people were annexed to Mangala province. Owing to the availability of resources in Päri, the DC in Torit requested for Lafon area be annexed to Torit which was granted. Today the Päri maintain the folk songs composed about the two great fights as they were passed to them orally by their ancestors.

The Arrival of Missionaries in Lafon

The penetration of south Sudan by Mohamed Ali the ruler of the Ottoman Empire in 1840 encouraged the missionaries who had been looking for the opportunity to introduce Christianity in the region. In 1846, the Catholics came to Sudan and settled in Khartoum, which was selected by Pope Gregory XVI to be the center of the Vicariate Apostolic of Central Africa. [24]

By 1850, Jesuit priests mostly Austrians began to work in the south Sudan. They established two stations; Gondokoro and the Holy Cross. Gondokoro was placed among the Bari while Holy Cross was built for the Dinka Tuic who lived along the Nile between Bor and Shambe. It was from Gondokoro in 1851 that Father Angelo Vinco ventured to the Päri country. After the exploratory visit of Father Vinco to the area, it took them almost seventy years (1851-1920) before Christianity began to establish its roots among the Päri people.

The spread of Christianity in south Sudan was greatly affected by a number of factors the important of which are; tropical diseases which killed many of the missionaries and the hostility of the tribes in the localities. These factors forced the missionaries to close down

---

24 (Dellagiacoma V., Missionaries in southern Sudan. 1900-1964, Khartoum 1986, p.7)

their mission stations at Gondokoro and the Holy Cross. And by 1863, all mission stations in south Sudan had been abandoned. The remaining missionaries decided to return to Khartoum their main base. After that the south Sudan remained without any kind of Christian activity.

When Sudan was reconquered by the Anglo-Egyptian forces in 1898, the Christian missionaries in Europe began to think of coming to revive their missionary work in Sudan. It was not, however, until 1900-1901 that the first missionaries proceeded to the south to survey their future areas of activities[25]. Following a suggestion made by the representatives of the Church Missionary Society (CMS) based in London and the Presbyterians, the Sudan government divided the areas south of parallel 10 degrees into three zones among the CMS, the Presbyterians and the Catholics.[26] This system of 'spheres of influence' was further improved by the codification of the missionary regulations in 1905. The territory east of Bahr el Jebel and the south of fifth parallel reserved for the British Missionary Societies. The country of the Päri lies above the fifth parallel, which had been allotted to the CMS in 1902. However, the Church Missionary Societies never extended their evangelical service to the inhabitants of the area. It was only in 1920 that Father Silvestri and Padrana of the Catholic Church mission first visited the area. The two priests came from Torit where the Catholic Church had been established. The colonial authority opposed this particular visit because it was contrary to their regulations of denominational sphere system, which has placed Lafon in the area allotted to the CMS. The Catholics were warned by the authority in Torit not to go to Päri again. But seeing the vacuum in the area, the Catholics insisted that they must bring the Päri to Christian faith. They expressed their intensions

---

25 Warburg, G. *(The Sudan under Wingate Administration in Anglo-Egyptian (era) 1899-1916.* London 1971, p.118.

26 ibid.

and seriousness to reach Lafon with the message of Jesus Christ by arguing with the authority verbally and through letters.

With the foundation of Torit mission in 1920, Lafon was included in that mission. And despite the government prohibitions, short visits were paid by a number of priests to the area. Fathers Padrana and Silverstri visited the area in Oct. 1920. Fr. Ghiotto arrived there in 1922; Fr. Gambaratto in 1923, Fr. Pelligrini who visited the area via Lopit arrived there in 1927.

After the recourse to Mr. Symes the Governor General of the Anglo-Egyptian Sudan, permission for Catholics foundation in Lafon was later granted[27].

As there was no competition from other Christian denominations for the Päri area, the Catholics who were encouraged by these favorable conditions went ahead with proselytization. By 1935, they had established a station in Lafon among Jo Päri. Between 1935 and 1947, the site was moved twice in an attempt to get the most suitable place for missionary operations. Initially the mission station was at 'Akwo' about a mile or so from the foot of Mount Lipul. Monsignor Zambonardi chose this place during his visit to Lafon in 1936. Immediately after the choice of the site, Brother Fanti started construction work. A chapel, school and the Fathers residence were built but all were grass thatched. Then the teaching of the catechumenate started.

Missionary Activities in Lafon

The objectives for the missionary education at the time were to produce literate members of the Päri community to be able to become catechists and teachers and some to proceed to the seminary

---

27 Dellagicoma V., *History of the Catholic Church in southern Sudan. 1900-1995.* Khartoum 1996, p. 64.

to pursue education for priesthood. Nevertheless, before the catholic missionary produced catechists from the school in Lafon in 1926, they brought a catechist from the Lotuko tribe. But because Lotuko language is different from that of Päri, communication proved difficult. Alternatively, three catechists from the Acholi tribe were brought to Lafon mission from Gulu in Uganda to instruct the catechumens in Acholi language which is similar with that of Päri. The Pari people were then entrusted to Palotaka. However, the two catechists could not bear living in Lafon on account of many challenges. But despite challenges, Dominiko continued giving instruction to the catechumens. After two years of instructions, the catechumens were taken to Palotaka for Baptism. On 10th of March 1935 the following catechumens were baptized:

> Leopoldo Ajiba, Mario Ajeri, Giovani Gilo, Paulo Aluri, Silvio Ucala, Filippo Abong, Arkadio Libaka, Bernardo Agole, Lorenzo Akwai, Marko Mongo, Dario Oryet, Ilario Ngila, Simone Urec, Andrea Jada, Celestino Uyo, Taddeo Alendo, Tomaso Aceri, Yakobo Uwitti, Petro Uywa Comboni Missionary (1963: 4)

This group was followed on 12th May 1935 by Yosefo Bila, Leone Odaha, Lino Okedi, and Maria Mwonga. In the meantime priests from Torit kept visiting the area. Fr. De Berti arrived there in 1935; fathers Cereda and Crazzolara were there in 1936. While at Lafon, Father Crazzolara carried out the research on the Luo. During this time, the response from the natives to Christianity was very poor. The Päri saw Christianity as a foreign culture challenging their own.

Despite of this, another batch of catechumens was baptized at Palotaka and they include: Bortholo Lopwonya (1936), Milkiore Ulum (1939), Enriko Bago (1941), and Gudio Adude (1942). In 1939, the site of the mission was transferred from Akwo to its present location right at the foot of the mountain in the land of Kɔɔr people. Fr. Gambaratto (with the help of Bro. Ejidio), constructed the school, chapel and the residence for the priests using grasses. After the building was completed, the school was opened in 1940 and run by Bernado Agole the first Päri teacher[28].

In 1945 Father Negrini took over the responsibility of Lafon mission station. During his time, another school was constructed at Wiatuo village. This school was run by Milkiore Ulum meanwhile the one at the mission was run by Lino Ukedi. In 1947, Lafon mission was finally established as Parish Church.

Lafon Catholic Mission fell under the ecclesiastical jurisdiction of Bahr el Jebel prefecture headed by a monsignor. During the administration of Sisto Mazzoldi in 1951, the Lopit areas of Lalanga, Yahi Yahi, up to Ngaboli were attached to the Lafon Catholic Mission.

Geographically, the Lopit is situated about twelve miles east of Lafon. The people live by the side or on top of the mountain. Their society is divided into sections: Ngotira east consists of: Ihirang, Emehejek, Mura Lopit, Habironge, Lohobohobo, and Lohinyang. Lomia/Omiega group comprises; Ibonni (Leilang, Imuluha, Ibahore, Ibele, and Atarrangi) Ohutok: Ifite, Sohot, Longerum, and Ofuluho. Lalanga: Mura, Obihiti, Idwa, Attolok, Woliwoli, and Laado. Dorrik: Oganawati (Obelo, Accarrok, Haba, and Lodo). Ngotira west: Yahiyahi, Abuhanga, Longiro, Lothurumo, Ohirri, Idali (Thabwor, Loson). Ngaboli: Loluro, Ohidomook, Omiorok, Lahomiling... The Ngotira section speak Lopit language and are regarded a true Lopit. The Lomia and Ohutok groups speak Lotuho language with some Lopit dialects. They originate from Lotuko proper.

It is to be noted that the evangelization of the Lopit started at the beginning of Torit Mission in 1920. However, the area has not been frequented by priests like Lafon. Priest could visit the areas only once or twice a year and in hurry, as the villages were many and the tour around the mountain very long.

---

28 *Comboni Missionary, History of Lafon Mission, Lafon 1963 p. 5*

With the establishment of Lafon mission, the Catholic clergymen introduced education in the area. Boys from the neighboring Lopit and Lotuko tribes were also brought in Lafon mission school. At first, the number of Päri children at school was great. But later, pulled back by their culture, their number reduced.

Generally, western educational system is not encouraged be the Päri people. Hence, the degree of illiteracy is very high almost 98% especially among women. Lack of education is basically due to the reluctance of the Päri people to accept foreign culture. In many cases, the Päri parents interfered with the education of their children and often withdrew them from schools to get married, rear cattle, goats/sheep or simply to go and scare birds in crops' fields. In the past, Lafon mission school was the center for primary education for the Lopit. But in 1961, the school was transferred to Imehejek in Lopit land due to irregularities of the Päri children in school attendance. Difference between Lino (a Pari) and Atilio (the school Director from Logir) over who should be the school director in Pari, forced Fr. Gambratto to transfer the school to Emehejek.

From Lafon primary school a few Päri students managed to go to Okaru Seminary to pursue priestly vocation. Among them are; Enriko Bago, Agustino Ulwar, Simplicio Kolong, Hilary Boma Umol, Andrew Adyang, Alesio Utho, Louis Liduba, Joseph Ukelo and Valente Upuri and many others. Of all who were accepted, only four became priest of the Catholic Church namely; Hilary Boma was ordained priest at Milan (Italy) by Cardinal G. Colombo on June 28th 1966; Andrea Adyang was ordained on May 14th 1967 by Bishop Mazzoldi in Moroto (Uganda), Valente Upuri was ordained at Lachor (Uganda) on Dec. 6th 1969 and Joseph Ukelo was ordained priest at Tivoli (Italy) by Bishop G. Gacquinta on April 23th 1972. Enriko Bago reached the Major Seminary in Uganda and arrived up to probation year and left.

Note, the four priests mentioned above were ordained outside Sudan. The first Päri son ordained in Sudan is Fr. Elias Uwodo Abuk ordained priest on 7th May 1995, by Archbishop Gabriel Zubeir Wako, Khartoum Sudan. He was followed by Fr. Anthony Ubeo Gilo ordained priest on 23rd June 2000 by Archbishop Gabriel Zubeir Wako, Khartom /Sudan. Fr. Andrew Lidu Ukuk ordained priest in July 2003, at Khartoum by Archbishop Gabriel Zubeir Wako. Fr. Mark Opere was ordained priest in Italy in 2012 by bishop Menegatti.

Generally, the response from the community regarding evangelization was not encouraging at first. From the time of the establishment of the mission in 1935 up to 1958, the number of persons baptized according to Fr. Tito was only four hundred from the population of five thousand people. Majority of those baptized were children and a few women. Men were not interested at first to accept Christian faith. As time went by, many men got convinced and eventually accepted Christianity.

It is worth mentioning the Päri sons who joined Kit Seminary to persue training for brotherhood and later consecrated included; Bro. John Likori. Bro. Ignazio Likudu ordained (1959), Bro. Lunjino Rex Ulum (1983), Sabastiano Landi (1986) and Bro. Anjelo Kidi Akaro (1993). Later, all of the above left their religious profession. Other Päri sons who got trained at technical school include; Aliardo Limunu who finished higher school and later joined and completed Polytechnique in Khartoum. Rogaziano Ukec, Paskwale Arii, Arkanjelo Ujwok, Filipo Likudu, and Patrizio Ujwok received missionary educational support.

Priests, Brothers and Sisters who served in Lafon Mission from 1920-1964 includes; Crazzolaro, Della Piazza, Fasolo, Gambaretto, Tito Giuntoli, Isidori, Lazzari, Martinato, Nani, Negrini, Pasquali, Rizzi, Simeoni, Soriani, Tognon, Vadovato, and Vignocchi. **Sisters** includes; Baronchelli, Piazza and Roncali[29]

---

29 See Dellagiacoma, V. (1986) Missionaries in Southern Sudan, (1900-1964) Khartoum, Sudan.

Benefits of Western Education

The benefits which the Päri realized from the introduction of missionary education in their area are seen in the persons of Dr. Benedetto Nyikalo a civi engineer, Marko Arii another civil engineer, Aliardo Limunu an engineer, Louis Liduba an agriculturalist and Enriko Bago who first became a province commissioner and later minister in the then Southern Sudan Regional government in Juba. Hon. Bago was instrumental in the building of Lafon primary school, the construction of Lafon Torit road built in 1977 with the help of the Norwegian Church Aid, and the drilling of bore holes for the community in all the six villages are accredited to him. The reopening of Lafon primary school was facilitated by Ex-priest, Fr. Valente Upuri in 1970.

As mentioned earlier, the objectives of the missionary education were to train the natives to become teachers and catechists, a philosophy adopted from Bishop Daniel Comboni who says, "Save Africa by Africans". Below is a list of Päri sons who were trained as teachers and catechists and served at Lafon Catholic Mission:

Table 4.1 Trained teachers and catechists

Bernardo Agole Likada	from Bura village
Lino Ukedi	from Wiatuo village
Milkiore Ulum	from Kɔɔr village
Luke Upieu	from Wiatuo village
Hilary Udoge	from Bura village
Gabriel Umana	from Wiatuo
Petronio Kolong	from Kɔɔr village
Roberto Ritho	from Pugäri village
Umberto Alodo	from Kɔɔr village
Ermano Yaani	from Pugäri village
Celestino Uyo (Amini)	from Pucwa village

Andrea Ungweenyi	from Pucwaa village
John Likori	from Angulumeere
Bortholo	from Angulumeere
Andrea Ukorikori	from Wiatuo
Simone Urec (Audo)	from Bura village
Lorensio Idia	from Pugäri village
Jorjo Angwee	from Kɔɔr village

Other Christian congregations

In 1940s, a Päri man named Jacob Lodu and popularly known as Lipeendakooyo came (after been converted to Christianity in Uganda) to Lafon to evangelize the people. He preached that the people should not drink beer for it was evil. This message angered the Päri people. For the Päri consider beer as food and for someone to condemn it signal a bad message. So, angered by this message, the Mojomiji passed a decision to kill the pastor publicly in the morning. But while waiting for the morning to come, the brothers of Jacob came at night, took the pastor out of the custody and accompanied him to the bush. There, they told him to go to the Anywaa country. When the mojomiji got up in the morning, they found Lodu had escaped. He went and instead of proceeding to the Anywaa country, he settled among the Murle community and preached the word of God there. The author met Pastor Lodu in 1984 in Malakal town and confirmed the same story from him. Since then, no protestant man ever came to preach the word of God in Päri. It was in 1993 that the African Inland Church (AIC) appeared in the area to propagate for the religion. This group was followed (in 2015) by Episcopal Church of Sudan (ECS). They established their churches after the SPLA war of liberation has ended and the CPA signed in 2005. However, both congregations had limited activities and hence have few followers.

Introduction of Islam in Päri Country

The violent struggle waged by foreigners who had ambition in southern Sudan was for many times challenged by the front-line tribes mainly the Shulluk and Dinka. These tribes controlled the White Nile gate way to south. Early, the Moslem Arab northerners had wanted to push far south beyond parallel thirteen in order to extend the Arabization and Islamization process in the region. But they could not manage due to the resistance of the Nilotic people (Shilluk) at the frontier[30]. It was not however, until 1840 that these people and other local resistances were ultimately overcome by the Turco-Egyptian under Mohamed Ali the Viceroy of Egypt.

Although the aim of Mohamed Ali to enter southern Sudan was to control gold and ivory trade and to some extent to get slaves, his soldiers also introduced Islam in the region. And already by 1870s before Mahdia insurrection, the Arabization and Islamization process made a considerable progress in many parts of southern Sudan. Islam religion was established in the garrison stations during the reign of Emin Pasha when he was the governor of Equatoria province (1878- 1889). Emin Pasha, a German medical Doctor and formerly a Christian with the name Edward Schnizter converted to Islam while in the Mid-East and entered the Sudan administration when already a Muslim. It was during his administration of Equatoria that the first Muslim school 'kalwa' and a mosque were constructed in Jebel Lado, the provincial capital. It has been reported that during his time Islam flourished in Equatoria. However, during the Mahdist era, Islam declined in the south in general and in Equatoria in particular, because the Mahdists were a brutal repressive force and never propagated for Islam.

Despite all these, the Päri remained untouched by Islamic influ-

---

30 *Sandersons, op.cit., p. 8*

ences until the period of Condominium rule. After the establishment of the Anglo-Egyptian administration in the southern Sudan in 1898, Islamization and Arabization was introduced by government officials and workers who were Muslims, traders and Egyptians administrators and military personnel. But with the introduction of Christianity in southern Sudan, the British colonial government administrators discouraged the progress of Islam, which they decreed in the Closed District Ordinance of 1920. As such, only individual southern Muslims who resisted these prohibitions carried its banner forward. It was only after the relaxation of the restriction on Islamization that southern Muslims, helped by their northern companions began to propagate the religion. Among the Päri, the work of Suliman Uciel will fit this context.

In 1945, immediately after the Second World War, Suliman Uciel the indigenous Päri man from Pucwaa village was appointed chief for the community. He was a devout Muslim and practiced his faith in Islam. When he was made chief, he introduced Islam to his fellow Päri people. He set up one kalwa at Pucwaa his residential village and invited parents to send their children there for instructions. And indeed, a few children did join the school. But since the people had already received Christianity, chief Suliman for the first time found it hard to get more converts into Islam. However, when he brought white uniforms for attendance of Koranic School, other children got converted and joined the school. Each day, while observing his duty as chief, Suliman spent his free time teaching Islamic subjects like the recitation of the Holy Kroan and how to pray. The children at that time used to march during drill singing 'la illa Ila Allah!' This exercise used to draw the admiration of the inhabitants of the area. Sometimes later, he built a mosque in Pugäri village for the people to pray in. Suliman Uciel left Lafon for Torit town following the mutiny by the Equatoria Corps, which took place on August 18th, 1955 in Torit itself. He could not stay long in Lafon because the situation was not favorable. Suleiman resigned on 1st June 1956. In 1958 when things became worst, he fled to Uganda and died there afterward.

Chief Suleiman Uciel

Suleiman comes from a kingship family in Pucwaa village. When his father, Uciel died, Suleiman's mother went to Gondokoro where she married a Nubi soldier called Gubara. Later, Gubara went with his wife to Uganda taking with him Suleiman. During the First World War, many young men and government chiefs were recruited to the King's African Rifles (K.A.R) to fight on behalf of the British army. As a grown-up man Suleiman needed to work for his livelihood. So, he enlisted in the King's African Rifles and served under Col. Lilley. On retirement he came to Torit and worked for a number of years as a cotton buyer and was generally praised for his honesty, ability and good conduct. When cotton buying ceased, Suleiman went to Kenya for a year or more, and later returned to Torit. Since it was a British criterion to choose officials from the newly retired warriors, Suleiman, an ex KAR veteran, became the favored candidate for chieftaincy. He was appointed chief on 26/6/1945[31].

At Lafon, Tax collectors used to charge people more than the law required. When a native failed to produce money, the officials would confisticate a cow or goats and sometimes the leopard skin as substitutes. This action angered the entire community very much. But they could not do anything about it. When Suleiman became chief, the first work he did was to stop unbearable taxes imposed by corrupt government officials on the Päri people. This

---

31 "Source: Torit District Monthly Diary". (TD/66. D. Tribal: Appointment & Dismissal of Chiefs, 1929-1948). Southern Sudan Office, Juba)

move really relieved the people and earned him great respect from the people.

Before the event of 1955 in Torit which affected the growth of Islam among the Päri, the idea of circumcision introduced by Suliman made the children abandoned the kalwa. The Päri in their culture despise circumcision and a circumcised man finds it difficult in traditional marriage. Despite persuasion by Suliman Uciel that circumcision was good for Muslims, but because the Päri are a people who cannot be easily convinced to adopt foreign culture, they rejected it outright. This attitude is common to Nilotic people like the Päri. A lot has been said about Nilotic attitude towards foreigners.

For example, Sandersons have this to say,

> Nilotic people throughout their recorded history have been very resistant to external influences of any kind; whether Arab or European, Muslim or Christian, and this cultural conservatism and independence has been bolstered by unshakable conviction that they are superior to all other men [32].

So Islam died in Päri country due to this issue of circumcision and the departure of Chief Suliman Uciel to Uganda escaping the mutineers. The mosque he built in his time stood there till 1974 when it fell down due to disuse. Although he is a Muslim, there are many songs praising him for his good chieftainship. One of the songs says;

> Päri bende bende wo koomu ru, tim madir motho na- *yä*gä licabiiru, yor tɔngwa *rɔgɔ gäälä*. *Rwäth* bɛ wor uciel ongida miji Pagilo luupa lummi tɔng.

---

[32] *Sanderson, Op cit. p.6*

Attack on Lafon by Sudan Armed Forces

On18th August 1955, members of the Equatorial Corps of the Sudan defence force mutinied in Torit, Equatoria. The mutiny was the outcome of the growing tension between northern and southern Sudanese in the lead up of the self-determination plebiscite on independence from Egypt and was the culmination of an escatlating series of violent confrontation between Southerners and the new northern Sudanese authorities[33]. The mutiny had a devasting effect on both Arab northerners and black southernes. Many people died during this fight. Nevertheless, the war did not take long. The mutineers left the town and the government soldiers with the assistance of the British took control of it.

Soon after retaking Torit town, the Arab led government in Khartoum called for peace to prevail in the country. So, peace compaign was then launched in Torit and other towns in eastern Equatoria. Flying with the helicopter and speaking in Arabic and Lotuko languages, the compaigners communicated the message to all the people in all villages of Eastern Equatoria. They were calling the mutineers to come back to resume their normal work. But that was a trick. The fact of the matter was, the government wanted to take revenge to pay for the Arab traders, their children, women and army killed during the disturbances. In that compaign, some soldiers got persuaded and came back. Others like Ukedi Limanyimoi refused to go back to resume their works. Those who responded to the call were arrested, court-martialled and killed in cold blood and their bodies dumped in a mass grave in Himodonge about nine miles south east of Torit town. Among Päri sons who were executed are:

- Henriko Ukal Butha from Bura village, killed in Torit

---

33   Source: South Sudan National Archives, Juba; File No. 36: A. 1

- Buul Luka Abo Agula from Pucwaa village, killed in Torit
- Ukwor Ngodi Mangath from Kɔɔr, killed in Torit
- Upieu Lijikimeeri Nyakalamoi, a police man from Bura village killed in Juba

After this event, a rebellion known as 'Anyanya Movement' started. The following guerrilla fighters pioneered the movenment: Ex-Priest Fr. Saturnino Ohure, William Deng, Ali Gbatala, Taping Odongi, Aggrey Jaden and others. At first, the rebellion was disorganized. It became organized and active in 1963 under the leadership of Joseph Lagu.

In 1965 (when Kwara age set were in power), a government army force came to Lafon to arrest a rebel soldier called Masimino Loguto. The army arrived in the late evening and surrounded the villages. The villagers however stayed ignorant of this move until morning when the people who had wanted to go to crop fields for work encountered the soldiers who ordered them to return to their houses. It was from here the news spread to all people that their villages had been besieged by the enemy. Immediately, members of ruling age set mobilized and sent a delegation to meet the invaders. The commander of the army told them to hand over Masimino Loguto or otherwise they would burn the area. The Päri refused to comply. And consequently, at sun rise, the army randomly started shooting. The children and women ran for cover leaving the mojomiji to defend the land. Although there were no human casualties in this attack, the houses of the clan of Nyikeeu (situated between Akoy and the Catholic Church) and the houses belonging to Atwo clan that lay between Bupi and Angulumeere were burned. The operation lasted three hours only and stopped. At 9:00 O'clock in the morning, the attackers withdrew and left for Torit.

Attack on Lafon by SPLA forces

The first town captured by Sudan People's Liberation Army (SPLA) forces in Equatoria soil was Lafon. The SPLA forces under the command of Arok Thon Arok came to the area in December 1985 and overrun it. The villagers responded positively to the SPLA campaign: women cook food and was shared with the soldiers while men joined in a large number as recruits. The number was so big that even Commander Arok complained to the local leaders to prevent more people from joining the movement. He told the mojomiji that if a family had three or more children, it could contribute one and leave the rest to care for the family. But such advice was not listened to. The youth continued pouring to the camp to be recruited. In the end, the Päri provided what can be called the first battalion of soldiers recruited by the SPLA from Equatoria. And indeed, President Salva Kiir in our meeting of 2nd July 2015, acknowledged the huge contribution provided by the Päri people in two great wars of the Sudan (Anyanya war and SPLA's) in which he both participated. The new recruits were then taken for training at the military bases in Ethiopia. In 1986, the battalion named 'tingili was graduated with Päri sons forming the largest number. While in Ethiopia, the government soldiers came and established a government garrison at Lafon. After training in Ethiopia, some Päri sons (about 70), returned as SPLA troops and attacked the government army garrison in Lafon in April 1986 and re-captured the town.

Lafon is considered militarily strategic by both the government army and the SPLA forces. In 1988, the SPLA set up a headquarters in Lafon. During that time, the villagers stayed neutral. The area never allied with the government forces and initially did not take sides when the Nasir group under Dr. Riak Macar attempted to oust Dr. Garang in August 1991. It is to be noted that some Equatorian commanders including Päri sons who were under Dr. Riak (when the incident happened) remained as part of the Nasir group.

In October 1992, when William Nyuon defected from the SPLA main faction, he took with him the Nuer and a number of Equatorians including Päri sons and en-camped in Lafon. Two weeks later, Riak Macar sent him a re-enforcement of troops from Nasir to face the SPLA – Garang faction who were pursuing Nyuon. However, the local authority refused to take sides in favour of either faction. The mojomiji attempted to make reconciliation of the two factions, but in vain. Consequently, on January 4th 1993, the SPLA Garang faction under the command of Isaac Obutu Mamur and Pieng Deng Kuol clashed with the forces of William Nyuon in Lafon which ended with the defeat of Nyuon forces. During the fight, the natives ran to the bushes or crop fields and made shelters and settled. Nyuon then withdrew and joined the government forces at Mugiri about forty miles west of Lafon. The SPLA Garang forces then looted properties and burnt down the six villages.

In April 1993, the Garang faction abandoned the town and the forces of William Nyuon entered the town again. While at Lafon, the SPLA main faction (Torit faction) sent Commander Ukec Alak (a Päri) with some soldiers to meet with the local authority demanding the expulsion of Nasir group from the area. But he was not listened to because the people had turned against the SPLA Garang faction for the great damage they had caused to the people by looting and destroying the houses. Before meeting the public, the mojomiji told them to go back to their bases or otherwise they would be mishandled. So Alak left and went back and joined his group.

Sometimes later, another group of Päri officers of Torit faction came to Lafon to see with their eyes the burnt villages. Upon their arrival, eleven of them were quickly arrested by Commander Peter Bol Kong (of Naser faction) with the collaboration of Madaan the ruling age set at the time. Shortly, after their arrest, the leadership of Nasir group issued an order for their execution.

Thus, the following officers were executed in cold blood:

Capt. Simon Ukac
1st Lt. Andrea Umo
1st Lt. Angelo Ukumu Ulum
1st Lt. George Urua Abuk
1st Lt. Galdino Uryeu
1st Agustino Alak Uyin
1st Lt. Henry Ujwok Gore Yapo
1st Lt. Pompeo Uwendo Jada
1st Silvio Munik
2nd Lt. Agustino Jang Abuk
R/SM. Valentino Ukongo

The death of these officers angered many Päri people. Fr. Joseph Ukelo (a Päri) saddened by this tragedy, decided to visit Lafon to raise his objection to the killings of the innocent soldiers. He addressed the people criticizing and pointing out the mistakes the mojomiji had done. Shortly after the function, he was arrested by the forces of Riak Macar under Peter Bol Kong. The priest was taken and locked in prison in Mugiri a government military garrison. It was after a serious pressure from the Church leaders that William Nyuon released the priest who was then transported to Nairobi.

Not long after this, commander Nyuon himself and his forces left Lafon and joined SPLA main faction under Dr. John Garang. The departure of Nyuon forces from the area enabled the army to come in and occupied Lafon garrison. Since April 1993, the Jebel remained under the control of the Sudan Armed Forces, until 2002 when it was recaptured by the SPLA Forces. The split of Naser faction from the SPLA mainstream in 1991 had devastating impact not only on humans, but on the political and military situation in the movement. This issue was so terrible that peace lovers demanded the warring parties to talk peace and be reconciled. In 1994, the movement for peace and unity between the SPLM/A main faction led by Dr. John Garang de Mabior and South Sudan Independent Movement SSIM/A faction led by Dr. Riak Macar kick started. On April 1995, the Lafon Declaration for the reconciliation, re-unification and re-integration of forces in the SPLM/A movement was signed by Dr. John Garang de Mabior and William Nyuon Bany on behalf of Dr. Riak Macar. In 2004, the SPLA leadership under Chairman, Dr John Garang de Mabior met to discuss over peace issue with the government in Khartoum. The meeting decided that a delegation be sent to Nairobi to engage in peace negotiation. Thereafter, the selected delegates were sent to Machacos for peace negotiation which ended up with the signing of the Comprehensive Peace Agreement (CPA) in 2005, in Kenya.

Chapter Five

Formation of Age Group (Laange)

Besides family and kinship, age system is one of the most important social institutions in Päri society. Usually, at an early stage of their growth (about six years old), young people of both sexes begin to form separate age groups. Children of approximately the same age in each village identify themselves with a common name that the whole group knows. In many cases, men adopt at later stage names of age groups chosen by a similar group in Wiatuo apparently because it is the largest and the most populated village in the Päri country. However, this rule does not apply to females. For example, the girls of Pucwaa may have a name different from their agemates in Bura village.

It must be noted that the Päri society classifies the youth according to different phases of their development. There are nine phases to be passed before an individual youth could be integrated into the ruling age set. The difference between one phase and another is usually three years. The distinction between one age group from another can be noticed during dances as well as in the camps 'baali'. Each age group has an independent camp where they reside and conduct their activities. During dances, each age group is decorated in distinct and special ornaments and body paints. No member of a specific age group is allowed to wear ornaments or decorate himself

Formation of Age Group (Laange)

in a style belonging to a group to which he is not a part. He who imitates another group style is sanctioned (beaten) by the group he is imitating.

Classification into phases of growth constitutes the basis of social advancement of the youth. It is reflected during käruma or buul dances. The first age group is composed of youngsters who are given the name, 'ayang- apiendi-nguny-kallo. Members of this group do not have a club' "baalu /baali". They are the first group to appear in the playground during käruma dances. The group is promoted to the second phase after completing three years. In the second stage, members of the age group use ashes to paint their feet white during the käruma dances. The Päri called this style of painting, 'buuti' (boots). The third phase consists of painting of heads and necks with a whitewash known as Läppi tar meaning white ocher. This symbol represents a type of bird known as 'buulu' (fish bird). In the fourth phase, members are identified by 'ligaande'. These are feathers of cocks specially designed for dances. They are worn on the head. The fifth phase in social advancement needs members of an age group to wear 'uthwonnhi'. In other words, they have to dress in feathers of a bishop bird which are woven and plaited for the purpose of käruma dances. The six phases is the 'athuol'. This is when members reach maturity. In this stage, they are entitled to courtship and thus, love affairs and marriages. The seventh stage is 'akuuru or ukook. The members of this group wear feathers of a bird called ukook (cattle egret). The eighth stage is 'agaal' or 'thorra' referring to the white Heron. Members of this group wear feathers of this bird to dance with. The ninth and the last stage are 'Jo col' referring to black people. Members of this group are called black because they do not wear arnaments on their bodies during the dance. When an age group has undergone all these phases, its members are thrown into a waiting stage. In other words, they remain in a stage of transition between the youth and the ruling age sets. They have to spend three years before they are integrated into the ruling age set. During this period, they are called *'läppi kwar'* meaning red soil.

Age set is headed by a prince (wä rwäth) and assisted by councilors (atielli) who act as messengers to the princes. Princes and councilors form a clique and are responsible for the administration of the whole group. To the Päri, laange are the institutions within which the youth grow and learn community functions, assimilates community values, norms and rules of the society; they build their own clubs in which they discuss their own affairs. They share their meals and organize dances. Also, they go for hunting wild animals spending several days in the bush to test their manhood. They compose songs about their hunting and competence of the group. They engage in physical fight with other age groups to test their strength and bravery and many more activities.

Elders in Päri society encourage youth inter-group fights using whips and sticks. The main purpose is to train young men to be brave. The youth are taught all tactics needed to face foreign aggression. Thus, fighting between one group and another is very common in all the Päri villages. The sum total of youth activities exposes the weak and the strong individuals within the group. Consequently, great runners, brave men, cowards, wrestlers, spokesmen emerged in Päri society during these activities. At the same time, the group develops a spirit of togetherness and love for one another strengthens ties as members of the age group grow.

Age sets are useful institutions in Päri society in as much as communal work is concerned. The responsibility of building assembly house (Kaboore), bringing firewood for elders to warm themselves during cold weather, cultivating and harvesting the fields of the rainmaker and that of the bird controller rest upon the youth. Youth participation in communal work is important. In 1976, the people of Kɔɔr managed their embankment (adiira) because of the support of the youth; the diversion of river kineiti in 1940s to make it flow directly to Päri territory was successfully carried out because of the support of the youth. Youth participation in various activities plays a major role in the Päri society. In fact, one is considered a youth until he is initiated into the Wegipach.

Classification of members of an Age Group

The theory of social stratification applies to the structure of age groups in Päri society. The principle of age group does not imply that members of an age group have strictly the same age. There are differences in age of individuals comprising an age group. Consequently, the Päri regroups a number of people who have approximately the same age into a stratum of the age group. These groups of people who have approximately of the same age are identified by specific titles. There are three groups making the general strata in an age group which are the following:

Wie. This term literally means the head. This group represents the most senior members of the age group

Koore. The word refers to the human body between the head and the limbs. This group is composed of all members of middle age in the age group.

Thare. This term is used to designate the lower part of human body below the waist. Indeed, this stratum comprises the youngest members of the group

However, there is an exception with respect to the general rule of classification of an age group. It applies only to two Päri villages, namely Wiatuo and Bura. To them, there are subgroups in the first two strata (wie and koore) of an age group which are subdivided as follows; the most senior members of the age group are subdivided into two categories:

Wie. Like in the general classification, this group is composed of the oldest members of an age group

Ucula. Although they are all senior members of an age group, the fact that their age is slightly less than those constituting the Wie, makes them the junior members within a senior age group.

Similarly, the stratum composed of middle age members of an age group is subdivided into two categories:

Koore. This category is composed of older members in the stratum of middle age members of an age group.

Paar. Members in this category are the youngest individuals in the middle group.

In Päri society, individuals within an age group are also classified according to their status. The status of an individual could be hereditary, prescribed or earned. The status of an individual is achieved when that individual distinguishes himself as a wrestler, brave man, and positive rhetoric (liloo). The first three classes of individuals are decorated differently in an age group. The bravest men are given red flags while those who are neither brave nor cowards, are given a flag decorated red and any other colour mixed together. A black flag known as 'allullu' is given to the most dedicated member of an age group. The qualification for this flag consists of the defense of the young members of the group against non-members in events of fighting. Also, the qualification must include bravery and physical strength. In the village of Bura and Wiatuo, this honour can be given to two individuals. The badges and honour are usually given by princes and councilors to those who qualify for the award. There are some exceptions in awarding this honour. No award is given to a prince however brave or strong he is in the age group. A councilor whose activities deserve an award can be decorated like any other ordinary members of a group.

It is worth mentioning that any individual who has been decorated for whatever social function is expected to demonstrate his ability to perform the functions accordingly. That is, he must not fear otherwise in a situation that endangers the community or a member of an age group. Should a decorated person fear when the enemies threaten the community or members of the age group, that particular individual is automatically sanctioned. The immediate sanction is the withdrawal of the badge representing his honour.

Privileges of Social Status

The stratification of an age group and the social status of each member of such a group play a significant role in several functions. For instance, an individual may decide to summon the youth to cultivate his field. This function necessitates the offer of a bull that will be slaughtered for this people to consume. The age group is remunerated by the distribution of the meat of the bull. There is a predetermined system of consumption and distribution, which corresponds to one's class in the age group and the title an individual, has acquired in the process of social activities in the group. The bull is always slaughtered after the group has completed the work of cultivation. On this day, two or three members of the group stay at home to slaughter the bull and supervise the cooking while the majority goes to finish the work. It must be noted that not all parts of the animal will be cooked and eaten by the whole group. The parts concerned are; the ribs, pancreas, liver, kidneys, lungs and bowels. Other parts are usually divided among members.

On return from the field, food is distributed according to the strata in an age group. The Wie group must take the whole liver and some meat. The Koore group is served the whole heart and their ration of meat. However, the Thare group is deprived from getting any special type of meat. They consume the ration of food that is meant for everybody. The phase of communal consumption ends here. The process of distribution of the bulk of the meat begins after everybody has eaten. The role of social categories and decorated individuals in the general stratification intervenes at this moment. The whole right hind leg (waadhi cwiic) of the animal is given to the Wie group. Members of the group will cut off the lower limb known as Lidang. Flesh will be removed from the leg leaving a little meat on the bone. The highest-ranking prince will take the bone called 'cuodho. If there two princes in the group with equal rank, they will divide the bone equally. The best runner takes the limb (lidang); ordinary members of the Wie group will divide the rest of meat removed from the hind leg. Ucula category of the wie appropriates the right fore leg (badi cwiic). The best runner in this category takes the limb cut away from the leg. The Ucula category offers the bone of the meat between the knee and the shoulder and gives it to the clan councilor (atiel). In addition, the chest called utukku is given to the bravest man in the Ucula a sub group of wie. The hip (baamo) is divided into two parts; the part with the tail is normally given to the wie group who in turn offer it to the holder of the black flag; the best wrestler takes the other part of the hip. The left hind leg (waadhi caam) is given to Koore group who will effect its distribution similar to that we have described above.

Unlike the case of the right hind leg, the left limb separated from the leg is given to the best runner of this group. The Thare group receives the left fore- leg (badi caam). This group will distribute this part of meat in a similar way the right fore leg was handled. The neck is distributed to the Thare group and divides it among them. The head is given to wegipaac (ruling age set). The waist (pier) is given to the beggars. In the absence of the beggars, Thare group will divide it among its members. Once the distribution is complete, each one takes home his ration of meat. This meat will be cooked and eaten by the group at breakfast time. Whoever, eats this meat alone, is sanctioned. Members can confiscate a quantity of dura or a goat which they kill and consume together including the man who is sanctioned.

Initiation Rites

Age groups undergo special ceremonies when they have satisfied all conditions during the phase of group formation. On the completion of the transitional period, the ruling age sets informs the group about its initiation and integration into the ruling age class. The age group is informed at the beginning of the cultivation season so that they could begin preparations. The motive behind the early information is to secure the approval of the concerned age group. When the group is not ready to be initiated, they may decline. For example, during the reign of Kilang, the Adeeyo age group (except that of Pucwass village) turned down the offer to join the ruling age set under the pretext that they were not prepared. A year after, they told the ruling age sets about their readiness to be initiated and integrated into the administration. But to their disappointment, the ruling age set rejected and cancelled the whole programme.

Preparations for initiation rites are composed of two basic items namely dancing decoration (Ngwaal) and food consumption. In the first place, each individual member of the age group must make sure that he has the right plaited black ostrich feathers known as 'litäängo' and secures leopard skin which is worn on the back. In addition, each member must dress in special beads that should cover the chest (tiiki kwac). Minor items such as puoda, ugari, eye glasses and others are also worn in their bodies. Should it happen that the family lacks these items, they can borrow one from friends and other families.

Modernization has nevertheless been influencing the process of decoration. The most notable influence is that each member of the group to be initiated has to buy a pair of shoes and stockings. The members of the group are allowed to put on decorated skirts and short sleep T-shirts upon which leopard skins are worn. Under this particular situation, members of the litäängo' group will smear mud decoration on parts of arms and legs which are not covered by clothes and stockings. Mud itself is a sign of entry of an adolescent into the groups of adults. In the meantime, wives and families of those to be initiated, prepare by making ingredients of beer which should be made ready waiting the day of the celebration. The dress prescribed for the ceremony consists of decorated goat skins skirts (duupe), aprons and beads worn around the waist, fore head, arms and other parts of the body.

The initiation ceremony has been undergoing considerable changes especially in the timing. It used to coincide with the ceremony of harvest (nyalam). Nowadays, the ceremony takes place before the feast of harvest. Initiation process starts at Wiatuo village where the members of this village are taken to a place called akwo (about two miles from the village) at dawn and the ritual performed. There, the senior group who had already been initiated is assembled separately from the new group. Elders then offer advice and instruct the new group about the administration of the people and land; defense of the community and property, as well as their duty to handle internal or external threats. In the meantime, elders smear mud on the incoming group, giving a sign of maturity. At the end of the ritual performance, one elder gets up, and tells the group that they are wasting time at the assembly point when the enemy is already attacking their families behind.

Formation of Age Group (Laange)

Nowadays a gun is fired. The speech or gunfire gives a signal that the group must race back to the village to defend the people and property. At this point the group burst into running. The first person that reaches the dancing ground is considered the best runner of the group.

While the group is running home, elders follow them in a procession (ipuura). The procession continues until the whole group reaches the dancing ground of Wiatuo. There, the people dance briefly and stop. The elders then enter the Assembly house, where they take their seats arranged in groups. Then the wives of the initiates bring in beer for elders to drink. The beer is distributed accordingly and then people start drinking. In the meantime, initiates disperse each taking his weapons back home and enjoy themselves while waiting for the evening to dance. In the evening people celebrate and enjoy themselves with food and drinks.

A similar function is concurrently performed by elders in each of the five villages. The only difference is the venue where initiation is conducted and the timing. Wiatuo elders conduct initiation rite at Akwo a few miles outside the villages while other villagers conduct the same to their counterparts in assembly house. In other words, the group to be initiated assembles in the Assembly house in the afternoon and receives same instructions and advice given to their counterparts at Akwo. Immediately after initiation rites performed, the group hurriedly goes to dress dance ornaments and march to Wiatuo village to participate in the great dances there. The celebration takes three days after which the group becomes junior partners of the ruling age set. Each member of this group is therefore, allowed to compose or make public his personal song called 'acira' which expresses sorrow or gratitude. During this time, no member of the youth can dispute their authority and action.

Women Age Grades

In Päri, women have age set of their own which corresponds to that of men. Like men, each group gives itself a name by which they are known. They conduct activities as a group; they organize nyikiro dances, collect firewood as a group and perform any work assigned to them by the ruling age set. However, when they marry, they join the age set of their husbands. Usually when they meet as wives of the same age set, they identify themselves with the name by which their husbands are called. For instances, the wives of Kwara say, *wana määndi Kwara*, meaning we are the wives of Kwara age set. In any occasion, they share responsibilities and act as co-wives. In this society, wives of the ruling age set are vested with powers to organize, direct and control women functions. They act as women leaders. In funeral places, for instance, they supervise the cooking, beer distribution to the mourners and receive visitors bringing gifts to the bereaved family.

The Päri categorise women into four stages of physical growth. *Nyakɔɔ (pl. nyakäwee)* is a young unmarried girl; *Juri (pl. juccee)* is a young woman who has produced one child or two; *mio(pl. mee)* is a woman of child bearing age and *Linnyo (pl. linyi)* refers to an old woman who can no longer produce a child. Men too are categorized in a similar manner. Awuobi (pl. awuope) is a young man; cidwong (pl. cidoongɛ) is an old man; janngo (pl. jaa) is a very old man and wuo (pl. wee) is a father;

Age set names

Age set names are sometimes associated with the concept of bravery and power. For example, a group of ageset in Wiatuo village called Morumaafi has named itself 'Israel'. Another group called 'Kilang' in Kɔɔr village named themselves as 'America'. And an age group in Bura village named themselves Mulle (Murle) a name of a tribe in Upper Nile. The significance of these names suggests the powereful and brave because Israel and America are powerful and courageous nations that can face their enemies without fear. Likewise, Murle is one of the strongest fighters in South Sudan. The *kwara* age set are also called 'madir'. This is a name by which the Päri call the British colonial army who defeated them in 1912. The group consider themselves strong and powerful like the British colonial forces. Further, names of fierce animals like, elephant, lion hyena, etc have also been used as names for an age set. For example, the people of Angulumɛɛrɛ are called 'Nyibworo' the lioness. That means they are wild and strong like the beast. And the current rulers called themselves 'Daaru or Daanu' a type of a poisonous snake. The names; Thomme (elephant), Ibou (hyena), Mura (village name in Lopit and Lotuko), Akaro (name for Toposa), and Kalang are of Lotuko origin.

Päri early names listed in Kurimoto, E. & S, Simonse (1998:39), (Table 2.5) and as quoted below, are Bari age-set names.[34]

Table 5.1 Pari age set names of Bari origin

Päri	Bari	Meaning in Bari
Kwe	Lokwe	Those who stick feathers in their hair
Akem	Akim	The overturners
Muura	Mura	The unripe
Amukwonyin	Mukkonyen	Those with closed eyes, because they fear nothing

---

34 Resonnance of Age Systems in southeastern Sudan. In Kurimoto, E. & S. Simonse (Eds), Conflict, Age & Power in North East Africa: Age system in Transition, PP 38-39. Oxford: James Currey. Nairobi E.A.E.P., Kampala: Foundation Publishers, Athens: Ohio University Press

Mirithigo	Mertiko	The intoxicated
Bongcut	Bonswot	The earshakers
Corogo	Soroko	The stabbers
Limojo	Limojong	Those who stay in their places
Amerkolong	Merkolong	Sun drunk
Alangore	Loungure	The bright-eyed who turn amorous glances on all women

The Päri started naming age sets in their language around 1930s. Below are the examples.

Table 5.2 Päri age set names and their meanings

Name   Meaning in Päri

Kuru	Young bees
Kalang	Foreign word
Wandi-tiɔ	Calabash for the bead(beads)
Ucwaada	Do something repetitively
Ukweer	Edible fruit
Lilaalɔ	Lyre, a substitute for salt
Kwara	Dried human faeces
Bondipala	Shaft/handle for a knife
Ithi-yio	Ear of a rat
Yulu	Green fly
Kilang	Foreign word
Thäängakwo	Half of Akwo forest
Ith-ucɔɔk (Anywaa)	Leave of a plant
Akɛɛo/Akɛɛyo	Type of vegetable
Maridi	A town in western Equatoria
Adeeo/Adeeyo	Burnt food at the bottom of a pot
Ithi-bule (Madaan)	Leave of bule tree

Formation of Age Group (Laange)

Boondikwɛɛri	Wooden handle for a hoe
Madir	Director/administraror (Arabic word)
Lidiit	Type of weaver bird
Kwodidhiɛng	Shield for cattle
Acaac	Red pepper
Agwiɛnɔ	Named after a hen (gwiɛno)
Adhiɛngɔ	Named after a cow (dhieng)
Sijuni	An Arabic word for prison warders
Buya	Name of Buya/larim tribe

While Päri have borrowed age set names from the neighbouring tribes, the Lokoya their neighbor to the south west have also borrowed and adopted age set names of the Päri. Names such as Kilang, Thäängakwo, Ith-ucɔɔk, Akɛɛo, Maridi, and Adeeo have been adopted as model by the Lokoya of Liria village.

Table 5.3 Names of generation sets (for both men and women groups) and their order of correspondence are listed below.

Women's names	Men age set names
Ithi-lworo	Kilang
Alilɛɛgi	Thäängakwo,
Ukwili	Ith-ucɔɔk
Ukuro	Akɛɛo/Akɛɛyo
Ugäbu (ith-ugäbu)	Maridi
Tiɔ	No counterpart
Biinnyo	Adeeo/Adeeyo
Ucɔl	No counterpart
Ithi-gwaana	Ithi-bule/Madaan
Ithi-kwäro	Boondikwɛɛri/morumaapi
Ithi-gooy	Madir
Ith-ubacca	Lidiit

Ith-ukɔndɔ(ugeengo wang yoo) Marik/ Kwodidhieng
Ithi-leero   Ith-acaac
Utwiila   Agwiɛnɔ
Bada-cagur   Adhiɛngɔ
utwilɔ   Sijuni
Kar-ingwäk   Buya

Historical Notes

Graded age system started among the Päri society a long time ago. It is not known whether the system was adapted before Luo migrations from Wipäri or that the community has copied their neighbors: Lopit, Lotuko, Lokoya, Bari, or the Toposa tribes. In this system, individual age group gives itself a name. But the ruling age set takes the name of the most senior age group. Historically, *Libuoceri* age set is remembered among the generations that lived before the new system of governance called 'wic' and popularly known as *mojomiji* was introduced in Päri society. This generation was well known for their inability to protect and defend the community against foreign aggression.

It is said that, whenever an enemy came, they could not resist but uttered such words; *culukɛɛu, culukɛɛu, ayak ayak*, a warning of alarm which was understood by the inhabitants that the enemy had come. And so, people ran to the mountain settlement to hide. The Päri began challenging their enemies during the time of 'Akara' age set who were children of Libuoceri. They fought and won several battles against their enemies. As a result, the community descended the mountain to dig their fields a mile or so from the foot of mount Lipul. It was during Akara that the Päri dug several surface ponds (aguule) for storing rainwater which they used in the winter when the water became scarce. Today, these ponds can still be seen in each

Formation of Age Group (Laange)

village's territory. In Bura, we find *agul adia*, Pucwaa has (*agula wɛɛndɔ*); Wiatuo has Jɔɔru and *Mɛɛnya*; Kɔɔr has *Rubugu* and *Licɔl*, Angulumɛɛrɛ has *wathe* and Pugäri has *agul Akara*. Akara warriors made the Päri well known to the neighbors and to the tribes beyond their borders. The subsequent generations later adopted their policies and thus made the community great.

Chapter Six

Political Institutions and Authority

All societies are organized into political and social institutions. It is through social organization that the flow of authority is regulated in accordance with the social pact that binds communities together in a given society. Sources of authority are determined by members of society and distributed among institutions, individuals or groups of individuals within the framework of a pact. In the real-world organized members of society tend to encroach on powers entrusted to political leaders. The practical example today is the case of the House of Commons, which grew slowly while taking away certain responsibilities from the monarchy. Similarly, the Päri society has been evolving while encroaching on powers of the monarchy. The Political structure of this society consists of the ruling age sets, the monarchy and the chief. Each of these structures exercises some kind of political authority, which is distributed unevenly among the existing institutions.

The Monarchy

The system of monarchy is the original political and social institution of the Päri society. All the other institutions came into existence through the evolution of the society and its contacts with the outside world. Each village in Päri society has a king who is recognized by the community as the legitimate leader and source of authority. This is a hereditary institution. When the village king dies, the son of the deceased king succeeds him. The Päri society is composed of six villages, which means there are six kings. However, the king of Wiatuo is the most important one among equals. The reason why this king is important is that, he is entrusted with the function of rain administration of the whole Päri society. No king besides him is allowed to make rain or own rain medicine. Further, the king of Wiatuo is the only king whose approval is sought by any organized prospective wegipaac aspiring to take over power from the age set in power.

In the past, the king could dictate to the people because he was an absolute monarch. Nobody could challenge his authority nor contest his decisions. The emergence of Wegipaac and the role of the government in establishing law and order and collection of taxes have contributed greatly to the decline in the authority of the kings. Consequently, authority and power are shared between the king and these new institutions in certain areas of competences. What is interesting is that, while powers of the kings as individuals have declined dramatically, the powers of weegipaac still remains in the hands of princes who are members of this institution.

Päri Kings

Below are the names of the kings in the six villages who ruled and died at Lafon (1700-2019) and the living kings.

Pugäri	Pucwaa	Wiatuo	Bura	Angulumɛɛrɛ	Kɔɔr
Dimo	Nyuunga	Uthienho	Mucuga	Uyuw	Ajuri
Alɛɛl	Libay	Lidu	Lidu	Jaal	Ranga
Gäri	Ukeelo 1	Udiek	Ujwok	Lidɛɛng	Col
Caai	Ukeelo 2	Alikoori	Laandi	Apido	Ukwoor
Unaam	Ukumu Ucala	Kidi	Nyamär	Udiingo	Ukwom Uluum
Uryeu	Udwaar	Ungang	Likonga Lithiiri	Agaakono	Okumu Liyiime
Amijo[1]	Pɛɛtha	Akaro Alwanya	Ngoomi Lithiiri	Ubote Ugäala	Urec Liyiime
Unam Uryeu	Awäälamuk	Fidele Unagang	Apira Lithiiri	Ujul Udingo	Matia Liyiime
Lithena Amijo	Biinyo Pɛɛtha	Nyibur	Paulino Pethamuge	Api Ulo	Atilio Ubur Libonya
Kabuy Unaam	Mugie Pɛɛtha	Akoligera Ungang			Ukelo Jabada
		Ubote Ukeelo			
Nyangabong	Apermoi	Uniepa Ajamoi			
Muthokori Licinga	Ukulo Mugie				
Angida	Ucen Aliema	Buul Ligwäälu			
Anguu Likono		Peter Upwoyo			
Abor Malanya		Mangisto Akaro			

Table 6.1 Päri Kings

Power struggle among princes

Päri kings marry many wives. And it is the Päri law of succession that the first son from the first wife becomes the successor in the event the king dies. Other brothers or stepbrothers from other wives are usually pushed aside and over time, they too branch and form separate clans. Figure 2.7 above which arrays Päri kings, illustrates that fully. In this particular case, I shall talk about power struggle among princes in Wiatuo village. Wiatuo is given special attention here because of the inner fighting for kingship position by princes. Päri law of succession maintains that the elder son born from the first wife of the king becomes a king. This law is sometimes not followed by the people of Wiatuo. For example, Uthienho who became the first king of Wiatuo took this position in violation of this rule. He is the youngest son but then his father chose him to be king. In Wiatuo, he married a number of wives. His first wife called Apieu bore him a son whom he named 'Lidu'. When he died, Lidu succeeded him in accordance to the law of successiion. Lidu also married as his first wife, a woman called 'Yigɛ who became the mother of Udiek. When Lidu died, his son Udiek succeeded him. Udiek married a woman called Adue and bore him a son called Ukoth Nyangiro (elder son) and Alikoori Uwitti the next born. Alikoori was known for his warlike attitude and a dictator. His father Udiek hates his behaviour. Before Udiek died, he noticed Alikoori's interest of becoming king in his place. But aware of the behaviors of Alikoori who was a war like; the father opposed such a move. He wanted Ukoth and not Alikoori to replace him. But after the death of king Udiek, Alikoori who was ambitious, worked out his own way and with the support of his age mates, he forced out Ukoth and became the rwäth of Wiatuo. Frustrated as he was, the deposed Ukoth later formed a sub clan now called 'Tung Ukoth Nyangiro' leaving Alikoori heading the royal clan. Alikoori himself had two sons; Liriathiigo born by a woman called nyingwe and Kidi Gumar born by a woman called Akuru. When king Alikoori died, people expected his first born (Liriathiigo) to replace him. But a similar drama happened. Kidi, who was younger, took over the power by force and became king. However, when Kidi died, his son 'Ungang' (born by a woman called Uywaa) succeeded him in accordance to the law.

King Alikoori Uwitti Nyilang

Alikoori is one of the notorious kings the community has ever had. Throughout his period of rule, the community never got good harvest. Persistent drought caused severe hunger and starvation. Yet, no one dared to complain. Whoever complained or talked about availability of food in another country, was seized and strangled. His guards used a wooden pole known as *arɛɛk* to kill his opponents. He showed no sympathy and grossly disregarded the feelings of his subjects. For example, if he learnt that a cow of Mr. so and so produced more milk, he sent his guards to bring the cow to his kraal. When he saw a beautiful girl or wife of somebody else, he ordered his guards to bring that girl or wife to become his own. Yet nobody could utter any word of complaint. If some one from any of the five villages (Pucwaa, Bura, Kɔɔr, Pugäri, and Angulumɛɛrɛ) committed a murder, Alikoori would order the people of Wiatuo to carry out punitive measures known as *ubutha* against the entire village where a crime has been committed. They would loot the properties, drive off cows or goats of that village, eat or distribute them among themselves. Alikoori one time ordered punitive measures against the people of Angulumɛɛrɛ during which the goats belonging to a man called Alappa were all killed and eaten. This action angered Alappa so much that he abandoned Lafon and migrated to Lokiri village of the Lotuko. There, before he died, he cursed the whole Päri community to suffer defeats from their enemies. And according to the legends, Alappa curse had a devastating effect on the people. This was proved when the people of Lokiri defeated the *Päri* during the Limojo era.

Alikoori is a leader who feels happy at the suffering of the people. At times he walked around the villages to know the mood of his opponents. Usually, when children saw him, they followed him singing songs expecting him to offer something to eat. The song reads,

> Nyilang (Alikoori) a-oo, kec bongo tin ooo, kec bongo tin ooo.
> Nyilang has come and so, there is no hunger today.

This song is repeated many times by the children. Amused by this song, Alikoori used to throw (to the children) some groundnuts and boiled nuts from higglig fruits known as *kɛɛk* which he carried in a bag (upir/ nyabonkoot) usually hung under the armpits. The children would then fight over the scattered groundnuts as he walked from village to village doing the same.

Alikoori's period of rule was marked by severe famine. People had nothing to eat and hence, they resorted to eating animals' hides (udweele) which they used as beds for sleeping on. This and many other ill treatment made many Päri people scatter to different places in search for better living conditions, Today you find Päri people living among the Otuho community identified as *'hang Päri (Päri clan).* A group of Päri who migrated to Mundari formed a clan known as *'käbura'*. The Bari nicknamed them as *Bori* and lives in Terekeka to this day. A sizeable number of Päri people live among the Lokoya of Lirya: specifically, the Opualang section which comprises the following camps: ohwaa, ongole, ohalla and ongorway. Two clans in Bilinyang village named *Boi* and *Bura* have actually originated from Päri. The year these people migrated there is not remembered.

Alikoori was a great fighter who led several battles against many tribes: Acholi, Bari, Madi, Lotuko, Longairo (section of Lotuko), Toposa, Lopit, and Tenet to mention a few. But despite military gains accorded to him, people felt discontented with his dictatorships, and hence, the most prominent elders in Wiatuo village agreed among themselves to depose him and install his son Kidi in his place. Kidi age mates' too gave their strong support for Alikoori removal from power. So, they instigated Kidi to takeover the kingship. In response to people's demand, Kidi who was ambitious for power agreed and ordered his father to step down or else, he could be eliminated. Afraid of his life, Alikoori accepted to step down. The next day, Kidi, accompanied by his guards, took his father to Mangala and handed him to the colonial authority telling them to keep him in exile.

This event was indeed reported by El Miralai R.C.R Owen Bey who in his words wrote;

> Sheikh Alikori, Head Sheikh of the Berri tribe, came to Mangalla with his son the morning of 21st May, bringing a present of one tusk to the government. The son, Kidi, had really brought his father, Alikori to Mangalla, complaining that all the tribe were angry with him because he held up the rain and refused to let it come down. Further, Kidi asked me to keep his father there for five months, as both he and all the tribe were very angry with him, and if he stayed at Lafone he would be killed, I am keeping Alikoori in Mangalla. Alikori's wife is also with him, and will stay here.[35]

Kidi left his father in Mangala and returned to Lafon on 22/5/1908.

---

35 See INTEL 6/5/18, NRO; Khartoum. SIR No 167 (June 1908); APPENDIX "D" Mangalla Inteligence Report; by El Miralai R.C.R Owen Bey, May 1908

With the end of Alikoori reign, the power passed in the hands of Kidi. Five months later, the colonial authority freed Alikoori and allowed him to return to Lafon. He came and lived in Lafon until his death in 1911[36]

Weegipaac (Ruling age set)

Weegipaac is a collective political institution in Päri society, which represents the highest source of authority. This institution is composed of alliance between groups of age sets. Weegipaac, which means fathers of the land, is popularly known as 'mojomiji'. This term was borrowed from the Lotuko tribe who pronounced it monyemiji. The Päri call them ' Jo wic' and literally means the headmen, apparently because of the bull's head which is the emblem of the ruling age set which takes power from its predecessors.The practice in power successions is that the groups of age sets, which take over the power, slaughter a bull for their occasion. The head of this particular bull is kept and hung up in a small hut which is located in a sacred place called 'lipunni'. This place is found in Wiatuo village, the residence of the king and the headquarters of the ruling age set. This symbol will remain in this sacred place until a new ruling group of age sets takes over power.

According to oral history, the weegipaac emerged as a result of interactions between the Päri and the Lopit tribe. Through Rwäth Ujwok from Bura village, the Päri borrowed the wic system of government from the Lopit and introduced considerable changes to enable it to be accommodated by their own culture. This is a system of government in which several age sets rule the community collectively. Weegipaac contrasts with the traditional power structure, which existed in Päri society. In fact, the king used to be absolute monarch. However, the emergence of weegipaac gave rise to

---

[36] Sudan Intelegence Report, No. 202 (May 1911). INTEL, 6/6/20. NRO: Khartoum

power sharing between the monarch and the ruling age sets. This process under went transformations to the extent that the weegipaac encroached on power of the monarch leaving this institution as a mere symbol of political and social leadership.

The generation which adopted the wic system, named themselves 'Thomme'. This term originates from the Lopit tribe. They pronounce it Tomme/Atomme which means elephant. The significance of this name suggests the powerful because elephants are huge and powerful. The Thomme was recognized as the established political power in the society. But they did not opt for the abolition of the monarchy. Therefore, these two institutions namely the Thomme and monarchy co-existed and worked hand in hand while exercising authority over the people.

The emergence of this new power structure in Päri society indicates that the people were dissatisfied with absolute monarchy. They wanted a system in which many people could participate in decision making and in the administration of the community such as that of the Lopit. Today, kings of the Päri people cannot decide or make orders without the knowledge of Weegipaac. All important decisions of kings must be approved first by the Weegipaac before they are implemented. For example, if a king wants his hut built or field to be cultivated, he has to channel this demand through the ruling age set who will then order the youth to do the work. Should the king undermine or deviate from conventional policies, he will be sanctioned. Such violations is construed an act of defiance, sorcery and the like. Such charges may result into beating or liquidation. Thomme who introduced the wic system of government were made up of two categories namely; the senior age group called 'cingi caam' left- hand side and their junior age group was called cingi cwiic right hand side. These two groups combined into one and called themselves Thomme. In wic system of government, the group in power had to exercise authority for a period of twenty-two years. This regulation was effectively applied only to the first and second generation namely, Thomme and Akeem. This arrangement was later interrupted after the third group known as Bongcuot was in power.

Previously, each ruling group was composed of two age groups, which we have already explained above. However, a new political development took place which was similar to a revolution on a small scale. It happened that another group of two age sets who were not due to claim power made a putsch. This group was called Limojo. They constituted a group, which established a new order in the wic system of government. Instead of ruling for twenty-two years, the new comers imposed the system of renewal (teengo). That is to say, the twenty-two years has to be shared between the two age sets and the group of newcomers. The newcomers namely *Limojo* and *Amirkolong* age sets demand was accepted by the Bongcuot authority with the condition that the renewal group of agesets should not throw away the head of the bull which is the emblem of the ruling age set. Their period of rule was considered a continuation of the old system of government already established by their predecessors. Their emblem could be hanged in the same hut the emblem of their predecessor was hung provided that the head of their bull is hung slightly below that of the two age set. All these heads will later be thrown out when a new group of two age set take over power.

There is a tendency among the renewal group to adopt an independent policy from those of the predecessors. When they take over power and are in a position to exercise their authority, they make their own policies. They also develop new relations with communities in the neighborhood. For example, the groups of renewal are able to change the date for planting crops. Similarly, they can cancel or promote commercial transactions with one or more neighbors who may be different from those who enjoyed certain privileges under the former regime.

Generally, the arrangement for taking over power from a particular ruling age set demonstrates some kind of regularity. There is nevertheless sufficient evidence indicating that a particular group of age sets is isolated from consultations intended for the overthrow of the age sets in power. For example, age groups such as the *Regemunu*, *kuru* and *ucwaada*, lost power sharing during their respective turns to overthrow their predecessors. This situation takes place when a particular age group fails to play an active and effective role in overthrowing the ruling age sets of the day. Such a group is usually integrated into the administrative system on the condition that its members do not take part in any top decision-making process. The Päri say, *laange amuony wicci* that is to say the age set has been swallowed by/ absorbed into the system. A similar thing would have happened to Lilaalo, the junior partner of Ukweer age set. That is, when Ukweer were preparing to takeover power from Kalang (who were the rulers at the time), the Lilaalo age set refused to participate. On the day the Ukweer went to lemungole to prepare for the next day to overthrow the rulers, all members of Lilaalo except one man called Umuutho (from Paraau clan) failed to turn up for the occasion in the hope that they would lead the revolution. In response to this conspiracy, the Ukweer leadership ignored all Lilaalo membership in the administration but then welcomed Umuutho as representative of the Lilaalo age group. In any gathering of the mojomiji, Umuutho was always called to speak on behalf of Lilaalo age set. The relation was later normalized after Lilaalo age set had acknowledged the leadership and joined the administration. Hence, Ukweer are in full control of power in the country. Although the group were accepted into the system, the leadership continued recognizing Umuutho as the legitimate and hence, the official representative of the whole group of Lilaalo.

Another salient feature of the wic organization consists of names of age sets. In principle, each a group gives itself a name. But the ruling age set is identified by the name of the senior age group. For example, the Kilang ruling age set consisted of Kilang which is the senior partner of the group and Thäängakwo the junior partner. But their collective name is Kilang. The following table illustrates this case in the whole system of government.

Table 6.2 The generations of the Wic system of governance.

	Groups	Identity	Date	Duration
1	a. Thomme	Leftists	1856-1878 @	22 years
	b. Ibou	Rightists		
2	a. Akeem.	Leftists	1878-1900 @	22 years
	b. Muura	Rightists		
3	a. Bongcuot	Leftists	1900-1911 @	11 years
	b. Cɔrɔgɔ	Rightists		
4	a. Limɔjɔ	Rightists	1911-1922 @	11 years
	b. Amerkolong ®	Leftists		
	c. Amerlwɛɛdo(regemunu)	Rightists		
5	a. Alangurre	Rightists	1922-1933 @	11 years
	b. Igaari	Leftists		
	c. Kuuru	Rightists		
6	a. Kalang	Leftists	1933-1948 @	15 years
	b. Wanditiɔ ®	Rightist		
	c. Ucwaada	Leftists		
7	a. Ukweer	Rightists	1948-1960 *	12 years
	b. Lilaalɔ	Leftists		
8	a. Kwara	Rightists	1960-1968 *	8 years
	b. Bondipala	Leftists		
	c. Ithi-yio ®	Rightists		
	d. Yulu	Leftists		

9	a. Kilang	Rightists	1968-1977 *	9 years
	b. Thäängakwo	Leftists		
10	a. Ith ucɔɔk (Anywaa)	Rightists	1977-1988 *	11 years
	b. Akɛɛyɔ ®	Leftists		
	c. Maridi	Rightists		
	d. Adeeyo	Leftists		
11	a. Ithi- bule (Madaan)	Rightists	1988-1999 *	11 years
	b. Mooru (Boondikwɛɛri)	Leftists		
12	a. Madir(Thomme)	Rightists	1999-2005 *	6 years
	b. Lidiit	Leftists		
13	a. Marik (Kwodidhiɛng)	Rightists	2005-2010 *	5 years
	b. Acaac	Leftists		
14	a. Agwiɛno (Akeem)	Rightists	2010- 2015	5 years
	b. Adhiɛngo	leftists		
15	a. Sijuni (Daaru)	Rightists	2015 - *	
	b. Buya	Leftists		

Key to the table:
* Exact dates and duration.
@ Estimates: 22 years in power applies to the first two generations; Thomme and Akeem
® Generations who renewed the administration of their predecessors
 Note; the generations numbered 12 and 14 are named after the 1st and 2nd generations.

a) The plot to take over Power

The process of succession of age sets is organized in secret consultations between corresponding age sets. In other words, an aspiring group of two age sets seeks the advice of the group of two age sets already retired. Similarly, the aspiring group of four age sets consults the group of four age sets retired on methods of removing a group of two age sets which is in power. For example, the Kilang age group sought advice from Ukweer while Anywaa (Ithi ucook) age group sought advice from Kwara.

This example is an oversimplification of the process. What happens actually is that the age sets are controlled by princes who are assisted by councilors (atielli). These classes of individuals who are an integral part of the age sets are responsible for making contacts with their counterparts in the retired ruling group for the purpose of overthrowing the ruling age sets of the day. These contacts are made in an absolute secrecy to avoid leakage to ruling age sets because such a leakage may result in a bloody reaction by the Wegipaac. All individuals who are known for their inability to keep secrets are isolated from these contacts.

The process of overthrowing the ruling age set starts in the village of Wiatuo, which is the residence of the paramount king. A special class of the senior age sets works out principles of the plot to take over power. This class is usually composed of princess and councilors. Once there is an agreement concerning this initiative, the senior age set will invite their counterparts in the junior age set for a joint meeting in which the issue of taking over power is the agenda. This meeting ends always in agreement. Such an agreement represents the first phase of the beginning of the plot in Wiatuo.

After this agreement, the next step is to make contact with the corresponding retired elders. Not all elders are eligible for these contacts. The plotters approach those individual councilors who in their era participated in the plot to over throw their predecessors. Usually the contact results in a preliminary understanding between the interested parties. These parties work out an appointment, which takes place in a particular house. The plotters choose the house for the meeting.

On the day of the meeting, only councilors of the plotters and the invited councilors among the elders take part in the discussion. The meeting starts before dawn (i.e. before cock craw). During the process, the plotters had informed their princes to wait in a specified home just as the selected councilors of elders had informed their princess in a similar manner. While the meeting is taking place, the princes are waiting indoors in the homes in which they are to wait for final outcome and resolution.

Before the meeting starts, the elders ask the prospective weegipaac to provide some tobacco, which is usually offered in sufficient quantities. The elders then begin to smoke and they invite those plotters who smoke to do so. It is after this formality that the elders ask the plotters for the agenda of the meeting. Then the plotters speak out all their intentions for taking over power from the ruling age sets. The main thing the plotters will seek is let the elders' advice on methods and techniques of removing the ruling age sets. During these meetings, the elders provide advice consisting mainly of three elements. The first element is that the plotters should make contacts with their corresponding age sets in all the remaining five villages: Bura, Pucwaa, Pugäri, Kɔɔr and Angulumeere, in order to work out jointly for the over throw of the ruling age set.

When these contacts are made successfully, the plotters will need to meet the king to declare their intentions and asses his position on the issue of overthrowing the group of age sets in power. Finally, the elders will always emphasize and stress the necessity of keeping such advice and consultations secret to protect themselves from the evil intentions of the wegipaac of the day.

It is at this moment that the plotters disperse while each goes immediately to inform their princes in homes in which they had been waiting secretly.

The next step consists of making contacts with groups of age mates in other villages. What happens is that the plotters at Wiatuo contact the chief prince in the senior age set, plus his councilor, and one chief prince in the junior age set and his councilor making a total of four people in one village. It means that the plotters will make contact with a similar number in all the other five Päri villages. However, the number of plotters in Wiatuo may be greater than that of the other villages.

The people so contacted are then summoned for a secret meeting, which takes place at night in Wiatuo. In hierarchy, the prince of the senior age set in Wiatuo is number one among equals. So he automatically becomes the chairman of the meeting of the plotters. In line with the advice they had received from elders, the meeting decides the year in which the plotters will take power. It will be determined during the same meeting what specific measure will be taken in the process of overthrowing the ruling group. They too determine when to demand the responsibility of 'Tuung' blowing horn/trumpet from the ruling age set. After the meeting, the participants go back to their respective villages with the message to be passed to their age mates. It is from here that the members of the aspiring plotting group will begin to know that they are already preparing to take over power. However, all are warned to keep this idea secret.

The first step the plotters usually will take is to approach the ruling age sets to beg them for permission to take care of the horn (tuung) which is usually blown to inform people to go for a communal services. At this moment, the ruling group will begin to understand that there is an underground movement intending to take over power from them. But they will not know when this will happen. The ruling age sets will always spot those individuals in the aspiring age sets that are likely to mastermind the plot. They will begin to threaten lives of such individuals by cures 'cien' or luook 'sorcery', which are conventional methods of eliminating potential rivals. Here, the plotters work out plans to meet the king on the issue of taking over power. But before the meeting, the plotters usually offer bribes to the king in the form of drinks, livestock and several other items so that one day when they ask for the over throw of the ruling group, he will not hesitate to keep his consent. When the plotters are sure that the king is happy with them, they will approach him and declare their intentions to take over power.

Bribery is also one instrument of the power struggle between the ruling group of age sets and their rivals. When the actual rulers sense that the aspiring age sets are making more offers to the king, they will try to maintain themselves in power by making more offers. Usually, natural disasters such as droughts leading to bad harvest or loss of wars by the Päri will precipitate the king's approval of the takeover by the aspiring group of age sets. After this phase, the chief aspiring prince in Wiatuo village is able to call general secret meetings comprising all members of the senior and junior age sets. These meetings are usually held at night at safe sites outside the villages. Three or four meetings may be held before taking over power. Themes of such meetings rotate around mutual encouragement (ayiemme). These meetings also determine when to meet elders so as to get technical advice and directives.

General secret meetings of the aspiring group of age sets with elders will intensify in all Päri villages. The councilors of the aspiring group in each village arrange to meet their elders. The focus of such meetings will be to explain the reasons for taking over power. These meetings will be held frequently in different homes of members of the aspiring group of age sets. This particular period is called duunyo. This term means entering. It describes the fact that people do enter from one house to another in their underground movement. After several meetings with the elders, the elders then disclose to the ruling age sets the new political development. And for three days, the councilors of elders and that of the ruling age sets will be discussing this matter. Finally, the ruling age set will be invited to attend a meeting in the house of one of the aspiring group of age sets. Such a message is usually communicated in the evening.

The next day, the three groups namely; the councilors of elders, that of the ruling age sets and the aspiring group, will meet in the house of appointment. Here, elders will advise the ruling group to hand over power to the aspiring group of age set in a peaceful manner. This aspiring group will accompany the elders to another house prepared for them where they will be entertained. However, the ruling age sets will be left behind with the plotters in the very house in which arrangements had been made in accordance with appointment of the previous day. These two groups will stay together to discuss modalities of hand over power. It is at this stage the Päri people will notice the development of power succession in the society.

As the period of power succession approaches, princes and councilors of the aspiring age sets organize visits (weelo) to their counterparts in the group of elders. During these visits an individual prince or councilor takes along with him some gifts which consist of a hoe, two cakes of tobacco and some beer conserved in a guard called ukool. In modern times, money has been introduced as part of the gift. This type of visits includes homes of princes and councilors that have already died. Concerning the dead, their families may own and consume these gifts except the beer. The family of the dead prince or councilor will always invite the age mates of the deceased to come and consume the beer on his behalf.

b) The Worship of Mount Lipul

The process of handing over power from one group of age sets to another one depends on specific conditions. The first condition is that there must be a good harvest, which would enable the wives of power seeking age sets to make sufficient beer for the ceremony of power succession. Secondly, there should be no outbreak of epidemic diseases such as cholera that would kill a large number of people. Once these conditions are satisfied, the ceremony of power succession can go ahead normally.

The determining factor in starting the ceremony is the shadow (tippo) of mount Lipul. The shadow must reach a predetermined point near the flour grinding stones of Pucwaa people. Specialists' elders from Pugäri who are the owners of this sacred hill monitor the position of the shadow during the month when the takeover of power will be organized usually in November after the harvest of crops. When this shadow reaches the exact point/site, these elders will inform the aspiring group of age sets. This information is circulated among members of this group who in turn fix the day for the beginning of the ceremony. When that day comes, the whole group assembles at the point of the shade in the afternoon hours. They sit down worshiping god while facing mount Lipul to the west. This siting and worship takes some minutes after which members disperse and return to their respective villages. The next day, the whole group assembles again in the afternoon in Wiatuo village. There, the prospective wegipaac divide themselves into two groups. The right-hand group consists of all members of the senior group while the left-hand composed of the junior group. These two groups have to walk in silence around the hill in opposite directions. In specific terns, the right hand group marches anti clockwise while the left hand group marches clockwise. When the two groups meet, members make gestures of warfare without talking to each other.

The round –the- hill tour goes on three times after that these groups assemble in Wiatuo village where they started then they will disperse each going to their respective villages.

The process of handing over power is closely associated with the star, which the Päri call ceci Nyalam (star of Nyalam). This star appears in the skies in November during the early morning hours before dawn. At this juncture, it is worth noting that the prospective group of ruling age sets waits for the appearance of this star to conduct the ceremony of taking over power because this group had already accomplished the phase of worship. So, members of the aspiring group of age sets organize themselves to watch the sky for the appearance of ceci nyalam. Once they have spotted this star, information is circulated among members of the group. After the confirmation that the star is the right one, the head prince will fix the day when the succession of power will take place.

It is the normal practice that the wife of the head prince will prepare beer in the palace of the king. This special beer known as *koongi laau* which means the beer of spittle will not be squeezed nor filtered like the normal beer. It is left in this form so that those elders should throw their spittle in the pots *dää* or *athää* for the beer. However, not all elders are eligible for this special rite. The elders needed are only the age mates of those who were contacted secretly when the aspiring group of age sets sought advice on how to overthrow the actual group of ruling age sets. The reason why these particular elders spit into beer is that they are blessing these new comers to exercise power with wisdom and to invoke prosperity for the Päri society during the reign of this group which is going to take over power in the immediate future.

When this beer has been prepared and is ready, all the eligible elders will be invited to perform the spittle rite, which takes place early in the morning. Parallel to the preparation of the beer as well as to the spittle rite, the aspiring group of age sets consults a divine oracle specialist ajwaa about the fate of their future while in power. These power diviners usually assure this group that prosperity will always prevail during the period of rule. It is also during this ritual period that these power contenders prepare their garments for the inauguration ceremony.

The actual ceremony of assuming power starts usually in the afternoon of the day in which the spittle rite was performed in the morning. Then all members of the power contending group assembles in the dancing court yard at the king's residence in Wiatuo village. The people who are preparing to assume power in a matter of hours are paraded in two lines in the court yard thworo all facing the king's palace where the pots of beer have been placed for the ceremony. The seniors who are the right hand group are lined up to the right while the juniors who are the left hand group are lined up to the left. The movement of members in the parade towards the pots of beer takes place in pairs. In other word, the pair is composed of one senior member and one junior member who go in turns to drink the beer. Upon reaching the pots, the pair kneels in front of the pot and drink. Once they have drunk, the pair returns to the court yard while the next pair continues the process. All pairs will go in turns until the pots are emptied of the stuff. What we should remember is that most hardened warriors are always lined up at the rear of the parade because they prefer to lick the thickest stuff of the spittle, which concentrates at the bottom of the pots. According to Likari Alwanya, some members close their eyes when drinking the beer because the sight of the spittle is so horrible that could trigger one to vomit.

Another decisive measure in the process of power succession is the lowering of the symbol of authority (head of the bull). It takes place after all the pots of beer have been emptied. What happens is that the elders who were engaged in this ceremony will go and remove their own symbol plus the one of those who renewed their administration and hand both of them to the new group who are about to take over power. Usually, two men come forward, one represents senior members and the other represents the junior age sets. Both men stand in front of the whole assembly waiting to receive the heads of the bulls. During the presentation of these symbols of the outgoing authority , the senior member will hold the right handed horns while the junior member hold the left handed horns. Then the junior will let go and the senior will run with the heads to the river and throw them into it. The whole assembly will accompany these symbols in a race until they are thrown into the river. Thereafter, all members of the new ruling group will disperse very hurriedly into their respective villages to perform the same removal of symbol of authority in the same way as it was conducted in Wiatuo. On this same day, the whole group will assemble and encamped in a place called lemungole about four miles away from the villages. This assembly takes place at night.

At lemungole, members stay segregated according to villages. It is at this time that individuals who have been living in other villages are made to join their own clansmen in their respective villages. Should a person fail to do so, he will be dismissed from the clan membership. All assets which are entitled to him, such as plot of land or agricultural/cultivatable land will be confiscated from him and given to the nearest relative. It is in Lemungole; the new ruling age sets through their appointed spokesmen review and make their policies. They discuss their trade relations with the Päri neighboring tribes; they set their policies with regards to the group they are removing from power; they declare the official number of cows for marriage settlement and the like. The discussions continue throughout the night. While the group is discussing various political issues some members who are known for their ability in identifying far objects will be made to stay up a tree to monitor and report the appearance of ceci nyalam. One man among them will be holding a horn (nowadays the gun is used). The moment the star appears, the horn is blown (or a gunmen will fire a shot in the air) as a signal to let the new rulers know that the star has finally appeared in the sky. The group then burst into yelling *twaaro* all expressing their readiness to take over power.

While the aspiring rulers are at Lemungole, the incumbent rulers gather in the dancing court yard of Wiatuo. They dance throughout the night claiming that nobody can remove them from power. This group threatens the new comers with hostile action until morning. They wait while armed with sticks and whips ready to fight what they called *jur* meaning strangers or enemy. Although the aspiring groups who are spending the night in the bush are armed with sticks, clubs (ulukki), jagged spears (ulaawwi), they are prohibited not to use them against the rulers. All they can do is to use shields to defend themselves. So often they wait for the morning to come to overrun the government seat.

c) The Process in the Transfer of Power

The transfer of power from the ruling age sets to the challengers is not a peaceful exercise. It involves a form of confrontation between the new rulers and the incumbent ruling group. The whole process includes the respect for special steps by the challengers and the attitude of the ruling group which resists relinquishing power to the challenging age sets.

After spending the night in the bush at lemungole and having seen the star of nyalam, the challengers assemble and parade in two lines at dawn. The senior age set takes the right hand line while the junior take the left. Based on this arrangement they start their march towards Wiatuo village where they have to confront the ruling group they are going to over throw. Members of the new rulers smear their bodies with ooze/mud, wearing ostrich feathers on their heads,

POLITICAL INSTITUTIONS AND AUTHORITY

leopards' skins on their backs, holding jagged spears, clubs and shields in their hands. The march is accompanied by war songs and songs of praise. As the prospective wegipaac advance towards the village of Pucwaa, another different group of juniors known as "Jo litäängo" joins the procession. This particular group neither claim power nor does it have any saying in political authority. They are the military wing of the ruling authority. The litäängo members are identified by black ostrich feathers which they wear on their heads. Meanwhile the prospective rulers decorate themselves in white ostrich feathers called licaaro. Both group members smear their bodies with ooze and have leopard skins on their backs. However, the litäängo members are not allowed to carry jagged spears.

The procession briefly stops in the zone of grinding stones in Pucwaa village to conduct worship in the area of the mountain shade. It is after this special rite that the whole group advances in a procession towards Wiatuo village. The outstanding rule during this march is that no person or animal should cross in front of this group. Otherwise that person or animal is speared to death. Another site of special rite is the tomb of Jogi, one of the elders of Booi clan. It follows that each member of the group of challengers picks a piece of stone and throws it on the tomb as a sign of respect. This tomb is just a short distance from the village of Wiatuo. When this particular rite is performed, the confrontation for taking over power is eminent.

While the challengers are preparing to assault the ruling group of age sets, the latter group prepares to prevent the challengers from taking over power. The resistance is organized in such a way that a few people from the ruling age group will be beating drums and dancing in the main court yard of Wiatuo. But the majority will have to lay in ambush on the predetermined main road leading to the court yard. The ambush is made along the main road in such a way that the senior age set lines up on the right hand side while the junior age set lines up on the opposite direction. Also, there is a group which blocks the road at the end of the ambush. The rationale behind this ambush is to prevent any member from penetrating into the court yard to beat the drums of the rulers.

When the preparations are over, the challenging group steps deliberately into the ambush and immediately, the ruling group begins to beat the new comers with whips, sticks and sometimes with clubs on both sides of the road. The golden rule is that the challengers though armed with spears, sticks and clubs should never retaliate but have to protect themselves with shields. However, serious injuries could be caused by an accident fall of a member of the defending group. Such an injury will not be done by the defending ruling group, but by the advancing group which will tread on the unfortunate victim. Another rule of engagement is that the group of the juniors decorated in black ostrich feathers should never be touched during the beating and the whipping. It is for this reason that this particular group is placed in the rear of the advancing group. The challengers always advance until they penetrate the defense of the ruling group to reach the drums. On rushing to the drums, the members of the senior age set will beat the biggest drum while the junior age set beats the second/next drum. Once the challengers have beaten the drums, all members of the outgoing group have to disappear from the courtyard. If one member of this group is seen in the courtyard and its vicinity, he is liable to real assault that could result in his death.

The actual transfer of power takes place when the outgoing age sets have been chased and dispersed when the drums have been taken over by the in-coming group of age sets. Once the later has taken control of the dance courtyard, a brief celebration of dances is performed singing about three songs. Then the procession (ipuura) moves to the royal common tomb. It is worth noting that all kings of Wiatuo are buried in one tomb since time immemorial. What happens is that when the reigning king dies, the tomb is dug, the bones of the preceding kings are exhumed and the body of the ruling king is buried at the bottom. Then the bones of the preceding kings are laid on the upper layer of the same tomb.

Upon reaching the tomb, every member of the ruling age sets which has just assumed power picks a stone and throws it on this royal tomb. This is the ceremonial way of paying respect to the royal spirits. After this rite, the new ruling group climbs up the Lafon Mountain until a specific site. This site is marked by a symbolic tree call adi-ngic. The new rulers sit down in the shade of this special tree to take rest. Wives of these new rulers bring beer and drinks, which have been prepared for this occasion. This resting place serves also as an assembly for re-organization. For example, two members from each village are selected to act as policemen, maintaining law and order in the society. Tradition provides extensive powers to the policing group. The group patrols day and night all villages to maintain discipline especially among the youth of both sexes. It is empowered to intervene in family disputes. While exercising police functions, no any victim should retaliate. Any retaliation results in sanction. The ruling age sets could order the killing of one bull of the offender or apply corporal punishment or both. Members of this police force are identified by whips in their hands and a bell that hangs on the shoulders. These selected people are paid in form of free food and drinks where ever they performed their functions. These police forces are called *lingololieri sing.pl.lingololierri.*

On the day of takeover, the new rulers do not participate in dances. Elders, liäängo members and the youth dance during this first day of celebration. Then there is a set of activities that must take place during the second day. All members of the ruling age sets assemble on a flat hill called wi-cule at dawn. The compound of the Catholic Church mission currently occupies part of the assembly ground. But the ceremonies continue to take place there without obstruction from the Church. The purpose of this assembly is to count all members of the ruling age sets in all the villages of the Päri country. When all have been counted, hardly warriors selected from among the new ruling age sets (representing all the Päri villages) are sent to bring a bull to be sacrificed for the occasion of the transfer of power. The system however has been changed during Madaan era. Instead of involving warriors from other five villages to participate in the exercise, the warriors from Wiatuo decided to rotate the bull round mount Lipul alone. And since then, the subsequent generations that tookover power could not challenge such a move but adopted it as system.

It is to be noted that during the plotting period, the head prince of the aspiring age sets (who comes from Wiatuo village) offered a bull to be sacrificed on the occasion day. This bull is kept secret. The reason behind this secrecy is based on belief. It is popularly believed that if the age sets in power know the bull in advance, they will apply sorcery to it or feed it with bad feeds that will incur misfortunes on their successors such as famine or outbreak of epidemic diseases .Such misfortunes do destabilized the period of the new group that takes over power.

Once the bull has been brought, the same group of warriors takes the bull at sunrise and rotates it around Lafon Mountain demonstrating it to the public in all the Päri villages. This rotation takes place three times in an anti-clock wise direction. When they have gone round the third time and return to the assembly, then the group leads the bull towards Bura village where it is to be slaughtered. It is at this moment that the whole assembly will rise up and follow the warriors in procession to the village of Bura which hosts the ceremony. In this village, the bull is handed over to a special group of merciless warriors who are already told by the elders the way of killing such sacrificial animals.

The slaughter of the bull must conform to special rules and procedures. First of all, the bull must not collapse on its left-handed side because this side is by belief, associated with misfortune. Secondly, the head should never touch the ground. Finally no human being or animal should come close to the slaughter area. Otherwise, such a thing or an individual would face death on the spot. Based on these rules many people hold the legs to direct its collapse to the right hand side during the process of killing by spears. Also several people are assigned to hold the horns and the head in such a way that it does not touch the ground at all. Observers usually watch these actions at a safe distance.

After killing the bull, its body is adjusted on its knees. Then the senior warrior sits on the back of the dead animal holding up the two horns while the junior warrior sits on the ground holding up the muzzle (dhi dhieng) to prevent it touching the ground. These two warriors must never make any movement even if bitten by any insect. For that reason, one warrior is assigned to chase away flies and biting insects from these two warriors. While the slaughter ceremony is taking place, the new rulers moves in procession towards the dance courtyard. They go round three times around the drums in a definite pattern. In practice the senior age sets rotates anti-clockwise and the junior age sets rotates clockwise. Then members in the procession are asked by elders to sit down in groups.

d) Making of Fire

Fire blessing is an important rite in the process of inaugurating the new ruling group. The purpose of this rite is to kindle a new fire by means of fire sticks to symbolize the beginning of a new political period. Special group of elders engage in kindling a fire while the high priest of mount Lipul and another group of elders from Pugäri, some from Wiatuo and Bura respectively must climb up the mountain to a specific point called liluuro. This is a place where the tomb of king Dimo is found. There, the high priest digs some earth from the tomb of king Dimo and passes the required quantity of earth to an elder from Wiatuo who sits near him with a calabash in hand. After this operation everybody climbs down the hill to Bura dance courtyard to join the elders engaged in the kindling fire. The high priest throws some of this sand on the fire board so that it facilitates the drilling process until fire is finally obtained during this operation. Once the fire is kindled, the elders will run towards the rulers showing a sign of achievement. And soon a new fire is made because firewood had already been prepared by the people of Bura for this purpose. The king of Wiatuo then mixes the balance of the sand brought from the tomb of Dimo with a considerable quantity of butter *buobo* collected from the cow. Then he throws this mixture on the new rulers which is also a form of blessing.

Another phase of blessing with the fire consists of lighting grass-touches known as *miilu* from the new fire. The king and some elders will go round the groups blessing and invoking spirits to bring prosperity during the term of office. In the meantime, the head of the bull is cut off and placed carefully on the stone. Then the butcher collects the prescribed flesh and parts, which are intended for the ruling group of age sets and put them aside. The meat and parts consists of the right front leg, the large intestine the lungs and the hump. The rest of the animal is left for the elders.

It is worth noting that the elders involved in the fire-blessing rite must not eat anything green before this occasion. It follows that each of these elders has to throw sputum three times on the muzzle of the sacrificial bull. Before doing this, warriors bring water for the elders to clean their mouths before spitting. This operation is closely supervised. The water used for washing the mouth must be spat down and inspected for the presence of green material. Abstention from eating green vegetables is the rule because green vegetables are assumed to be a harm or curse of the term of office of the new ruling group. Finally the elders will return to the place where the fire has been kindled. This marks the end of the blessing process. Then the rulers are requested to evacuate the dance courtyard. Immediately, the litäängo group will take off running. The representatives of the new ruling group handle the new fire which is taken to the camping site called *ajwaa* about three miles away from the village. When they reach there, one senior and junior member will climb on a specific rock with fire. Then the litäängo members will collect the firewood and the fire is lit.

While fire is being lit on the rock, the procession of rulers passes through the slaughter site to take their share of the sacrifices. The eldest man among the new rulers carries the head of the bull while the procession follows behind. There the symbol of the group (antler) will be removed and put aside. The head and all the parts brought here will be roasted. Also, all members of the ruling class spit on the lungs before women join them. Lungs symbolize fear. They are roasted and cut into small pieces/bits to be distributed to women. This part of the animal must be consumed immediately by women. The idea behind this rite is that women are delicate as the lungs. The consumption of this organ will make women fear men when a quarrel happens between husbands and wives. After women have arrived with beer and drinks, small pieces of roasted skin of the head is distributed to everybody including women. A small piece of lung is added to the ration of women so that those women consume it as well. Then the other parts of the meat are divided as follows:

- The hump (*kwom*) is offered to the senior prince who will invite all princes of other villages to take the meal.
- The turn of the right front leg comes for distribution. The upper part of the leg *baac* is given to the senior group of the ruling age sets; the junior takes the part between the elbow and below the shoulder. The part between the elbow and the hoof is given to the senior members of litäängo group while their junior partners take the hoof and wrist.

- The large intestine is divided in such a way that the senior age group takes the upper part while the junior takes the lower part of the intestine.
- For the period of three years, the brain is eaten only by the senior members of the rulers. The junior group will participate in the consumption of brain of any animal after three years have elapsed.
- The elder person among the junior group of age sets will eat the nose below the eyes and the upper jaw known as ngarngwaadhi
- Concerning the eyes, ears, the right eye and right ear will be given to the senior group while the opposite parts will be offered to the junior group of age sets.
- The jawbones are divided in a similar manner as the eyes and the ears.
- The tongue is given to the senior age group of the ruling age sets.

Once the share of the sacrificed animal has been divided and eaten, the whole group begins to take beer. It is during this period that individuals who ate the brain in the skull and the muzzle will retreat from the group and at a good distance they burry these bones respectively. On return of these two individuals to rejoin the group, the procession starts moving to Wiatuo village. There the **antler** will be hung on the top of the ebony poles affixed together right at the center of the court yard known to Päri as balacaar.

The ceremony of the day ends with the fixing of the head of the bull on the poles. So a general curfew is declared which prevents people from crossing the court yard (thworo). Precautions are made to avoid losing the symbol of authority (antler) as it occurred to the Limojo during their era in which prince Nyangiro stole the antler wishing this group to fail in the administration of the people. When he realized that the rulers were looking for him, he ran to the compound of king Gumar to hide. When Gumar saw him hiding in the veranda (dooro) he asked, 'why did you come here? We would have killed you and throw your body to birds'. However, he felt a pity on him and begged the rulers to pardon him and the rullers forgave and set him free. Since then it has become a rule that whenever there is a change of power, a curfew is to be declared, guards are appointed from among the members of the rulers and assigned to protect the symbol of authority and thus, prevent jealous individuals from humiliating the rulers by depriving them the head of the bull which has a significance of power. Any person violating the curfew is subject to sanction which can be death penalty. In 1988, Madaan rulers killed Lilɛɛrɔ and his brother Ujiingi for having broken this rule.

The next stage in the ceremony of transfer of power starts when the head of the bull (antler) is untied from the balacaar. On this day the entire ruling age sets together with their wives assemble at dawn in the dancing yard of Wiatuo. Then the antler is untied from the Balacaar and given to the most senior leader from the senior age sets to carry on his head as the group rotate/ move round the Lafon hill in silence. The movement is organized in such a way that members of the senior age group go around the hill in anticlockwise direction while their juniors take clockwise direction. All the two groups are accompanied by their wives. These movements are made in such a way that each group go three rounds. Each time the two groups meet, they make gestures of power victory without exchanging any word. The whole movement will take place three times. During this movement, wives carry jagged spears (ulaawwi) of their husbands leaving men carry shields *koodo (sing. kwod)* and clubs *ulukki* in their hands. Unmarried members of the ruling age sets carry all the required weapons because they don't have wives to help them in carrying these weapons.

On arrival in Wiatuo for the third round, they go round the *balacaar* in the same way they did in making rotation around Lafon Mountain. Then the ruling age sets together with their wives dance briefly to the tune of three songs which are composed for the purpose. It is after this symbolic gesture that the head of the bull will be taken for storage in the sacred hut known as *lipunni* situated by the side of the hill. The arrival of the ruling age sets from the hill precipitates dances. Thus, everybody joins the dance. This will continue for three days during which people enjoy food and drink beer.

The last day of the ceremony is important. It is the day the new rulers declare their policies. Such policies cover all aspects of life of the community. On the first day of the occasion the rulers allow elders to say their opinions. They would be followed the next day by the group they have just overthrown. The third day is their turn. So often, people pay greater attention as they listen to the spokesmen announcing the new policies. Traditionally, the spokesman from the senior ruling group starts announcing the policies. The policy cover; trade relations with the neighbors, planting periods, the bride wealth, the security of the community as well as the protection of properties against the enemy and the like. This declaration is actually made in the afternoon before sunset. It is to be noted that the Pӓri community normally pray for the well being of their community and curses their enemies and wild beasts which endanger their lives and the lives of their animals. Thus, the proclamation of new policies ends with prayers **lam** which means invocation. The following words are often said during prayers on such ocassions:

Kwän u-ooe	let there be food,
Kɔth u-ooe,	let there be rain,
Jwɔk uci wɔgɔ	let diseases go away
Mään unywonde	may women produce
Bɛɛl ucieke	let grain ripe

Each time the spokesman says a prayer, the people echo his words jointly. Just as the spokesman for the senior age sets concluds his speech, the representative of the junior ruling age sets steps in and as a tradition; he goes round the drums poles three times and then pronounces the same policies of the new rulers. And people respond accordingly.

Another event which marks the end of the transfer of power is a marathon. Participants in this marathon are usually the young men comprising the litäängo group. They race for a long distance to a predetermined destination. It is a test to know the fastest young man in the community. While the marathon is taking place, elders, the ruling age group and the teenagers dance in the court yard. When the marathon runners return, they will immediately interrupt the dance of the ruling group and elders which has been going on when they were on the race. Their prince beat the drum while the members sing a song and all together the people join the dance. People dance until mid-night when the ceremony ends. In the morning, the drums are

The ruling age set and their wives celebrating the occasion of the establishments of Lafon County, on June 20th 2016

taken back to the drum house for custody. This marks the end of the ceremony. The new rulers then assume fully the political and social responsibilities of the community. Soon, after this event the ruling age sets disperse to their respective villages. It is the beginning of decentralized ceremony and enjoyment at the village level.

Taking into consideration that the transfer of power takes place between November and December, the period before the next cultivation seasons is that of relaxation and enjoyment. In other words, the ruling age sets congregates at homes of their colleagues in turns. Members of the senior ruling age sets and those of the junior arrange to stay together and are served the best dishes of the community. Their wives then pool dishes at one home where their husbands gather to eat and drink beer. This type of enjoyment continues in different homes in all the villages until the rainy season approaches.

Ipura dance

For ladies, smartness is the rule of the day. So, wives of the new rulers have to dress or wear attractive traditional leather skirts (duupe) during the service. Moreover, ladies have to show great humility and respect towards their husbands. Any lady who does not observe this rule is barred from entering the home of congregation. In that regards, the disobedient lady can be beaten by the husband for this humiliation. Within the same period of enjoyment, the ruling age set may declare a feast of goat eating day *lwaak cämo ki jeethe* (jeedhi for singular). On this occasion, members of each clan in the ruling age sets assemble together, go collectively and seize goats or rams belonging to their sons-in-law known to Päri as *cinyitte*. They seize these animals, slaughter them and eat it together with the elders. In case a son-in-law has no goat or ram, a quantity of dura/sorghum equivalent to the value of a goat or ram will have to be offered as a substitute. Today the system is no longer in use. The practice ended after the regime of kwara ruling age sets in sixties.

Tradition does not allow the new rulers to enter the Assembly house immediately after assuming the authority. The reason why these new rulers abstain from the Assembly House is that they have to work hard in their fields in order to prepare for the consecration. The latter takes place normally after the harvest since the transfer of power. Then it will be logical to provide a brief description of the Assembly House that the Päri called Kaboore.

Chapter Seven

Institutions of Power, Relational Linkages and Justice

a) Assembly House (Kaboore)

The entire Päri people are organized into groups better known as laange. Every village comprises various age groups and each group has its baalu (pl. baali). This term means a camp/club. This word is foreign to the Päri; the equivalent word for this term is 'wi-maac'. In addition, clan groups in each village have their own clubs where clan members discuss issues of interest. The largest club is the one called Kaboore. It is the official administrative center found in every village. It is always built at the edge of the dance court yard (thwɔrɔ). The village king stays there during the day. Once there is an issue of common concern/ interest in the village, all clan elders and the ruling age sets for that clan are summoned to the Kaboore for the deliberations.

One salient feature of this administrative center is that it must be the highest building in the whole village. Unlike the other constructions built with mud walls, the walls of the Kaboore are made of ebony wood posts called loodi, which support the roof. The thatch of this building is made of bamboo and covered with grass. Inside this building is an elevated platform called *peedhe* where drums are laid on. Sometimes people do sleep in this building. Kaboore is surrounded by wooden fence called *ligaani* and has two opening gates.

Another peculiar scene of the Kaboore is that people sit inside the building according to age groups. Each age group has its hearth called *wi-maac*. There is a pattern in the placement of the hearths. For example, the ruling age sets have their hearth placed close to the main gate that opens to the dancing ground *thwooro*, and the next to them is that of the age set they overthrew and so forth. Usually, beer drinks and meat are divided in accordance with the seating arrangement. The ruling age sets may raise an issue that calls for the group discussions. Each group wishing to express an opinion must talk loudly while keeping together round their hearth. Although elders are allowed to participate in the discussions, all decisions are made by the ruling age sets. The opinions from elders are treated as advice which may or may not be considered.

We have already mentioned that the new ruling age sets will not enter the Assembly House until they have ascertained that the harvest has been successful during that cultivation season. The reason for this delay is that wives of the new rulers are expected to prepare beer for the entertainment of the elders. Consequently, the timing of the entry into Kaboore is not uniform because it depends on the success of the harvest and absence of misfortunes such as epidemics. Sometimes the new rulers may wait for a year or so before they can enter Assembly House and join the elders. The entry of the ruling age sets into the Assembly House is an important event in Päri society. The new rulers will inform all elders in the village in advance and specify when the ceremony will take place. Meanwhile, wives of the new rulers prepare large quantities of beer (koongo) for the occasion. When preparations are ready, the seats *peedhe* belonging to the new rulers are then transferred to the village administrative Center (Assembly House) where they will be fixed to the ground. On the day of the ceremony, the wives of the rulers bring drinks in big quantities and pour it into large pots (nowadays, barrels are used). Each group sitting around the hearth receives its ration. The elders then bless the new rulers and wish them a prosperous life. After blessings, people start drinking. Elders from other villages do come and join the celebrations and enjoyment. People dance and conclude it after three days. The new rulers will then be confirmed as the political authority of the community.

b) Relationship between the Ruling age sets and the King

There is a need to explain the relationship between the ruling age sets and the king. The former authorizes the king to make rain at specified periods such as during the planting period. Relationship between the rulers and the rainmaker depends on the success of crop season. In other words, the rulers are always happy with the rainmaker when the cultivation season is successful. Hence, they do offer gifts in the form of cattle, goats, fish and the like. Relationship deteriorates sharply when the Pari land experiences serious persistent drought or when heavy rains destroy people's crops in the fields. In such circumstances, the king is summoned, interrogated and if found wrong receives a punishment. The punishment includes, beating the king with whips and clubs which may results into his death. In late 1966, when Kwara age sets were in power, the wife of prince Nyangiro by name Apiidhi was put to death. She was held responsible for the failure of rains during the crops season. Similarly, during the reign of Anywaa age sets, the rain queen called Nyibur (who took over rain administration in May 1980 following the death of her husband king Fidele) was held responsible for the persistent drought in 1984 which resulted in the total failure of crops. The rain queen was held responsible for that misfortune and was beaten to death. In 1993, the Madaan ruling agesets alleged that the king of Pucwaa village called Apermoi Mugie was responsible for the destruction of crops by unprecedented floods. In other words, he performed sorcery which brought much more rain than people needed and so he was executed publicly. During the reign of Thomme, the rain king called Ubote Ukeelo was expelled in March 2001 to Juba and warned not to come back to Lafon until crops have been harvested. In August 2001, he returned to Lafon in defiance of the warning and the ruling age set killed him by fire squard.

c) Relationship between Ruling age sets and Bird Controller

The Päri have an eminent person who is the bird controller. He is responsible for performing rites which deter the bird pest during the annual harvests. It is his duty to prevent birds from destroying harvest. Should it happen that there is a bird pest which has affected the Päri peasants; the bird controller is immediately sanctioned by the ruling age sets. The sanction includes beating and in extreme cases, punishment by death. In late 1967, when Kwara age sets were in power, the son of a bird controller called Agirarii Aruarith was accused of sending swarms of birds which destroyed people's crops. He was executed in front of the public. But the reason for sparing the life of his father called Aruarith who was the actual bird controller remains a mystery. Before Kilang ageset tookover power from Kwara (in 1968), a man called Arogomoi and his wife were executed for having murdered Urogokolong a member of the prospective ruling ageset. In 1996, when Madaan age sets was ruling the country, the daughter of the bird controller called Nyimuri Ukwiri was accused for being the cause of birds' pest that year, and consequently she got murdered. Recently (25.8.2015), another bird controller named Coono Liminikwac was murdered by the new ruling age sets called Daaru for allegedly failing to control bird pests which destroyed the fields belonging to Wiatuo people. The ruling age sets of that village killed him at once.

d) Social Sanction

Like any other deviant, a King can be executed or expelled from the Päri land by the ruling age set if accused of committing an act of sorcery, treason and the like. In 1981, the king of Kɔɔr village called Matia was exiled to Torit because he was accused of being involved in the act of sorcery that resulted to the failure of crops by making rain to fail. In 1982, the villagers of Wiatuo beat to death three persons from the village of Bura. The two men Alara and Abuakono were accused of having conducted sorcery against the people of Wiatuo wishing their crops to fail and consequently to starve. And so they were beaten to death. Moreover, the diviner named Nyakiilu whom they contacted for advice was also murdered by the same people. Similarly, a man named Anyala Ukoth who belongs to the royal family in Wiatuo village was beaten almost to death by the Anywaa ruling age sets. The rain maker called Fidele Ungang accused him for making sorcery that prevented rain to fall and which caused drought that year. After he was beaten, his relatives took him to Torit hospital where he was treated. The ruling age sets in Wiatuo village warned that he could still be executed if he returned. Anyala remained in exile until his death in Yei in early 1990s. When Madaan age set was in power, the rain maker called Akoligera was expelled to Juba accused of causing rain to fail. The mojomiji warned him not to come back to Lafon lest he would lose his life. And indeed, he remained in Juba until his death in the year 2000.

During the reign of Kwodidhieng, a man called Akaanni was accused of being a sorcerer wishing crops to fail and the people to starve and so he was killed. A man called Ariega Limunu was also murdered by Kwodidhieng ruling age set for allegedly wished the youngsters in Wiatuo village to die. During the reign of Akeem, Prince Aruoca Linyang was murdered but without a clear reason stated to the people. Zachariah Uceng Thaanga who died in Juba met a similar fate when his relative took his body to Lafon for burial. That is, the ruling age set called Akeem suspected him of having cursed the society and burnt the corpse instantly. Now, the present rulers called Daaru have also executed Limootho in May 2014. He was accused of having conducted sorcery wishing rain to fail. The same rulers killed Upala in Upuo Boma of Kɔɔr village accusing him of the same sorcery.

Troublemakers within the society can also be chased out of the village or executed by the ruling age set if their actions proved a threat to people's welfare. During the reign of Kwara, a man called Winjawiin was indirectly chased away by the Kwara authority to Uganda. He was found to be very nuisant, disrespecting members of the ruling ageset. First, the authority thought to eliminate him by way of curse (cien). But then the mojomiji changed their minds. Instead they assigned him to carry out sorcery on the crop's fields of the neighbouring Lopit tribe to make their crops fail so that they could bring their cattle, goats and other valuable materials to Pari to be exchanged for dura. He successfully performed the function as directed and then proceeded to Uganda where he stayed for a considerable number of years. Consequently, the Lopit suffered serious famine and brought their domestic animals and other goods to Lafon that was exchanged with dura. In the early seventies, Winjawiin returned to Lafon and was praised for his work.

Renewal Group (Jo teengo)

The phrase Jo teengo refers to a group of age sets who plot to overthrow the ruling age sets (two age sets) of the day but without necessarily denouncing their symbol of authority (antler). They do not build a new hut to store the sacrificed bull. They only rethatched the roof. Thus, their period of rule is considered a continuation of the old administration but with new and improved system of governance. The renewal groups plot in the same way the two-age sets proceeds to take over power from the age sets in power. Nevertheless, there are variations with regards the location where the new rulers would assemble to make their policies and also the slaughter sites for the sacrificial bull. Traditionally, the renewal groups assemble at *dhi-gär* in Bura territory whereas the two age sets assemble at *lemungole* in Pucwaa territory. Another difference pertains to the place where the bull is slaughtered. The two age sets slaughter their bull in Bura whereas the renewal groups have their bull slaughtered at Wiatuo village. Further, the renewal groups do not confront the group they are overthrowing. The two age sets involve in a physical confrontation with the ruling age sets resulting in beating with whips and sticks and sometimes clubs are used. Today, the system of authority has changed infavour of two age sets. This system was brought back by Kwodidhieng after they refused to join their ranks withThomme age group. Their action forced Madir and Lidit age groups to go to Lemungole from where they named their group 'Thomme'. When Kwodidhieng tookover power from Thomme in 2005, elders officially declared that the administration of mojomiji system of governance would then be run by two agesets and not more. This is to allow all age groups participate in governance unlike the previous system when others were treated as juniors and therefore are deprived from participating actively in power exercise.

The distribution of meat of slaughtered bull

In Päri society, when some one commits a serious crime, such as wounding or spearing a person to death or destroying a community asset, the ruling age set punishes that individual by slaughtering his bull or bulls. For example, when the youth engage in a stick fight(between corresponding age sets), the ruling age set usually identify ring leaders and punish them by killing their bulls, The meat of the slaughtered bulls would then be distributed in the following way: The ruling age set takes the head, right foreleg (badiwic), heart (aduundo), gut (likwεεthilith), buɔb, chest and waist (piεr); the left foreleg and ribs (badi ngeed) is given to the immediate retired rulers; right hind leg and the hip (waadhi baam) given to the old retired rulers; the left hind leg and liver (waadhi cwiiny) is given to the oldest retired rulers. The neck is allotted to the litäängo group 'nyingudi' the junior partners of the rulers; the hump is allotted to the king. In 1999, however, Thomme ruling age set changed the system. They added the neck of the bull to their ration. They did that because the junior partners known as Kwodidhieng age set who were due to share in the administration rejected to be part of the administration because they wanted to run their administration independent from that of Thomme. From that time, the subsequent rulers followed Thomme by adding the neck to their ration.

e) Chieftaincy

The Päri word for a chief or king is rwäth. For distinctive purposes, a king is referred to as rwädhi paac (chief of the village) paac being the village or home. A chief is referred to as rwädhi gäala meaning (the chief for the government). In other words, he is a government agent. The position of a chief is got by election whereas that of a king is hereditary succession. The duty of a chief is to collect taxes (*mucooro*), deal with all sorts of criminal offences such as girls' seductions, disputes, theft, raping and so forth. This work is carried out with the assistance from sub-chiefs known as *mukungu (pl. mukungi)* who are distributed equally in every village.

The sub chief of the village works with a secretary known as *karan* and assisted by two *nyampara*. The work of nyampara is mainly to take summons to the accused ordering him/her to come to the court. The sub chief solves all cases brought before him. First, he summons the accused to appear before the court and after a hearing, he decides the case. Should there be an appeal by a party to the conflict; the sub chief will forward the case to the higher court.

Chieftaincy was introduced in the Päri society by the Anglo Egyptian government in the Sudan in 1930s. The main purpose for instituting this structure was to help the government in its administration and maintenance of law and order. Each community must have a chief who represents the government there. While it is understood in this sense, the Päri understands it differently. For them the chief and sub chiefs are referred to as gäála meaning government rather than their own rulers. So, the Päri consider chieftaincy as foreign and an additional structure in their political set up. However, political developments in the Sudan have been re-enforcing progressively the authority and powers of the chiefs. For example, the government has given chiefs considerable administrative and judicial powers. Chiefs can punish anybody including members of the ruling age sets by lashes or putting them in jail if they fail to obey the law. A paramount chief works with strong men drawn from each village. These men are called surkali. They are tasked to enforce the law and order.

Chiefs have powers to make changes in the society. For example, chief Albano was able to change the traditional mode of dressing of the Päri people from the use of leather skirts, to western clothes. Earlier, majority of men went naked while women wore leather skirts made of goat's skin and apron called Päri made of goat or calfskin. In 1950s, skirts made of cloth known as thanura and a garment called abaanda were introduced to Päri women. Yet, the Päri girls or women remained traditionally bare- breasted. After the Addis Ababa Peace Agreement of 1972, which ended the civil strife in the southern Sudan, Albano Urua was appointed by the inspector of local government in Torit following his selection by the Päri as their paramount chief. He enforced the law, which stipulated that all men must wear clothes and any one found naked was lashed and warned that he would receive more punishment if he were found naked again. Today all Päri people wear clothes. Because chiefs apply justice when solving people's cases, their importance is recognized and feared by the common men. Today, when two persons fight or get into disputes over the issue of cattle or land, the weak in many cases seeks justices from the sub chief. Thus, phrases like, *I citha ki bang gääla* meaning, I will sue you to court or report to the police is commonly heard.

The position of a chief is got by election. He can remain in office as long as he cooperates with the ruling age sets. If he fails to cooperate, the weegipaac in power may use their influence to remove him from the post. This is done by general mobilization of the community condemning the chief and calling for his replacement. They usually forward their complaints to local government who examine the complaints and take appropriate action which may include election of a new chief.

Table 7.1 Names of the chiefs who ruled the country from 1909-2019.

Name	Year	Village
Lidu likide	1909	Wiatuo
Kidi Gumar	1909-	Wiatuo
Ungang Kidi Gumar[3]	? 1938	Wiatuo
Liyiime Ukwom Ukumu	1938-1939	Kɔɔr
Akaro Gumar Alwanya	1939-1945	Wiatuo
Suleiman Uciel	1945-1956	Pucwaa
Karlo Kidi Ujure	1956-1967	Wiatuo
Ubur Unyangameeri	1967-1968	Kɔɔr
Fidele Ungang	1968-1973	Wiatuo
Albano Urua Aciega	1973-1977	Pucwaa
Timon Arugo	1977-1978	Pugäri
Valentino Ukongo	1978-1981	Wiatuo
Ubote Ugäälä	1981-1982	Angulumɛɛrɛ
Paskwale Ungang Bule	1982-2019	Wiatuo

Since chieftaincy was introduced into Päri system of administration, the position of a chief has always been held by a member from the royal clan. As you can see above, the only chiefs who do not belong to a royal clan are; Albano Urua, Timon Arugo and Paskwale Ungang. The rest came from royal clans.

Note: Chief Ungang was dismissed and imprisoned at the end of 1938 for complicity in the murder of ten Lopit by the three men of the Lafon villages in December 1937. Therefore, Okumu was told to carry on until a new chief would be appointed. And in 1939 Akaro was appointed to replace Ungang[37].

---

37 .Source: TD/66-H-1 From DC to Gov. 4/2/39, Notes on chief Ungang

Chief Lidu Likide was the first chief to serve in Päri country as government agent after the British colonial administration instituted the chieftainship in Southern Sudan. Initially the government policy was to appoint influential people from the royal family to work as government agents. So, they asked chiefs to nominate and send the candidates to Mangalla to be made chiefs. When information reached Lafon, rwäth Kidi nominated Lidu Likide. According to Kidi, the people so wanted would either be killed or imprisoned. He chose Lidu because he originally comes from Bari and adopted as a son by his father. He thought it was better to send him rather than a true son or brother to Mangalla. So, Lidu Likide was sent to Mangala and got trained there. After training, he was given a bicycle, pair of kaki shots, shoes, stockings and a hat and sent back to Lafon to be in charge of the administration. When Kidi saw Lidu riding on a bicycle, dressed in uniform with the hat on head, he got surprised. It was here he came to know that government had vested more power on the chief than that of the local. Instead of congratulating the chief Likide, Kidi and his brothers became jealous of him and planned to eliminate him. According to the legend, Likide suddenly knocked his toe against the rock and swelled until the wound killed him. When chief Likide died, Kidi immediately took over and became both the chief and king. He appointed sub chiefs (mukungi) who must also come from royal clans. Such a policy was later followed by his son called Ongang who tookover from him. It was in 1970s that a common man was elected to serve as a chief.

f) Juridical Settlement of Disputes (Likwɛɛri)

The Päri people have a well-established system of traditional justice which centers around a court known as Likwɛɛri. The administration of this court conforms to the laws of the government especially court proceedings. The Likweɛri court deals with two types of cases. Firstly, murder falls within the competent of the court. Secondly, the court is responsible for handling disputes that may arise between one village and another. The king is the president of the court. He works with panel of judges who come from particular clans. The criteria for selecting these judges consist primarily of a strict loyalty to the king, wisdom and above all, the ability of the individual to speak eloquently in public. There are two sticks in Päri believed to have magic powers: *Tingidik* belonging to Kɔɔr village and *Gar* belonging to Wiatuo village. These sticks which are also named Likweeri are used as charms to bring good luck.

In the past the king of Kɔɔr village was the one holding the responsibility for administration of justice in the whole society. But later, the king of Wiatuo was vested with similar powers. The reason for devolving the administration of justice in this manner is that there was need for neutrality in the settlement of disputes. It was one way of reducing injustice or bias of the sole president of the court. For example, if a conflict arose between residents of Kɔɔr and any other village, there was a probability that the king of Kɔɔr may be biased in favour of his own subjects. What must be made clear is that the king of Kɔɔr settles all inter-village conflicts not involving Jo Kɔɔr. However, when a conflict opposes Kɔɔr villagers to any other villagers, the case must be settled by the court of likweeri which is presided over by the king of Wiatuo.

Concerning murder cases, there is an action to be taken in accordance with traditions. The normal practice is that the offender has to seek protection from the king of Kɔɔr or that of Wiatuo. It means that the murderer must escape revenge and has to declare himself to the custodian of likweeri. Supposing that the murder is committed in Kɔɔr, the offender must seek the protection of the king of Wiatuo and vice versa.

It is worth mentioning that for protection, the offender must have a goat slaughtered on his behalf before he is allowed to enter the compound of the king. The purpose of slaughtering the goat is to perform a purification rite on the offender. It is believed that the people in the compound where the offender takes refuge could contract leprosy if he is not purified. The purification process is done by painting the murderer with *wɛɛɲyi* that is the content of the guts (chyme). A sample of chyme is smeared on the forehead, shoulders, knees and the feet. There after, the murderer will be allowed to enter the king's compound and enjoys protection. During this time, no one can dare to take revenge on his life. People fear that a misfortune would strike the family of the person who would do so. However, for mere precaution, panel of judges strictly escort the murderer whenever he goes out during the first week of the murder. After some times, when the temper of the relatives of the deceased have subsided, the offender enjoys a kind of liberty he needed. He can join the company of his age mates and participate in all activities in the village of protection while waiting the judgement of his case.

When the day of court hearing comes, the panel of judges will summon the parent of both the deceased and the murderer to attend the court. The clansmen of two parties in conflict will accompany the parents to the court. Interested elders in other villages do participate in the hearing. Initially, the offender is questioned on how the murder took place, who were the witnesses and other key information are sought. Then the panel of judges asks the attendees to make their opinion on what kind of judgment could be passed.

It must be understood that the killing of the murderer is prohibited in court verdicts. Nevertheless, Likweere court does ask the parents of the deceased to tell what kind of compensation they would want their love one be compensated with. The choice is restricted to two: either cattle or human being (lääy or cuo). Whatever choice the deceased parents make is considered and passed. The court then sets the period in which the compensation should be completed.

The compensation made for the dead person is known as *kwoor*. Normally, the court keeps the murderer until kwoor payment is made.

In case the parents of the victim have settled for compensation in form of a human being, that person must be perfect without visible defects. In practice, Päri people take the female for compensation. The female selected for compensation, must be a virgin girl. Her parents must procure all kinds of dance ornaments such as beads, leather skirts, and other important onarments.

On the day she is to be presented to the court, the parents dress her with dance ornament. Her best friends who also wear dance ornaments accompany her to the court. Usually, before the girl is handed over to the parents of the victim, the panel of judges must inspect her. The girl must be perfect without any defect on her body. The reason why the judges have to check the girl or animals presented for compensation is to convince the parents of the dead to accept the offer without reservations. This is because every child is perfect in the eyes of his/her parents. Consequently, a perfect human being can only be determined by a neutral person. Even when the person killed is disabled, the person given to replace him must satisfy the criterion of perfection. When this condition is met, the panels of judges receive the girl or animals for that matter and bless her wishing her to stay well and produce many children. After the prayers, the girl is handed over to the parents of the deceased family who takes her home. There one of the brothers of the deceased will take her as his wife to produce children. But the children they produce in this type of marriage belong to the dead person. Nowadays, the government is discouraging this form of compensation and warns tribes practicing this to abandon the act.

At times the family of the dead chooses compensation in the form of cattle. In such a case, the responsibility will fall on the whole clan members of the murderer. Each member, including the family of the murderer, will have to contribute a required number of cattle for compensation. After getting them, they send a message informing the panels (Jo likweeri) that they have in their possessions the needed heads of cattle for compensation and are ready for delivery. The king and the panel of judges will then decide the day when these cattle would be handed over to the family of the deceased. Hence, they inform the later of the day of the court.

There is a strict checking of the cattle by the panel of judges before they hand them to the family of the deceased. All animals that demonstrate any kind of defect are immediately rejected and returned with the condition that they must be replaced without delay. So their mouths, noses, eyes, ears, horns, tails, and hoofs are thoroughly checked. When all the cattle have met the condition of perfection, the king and the panel of judges bless them after which they hand them to the brothers of the deceased who will drive them home. In addition to the cattle, the clansmen of the murderer must offer a number of goats to Jo likweeri who will slaughter one to smear the chyme on the stick, which is also called likweeri. The remaining goats will then be divided among the panel of judges and the king. Therefore, the murderer is set free. He can then choose to go where he committed the murder without any fear of revenge. Some free murderers choose to live with the king and become an adopted son. The cattle given for compensation are always used to marry a wife for the dead person. The children born by one of the brothers are legitimate offspring of the deceased.

CHAPTER EIGHT

Marriage

Every Päri person shares the idea that every female is born to be married. For that matter, all women whether blind, deaf, lame, cripple or abnormal are married in Päri society. A woman is married to produce children who are wished to continue the family name. The children are expected to protect the society and help their parents with work when they become old.

Päri men marry their wives almost at any age after they have reached maturity. Foremost, young men of 18 years begin to marry their wives at the time the group has reached the stage of *Athwol* (i.e. an ornament used by the youth during *Käruma* traditional dances*).* Other individuals marry their wives after they have passed that stage. Similarly, the right time for a girl to be married is when her breasts start protruding and others after that. Marriage involves transfer of bride wealth from the bridegroom's family to that of the bride. This involves payment of cattle, goats or sheep. Once these animals are given to the parents of the girl, marriage becomes established.

Betrothal

In normal circumstances, most Päri men prefer direct talks with a girl one may wish to marry. Engagement takes place at particular centers or homes. These centers are spread all over the villages and usually in the home of either the mother to one of the members or in the home of an old woman related to one of the members. It is in such homes that men come for engagement. At engagement centers, girls often sit on wooden benches arranged in rows. When a man comes, he chooses one girl from the group and in an isolated corner they talk words of love. If a girl accepts the words of the boy and made commitment, the boy will later ask the girl to let them make sexual intercourse.

Girls' age at the start of love affairs.

Premarital sex

Making first physical love with a Päri girl involves serious negotiation. A girl always wonders whether a boy is really sincere or just wanting to use her. To know if in fact a boy is sincere or exploiters, most girls often attach conditions to such requests. A girl may ask a boyfriend to present marriage request to her parents before accepting sexual intercourse. But young men want to test the virginity of a woman before marriage. They often insist that to make sexual intercourse with a girl truly confirms the existence of love between the two partners. Here, if a girl is rigid, the relationship may break. If she gives in, it won't be done without wrestling either. Often a girl resists and in due course, the two will always wrestle. And unless a girl is overpowered by the boy real physical intercourse will not take place. Päri girls behave in this way for the general belief that a girl who never resists during the first physical intercourse will bear a weak and abnormal baby. Nevertheless, after the first physical intercourse with a girl, a boy/man becomes confident of his lover and may eventually start the process of marriage.

Marriage Talks

A Päri boy never talks directly to his parents about the girl he loves and hopes to marry. Often, he uses his intimate friend to tell his parents about the girl he may wish to marry. When the parents learn of the issue, they discuss the matter. First, they trace out if there are barriers that will not allow a normal marriage to take place between the two families. For instance, the parents must make sure that no enmity exists between the two families; the parents of the girl should not be trouble makers, nor engaged in the practice of sorcery, witchcraft and the like. Concerning the girl, she must be a hard working, obedient and to some extent, beautiful. When these and other negative aspects are non-existent, the parents arrange for the marriage of their son.

The process always starts by selecting and assigning a mediator (Nyi*yoo)* to pass the message of marriage to the parents of the girl. This is because both parents do not engage in direct talks. Customarily, a mediator does not enter the house of the in-laws before sunset. He enters there after the sun has disappeared from the horizon. And before a mediator enters the compound of the in-laws, he has to send a neighbor to let the parents not to be taken by surprise. Such information is always necessary so as to enable the in-laws make some preparation, such as, cleaning the compound, preparing the stools or a bed for the visitor to sit on. Usually after preparation, the mediator is let in and welcomed on the bed. Then he will tell the father of the girl about the desires of the boy to marry his daughter. But since both parents do not involve themselves in direct discussions, the father of the girl will always tell the mediator to go back and return the next day.

While alone with his wife, the father calls his daughter and asks her as to whether she really loves the boy mentioned. If the answer is yes, the parents send out their daughter and remain behind discussing the matter. They trace out the boy's background with special regards to his behavior and that of his parents; bad characters such as stealing, quarrelling, sorcery, etc can block marriage relationships. There should not be enmity between the two families either. And insufficient cattle and goats to pay for the bride wealth make marriage talks difficult to continue.

After this survey, the father of the girl consults his brothers to know if there are barriers, which will not allow a normal marriage. The mother will make a similar contact with her brothers. These consultations are necessary to avoid misunderstanding, which could lead to a total break of relationship among brothers and sisters. However, when no barriers exist, marriage can be conducted successfully. But if there are bars, it may not succeed.

Whatever the case may be, when the mediator of the boy's parents comes back for the second round of talks, he will be met by the mediator of the girl's parents. The two mediators, who are well instructed of what to say during the negotiation, begin their talks. Often, talks cover the actual number of cattle, goats and any other issue of importance. The mediator on the side of the boy's parents must mention the colours of those cows and bulls for the dowry.

Usually, when the demands of the parents of the girl are met, a hoe (which is a sign of covenant) is received from the mediator of the boy's parent. That means marriage talks have been successful. From there the mediator is told to convey a message to the parents of the boy that members of both families should now observe mutual respect. Customarily the husband must avoid meeting face to face with the father-in-law or mother-in-law. Avoidance is an extreme form of respect. A good son-in-law hides himself from the mother-in-law whenever he sees him/her coming towards. If a son –in-law fails to observe this custom, it may lead to the break up of marriage relationship. These days, the youth are not observing this custom. Instead of running away from the mother-in-laws, they make physical contacts with them by shaking hands.

It is to be noted that bride wealth is not paid immediately to the father of the girl just as marriage agreement has been reached. The dowry remains under the care of the boy's parents until the day the father of the girl demands them. So, it is necessary to mention the number and colours of those cows and bulls to be remembered and proved later. This is to avoid any future confusion when these animals are physically shown. Actually, parents fear that if the actual number and colours of cows and bulls are not declared during marriage talks, the father of the boy may change his mind later on when those animals are physically seen, but then give different cattle or goats which may not be in the interest of the father of the girl.

Exchange of Visits

In Päri society, a newly married woman is never handed to the husband immediately after the marriage covenant has been reached. Usually she remains in the care of her parents for a period of time. In the past, a new wife used to stay with her parents for a period of three years before giving her freedom to start a new family. Nowadays, the period has been reduced to a year. During her stay with her parents, she is allowed to visit the family of the husband as many times as she likes. Unlike the wife, the husband does not frequently visit the family house of his wife. He can go there only if a member of that family is sick or when his wife has brought in a newborn child. He can also go there when called to do house- work services such as building the hut or fence.

When a wife pays a visit to the family of her husband, she often goes in the company of her best friends (about two or three girls). When they go, they usually take along with them some flour and drinking water as gifts to be presented to the family. The moment they arrive, they are welcomed and entertained by clan sisters and girls from the neighbourhood. In the evening, they return to their homes with a goat or money as gifts from the parents of the husband. In fact, money has only been introduced recently in the 1970s. Previously people used goats to settle such issues.

Bride Wealth Payments

As mentioned earlier, cattle and goats are not handed to the father of the girl immediately the marriage agreement has been reached. Often these animals are left for a period for time under the care of the boy's parents until the day the parents of the girl want to take them. When the day comes for taking the bride wealth, both mediators are called to witness the hand over. The mediators must prove the number and colours of cows or bulls are the same as described in the agreement reached during the talks. When everything is proved true, the cattle and goats are then received by the father of the girl, who will take them to his kraal (kaalo). From here the marriage of the couple is established. But if contradiction occurs, for example, if the number of cattle shown is less than the ones agreed upon or that the colours stated during negotiations are different, marriage can be broken.

Extra Wealth payments

To Päri, when a daughter is married, the maternal uncle (even though he has taken all the cattle required for marriage from his brother-in-law), asks to be given a cow or a bull. He needs this cow to offer his final blessings upon his sister's daughter. This is what the Päri call *nguti piny* meaning to spit down the saliva. That means, if a sister has many daughters the uncle demands one cow or bull from the wealth paid for each. However, before an uncle asks the in-laws to be given such a cow, he offers beer to the in-laws as a bribe. Without beer, some in-laws refuse to give a cow or a bull to the maternal uncle of the wife (nääro).

End of bride wealth payments

Legally, after the bride wealth has all been paid to the girl's father, the son-in-law has the right to demand one cow back from the father-in-law. Such a cow is known as *deedi*. This word derives from the verb *deed* meaning to close or block. When this cow is given, marriage payments end.

Married Couple Work-Test

After marriage has been established, the entire responsibility of fieldwork: cultivation, sowing, weeding, harvesting of the crops, building and renovating the huts of the in-laws and many other services are put on the shoulders of the husband. These services are termed '*kony*', meaning help. Actually, the husband is doing this to pay for all the parents of the girl had done to bring up their daughter. In the past, a husband used to labour for the in-laws for a period not less than three years before the couple are allowed to form their family. However, in the late 1970's, most young men began challenging this long period of hard labour and decided to work for only one or two years and then demand their wives. The reduction in the period of services made the ruling authority (*madaan*) to increase one cow on top of the official number of cattle needed for marriage. This additional cow known as 'dhieng puur' is given as compensation for the services the husband would have given to the family of his wife. This is a change of policy. In the past, if the husband failed to accomplish these tests, marriage was broken and the woman remarried to another person.

The test for obedience and hard work is not applied to a husband alone. A new wife is also subjected to such tests. Normally, if the parents of the boy want to know whether the wife of their son is a hard-working woman and obedient, they invite her to do house work service. The moment the message of invitation reaches the new wife, she informs two or three of her best friends to accompany her to the husband father's house. When they arrive in the house, they will be welcomed and entertained by clan sisters and girls from the neighbourhood. After some time, the girls who escorted the new wife return to their homes. The parents of the husband offer them some gifts in the form of a goat or money. After the girls have gone, the new wife starts the work she is being called for.

Usually before she starts the work, the mother of the boy introduces the housework. She will be shown various calabashes in which each family member gets his/her ration put in and all the kitchen works. After introduction, the new wife is left alone to do the work. She will do everything without getting help from anyone. Every day she grinds grain into flour, brings drinking water, gives bathing water to every family member, cooks food and serves every member of the household during each meal.

Customarily, a new wife (anyääno) never tastes the broth she cooks nor eats the food she cooks in the husband's father's house. Whenever she wants to know whether the salt she has put in the broth is tasty, she calls another person to do so. If a new wife eats food in the house of the in-laws, people will insult her as a greedy, glutton or, disrespectful woman. However, during her stay in the family house of the husband, neighbours and relatives of the husband keep on bringing food to share with her. She can eat food cooked by a non-relative of the husband and rejects food cooked by a relative to the husband. Unless a goat is slaughtered and a ritual performed and blood sprinkled on her, she won't eat food there at all.

The Daily Meals

Generally, the Päri eat twice in a day: breakfast and super. In each meal, the newly married man is served more food than any other member of the household. At breakfast time, while each member gets one ration, the husband alone is served two rations. He shares one ration with his best friend and another ration is served to the age group. At super times, he gets three rations. One ration is served to his age group and shares another one with his best friend. Later at midnight before he sleeps, the wife serves him with a special meal known as *ugän*.

Traditionally the food cooked by a new wife is always the first to be eaten by members of an age group. Usually, the agemates go to the house before sunset with the expectation that the new wife has already prepared the food. If they find the food not ready, they can level the new wife lazy. Such remaks may lead the husband disqualifying the new wife. To avoid humiliation and embarrassment when found unprepared, a new wife takes it a duty to prepare the meal much earlier than the rest of women. When members of an age group come to eat the meal, a new wife welcomes them and serves them with stools (*Liguutte)* or chairs (*kɔɔmi*). After they have settled, she serves them with warm water put in a gourd (*ukool*). During this service a new wife moves on her knees. She must make sure each member washes his mouth before eating the food. When all have washed their mouths, the wife returns to the kitchen to bring more water for washing their hands and then serves every individual as she passes from one man to the next. After this she goes back to the kitchen again to bring food. Customarily, a new wife should not walk but moves on her knees when bringing food to the age group. Often, a new wife has to make sure the thick porridge (*kwän*) and broth (*kadɔ*) filled in a bowl should not spill over to the ground. Any careless movement causing food to spill over disqualifies the woman and paves the way to divorce.

When the food is finally placed in the centre of the group it is eaten. While eating, the new wife hides herself in the kitchen to avoid seeing people eat the food. According to Päri tradition, the food cooked by Anyääno should not be eaten completely. Some food must always be left purposely in the dish even if the people are still hungry. The reason for doing this is that, the age groups fear being called by the woman as great eaters. And to be called a great eater is a bad insult to a Päri man.

After eating, the group returns to their camp to wait for a while before moving to share their other meals. Behind here, the new wife continues serving other household members. In the meantime, neighbours and relatives come in bringing food to share with the new wife. They will then share the meals with the neighbours. After the meals, they converse and disperse a few hours later the neighbours return to their homes. The work of the day ends here. This will be repeated every day until the period specified by the parents of the husband expires. This period varies from family to family. It may take seven or fourteen days before the new wife is allowed to return to their home. During this period the parents of the husband are able to know the character of the wife of their son. If they are satisfied with her manners, they bless the marriage. If not, they ask their son to look for another wife and abandon the woman.

Building a family home

After a husband and wife have completed the period of work test the couple plans to form their independent home. Here, a lot of preparations will be needed. This includes, cultivating a large field to produce enough grain so that some of the grain will later be made into beer for the people who would help in the work of the house. Other preparations include getting building materials. The materials for building a house are obtained through contributions by members of both families. In practice, the brothers of the wife cut poles for the wall known as coothe and also keede (type of wood). The husband brings bundles of bamboos for roofing, tying ropes, bundles of thatched grass to cover the bamboos and cuts ebony poles (aredo) known as loodi which are fixed on the ground in a circle upon which are tied bamboos to support the roof from falling. The roof is thatched by people who would be offered beer and food for their work.

When everything is ready, the husband chooses a site to build in the house. However, before building a hut, a diviner's advice is always sought to guarantee the safety of household members after they have settled there. If a diviner predicts that a misfortune may occur to the family after settlement in the new house, the location is changed to a safer place. If everything is okay, the building can go ahead until it is completed. After, the hut has been thatched; clan women on the side of the wife come and plaster the walls. After plastering, they flatten the floor with broken pots known as athää to make it smooth and splendid. In the meantime, the wife cuts woods for the fence (kallɔ). The sisters of the husband will help bring them home. When the work of building is completed, the couple waits for the new harvest to come and enter their new house. In the meantime, the parent of the wife buys a number of properties for their daughter. These include cooking pots, calabashes and sleeping beds. [38]

Early life in a new home

People celebrate when a new couple enters their new home. Often, this occasion takes place in the evening before sun set. In the compound, invited members are made to sit in groups according to clans. In this siting, the wife joins her parents and so do the husband. Talks center on the proper management of the family affairs. Initially, a mediator from the side of the wife stands up, welcomes the couple in their new home and relates the background of the wife. He will talk about the daughter being obedient, hardworking, and kind hearted woman. He concludes his speech by advicing the parents of the boy to teach their son to behave himself and avoid beating or mistreating their daughter. A similar speech will be repeated by the step mother of the wife, all stressing the need for the couple to live a peaceful life. After this, the mediator for the boy's family speaks about the background of the man. He will testify that their son is obedient, hard worker and that his mother cooks well for him. They will regret if the new wife fails to take care of his stomach. In most of the occasions I attended, parents

---

38 *Note: the early Päri people used cowhides as beds to sleep on. But in 1970s, mats and iron beds with mattresses were first introduced.*

never disclose the weakness of their son or daughter. Always they talk about the positive side of their sons or daughters.

After the mediators have spoken, elders advise the wife and the husband to behave themselves in their home. They are told to avoid quarrelling or fighting each other in the house. The wife should cook food to her husband regularly. She must respect the husband and all his relatives, brothers and sisters. Equally the same the husband is advised to treat brothers, sisters and relatives of his wife on equal basis as his own. He should also satisfy the needs of the wife. At the end of the talks, drinks are served to the people and everyone enjoys beer and dance as well. When night time comes, the people disperse each one going to his or her house leaving the couple start their new life. In the morning, old women come to say hallo to the couple. They will be welcomed and served food and drinks. For the first two to three weeks, a new wife has to labour a lot. At cockcraw, before the busband goes to work in the field, she prepares special food known as *nyakor gwieno* and gives it to the husband to eat. While in the field, his age group come and are served breakfast meal. For a number of days, the age mates continue to come regularly to have their meals in the house.

At the early years in the house the wife fears to eat food with her husband even though they are alone. Not only that, she even fears to eat food with the brothers or friends of her husband. It is only after a period of time (10-15 years) that a wife may develop courage to eat food with her husband but only when there are no visitors in the house. For this society, a woman is married for the whole clan. She should serve whoever comes to the house. The brother of the husband can command the wife of his brother to cook for him when he is hungry. The woman should not refuse. That's why a brother or friend addresses the wife of his brother as his wife.

Types of marriages

Every Päri man belongs to one of a number of exogamous (marriage outside) clans. And by rules of exogamy that regulates the choice of a wife, a man may not marry a girl of his own clan nor may he marry a girl belonging to the clan of his mother. There is a general believe that God does not give children to a married couple who are related by blood. Whenever a child is born, that child will always die. But at times, out of ignorance, a boy may enter into love affairs with his distant sister. Situation like this happens when both families do not exchange visits. And as time passes, some relatives become more distant than others do. Consequently, a boy can possibly get into love affairs with his sister. There are five types of marriages;

Marrying a distant sister

When a Päri man falls in love with his distant sister and would like to marry her, parents always refuse such a union on account of blood relationship. But some boys do ignore such beliefs and insist on marrying their lovers despite their parental refusal. When that happens, relationships break and the two families will not regard themselves relatives any more. Usually marriage of this kind keeps both parents in a state of anxiety. Parents doubt the couple may not get children in their life time. For the first six months or so, they wait anxiously for the woman to get pregnant. If the wife never conceives or that a child born dies, a diviner advice is sought immediately to discover the cause of the problem. If the reason is linked to the blood relationship, the parents of the couple organize an official break of their state of relationship. So, a ritual is performed in which God is prayed to bless the separation of these kinsmen and thus give them children.

The people invited for this ritual are; the clansmen and maternal uncles (*näree*) of the husband and the clansmen and maternal uncles of the wife. The maternal uncles from the couple make special ornaments called *atheere* made of alluminium metal. Each group produces four pieces of this metal to be dressed on the legs of the wife and the husband. The ritual is often performed in the morning in the homestead of the married couple. It begins with the narration of the genealogy of these kinsmen and ends with prayers. The people ask God to accept the official break of relationship between the wife and the husband. After this, *atheere* are tied with ropes on the legs of the wife and the husband. The atheere prepared by the maternal uncles of the wife are tied on the legs of the husband. And the ones made by the uncles of the husband are tied on the legs of the wife. Thereafter, the people start drinking beer prepared for the ocassion and disperse afterwards. The two married persons are no longer considered relatives any more and are expected to live a normal life.

Marrying a close sister

The situation slightly differs in the case when a son insists on marring what the parents consider a close sister. In this situation, a ritual known as *Tökran* is performed. According to this ritual, a ram or goat is brought and slaughtered. Its intestine is then removed and cooked whole without cutting it into parts. When the meat is ready, it is taken out from the cooking pot. In the meantime, the wife and the husband are made to climb up the roof of their hut each served with whips to beat each other. Up there on the roof, they stand facing each other, and down below the relatives are divided into two. The clansmen and maternal uncles of the wife stay as a group and position themselves behind (in the direction of their daughter). The clansmen and maternal uncles of the husband will make a similar arrangement. In other words, each group stays behind their person.

Very soon, the intestine is given to the couple up there on the roof. Then each of them is told to bite the long intestine from either ends and start pulling it towards each other. So the couple begins pulling the intestine with their mouths and not with their hands while at the same time beating each other with the whips. They too ask each other this question;' what relation do we have? ' ɔ rɔmba kɛɛ ki iini? The couple must deny their blood relationship before the relatives for god to accept and bless their union. The moment the intestine cuts into two parts, each one takes his or her portion and hurriedly climbs down. Upon reaching the ground, they immediately enter the room and close the door behind them

A few minutes later, a man from the husband side calls this people to come out. So, he knocks the door three times but the door will not be opened. When the person from the side of the wife knocks the door four times, the wife opens the door and both the wife and the husband are told to eat the intestine. After completing the meal, they come out to join the group in the compound. Soon the maternal uncles of the wife come and tie their atheere on the legs of the husband while their counterparts tie their atheere on the legs of the wife. After performing this ritual, the people are served with food and beer. But, the wife and the husband will not take part in this meal. After eating and drinking, the participants disperse leaving the couple in their house.

Co-wives (Nyää/Nyäkke)

The tradition of marrying more wives is still being practiced by many people in most African societies including the Päri. Marriages of this kind are made with the aim of producing more children so that in the future, these children are expected to help their parents with work and protect the community against outside aggression. In the case of female children, they are expected to bring riches into the family when they are married with cattle and goats.

But in real life, more wives create problems to husbands than good. There are instances in which co-wives make the life of their husband difficult and hateful. In this study, we have found out that most elder wives want the new wife to show a particular respect to them. If a new wife tries to develop independent thinking not wanted by the first wife, tensions arise in the family. And any slight favoritism to the new wife by the husband worsens the problem. Another common problem, which occurs among co-wives relates to the husband's time table for sleeping in the house of his wives. Co-wives want the husband to divide his days equally for sleeping in the house of both wives. He should not sleep consecutively in the house of one wife nor work consecutively in the field of one wife. If this rule is not followed, the wife who feels neglected becomes jealous and can cause trouble to the husband. Similarly, when a man goes for hunting and brought some meat home, he should call his wives together and divide the meat equally. Should he divide the meat in the absence of another; the absentee can accuse the husband for being unjust and this may result into confrontation. And the more tension increases the more family disintegrates.

Forced marriage (Rwɛɛc)

Not all marriages in Päri society are carried out on the basis of mutual agreement between a wife and a husband. Some marriages are forced. The Päri called this *Rwɛɛc*. In this type of marriage, the parents of the boy arrange with the parents of the girl for marriage but without the consent of the girl. This often brings disagreement between a girl and her parents. Consequently, a father resorts to the use of force. He does this by ordering his sons (if any) and young men of the clan to bring some whips with which to beat the girl. When the whips are brought, the young men force the girl to walk to the house of the man who has brought wealth into the family. As they walk, they make sure the girl does not resist. Any resistance will be met with severe beating. They beat her right from home all along the way to the house of the man. When they reach the house, they return leaving their sister to live with the man she otherwise hates very much. Most girls treated like this sometimes commit suicide. Others give up their resistance and conditionally accept such a marriage.

Another form of forced marriage is known as *Tingi dhaagɔ*. This is where a husband, supported by friends, seizes a woman and takes her to his house by force. This happens after the husband has paid the required cattle to the father of the girl and that the parents of the girl had given him freedom to posses her. This is not always an easy exercise. A girl usually fights back. In the course of the struggle, strong men are made to drag her on the ground or raise and carry her on the back. This is what the Päri called *Tingi Dhaagɔ* the raising up of a woman. In the house, the cohorts make sure the girl willingly accepts to have sexual intercourse with the husband. If not, they intervene by throwing her down, spread her legs open while pressing her hands down and make the husband rape her. After this, the group leaves them alone. The woman may stay in this house for some days before she returns to her parent's home. From 1970s, however, the attitudes of people towards this form of marriage have changed. Many people began condemning it as a bad system. The youth of today prefer marriage based on mutual agreement between a girl and a boy rather than arranged formed of marriage.

Elopement of a Girl (kandi dhaagɔ)

Another way by which some Päri men marry their wives is by means of elopement. Elopement means running away with a girl from the village to another place to hide from her parents. Usually, before running away with a girl, the parents of the boy send their mediator to the parents of the girl informing them about the desire of the boy to marry their daughter. When the parents of the girl reject owing to some reasons, the boy and his girlfriend take as a last resort to run away to an unknown place in order to hide from the parents and relatives of the girl. Men take this as an alternative method to force the parents of the girl to surrender their daughter in marriage. While living in the place of hiding, the intimate friend who helped in the process of elopement keeps communicating with the lovers. He brings information concerning the reactions and attitudes of the parents of the girl to his friend. And as long as the attitudes of the parents of the girl remain hostile, the run away couple will stay in hiding. When the anger has subsided, the lovers return and resume their normal lives. In many cases, after pregnancy, some lovers opt to return home and expose themselves. In such a situation, some parents do reconsider their previous stand and accept marriage to take place. Others maintain their rejection and return their daughter under their care but demand one cow for breaking the viginity of the girl.

Isolated wife (Ajäära)

Earlier, divorce can hardly be approved by elders in Päri society particularly when a woman has produced male children. Thus, most men resort to isolate a woman considered notorious and troublesome and opt to live with a fairly good-mannered wife. The isolated wife will then undergo some punishment for her misbehaviour. To enforce this punishment, the husband instructs his brothers, sisters and relatives to stay away from this woman. No one should give any assistance to her. She is left to wander about trying to survive. The main purpose for this punishment is to rehabilitate the woman's behaviours to become good again. A woman treated like this is called Ajäära meaning the isolated wife. Unless the isolated woman reforms herself, she will remain in this desperate condition until her children become mature enough to help her with work. During the period of isolation, she is not allowed to make sexual intercourse with another man. If she commits adultery with another individual, that person will be sued to court and fined with two cows and a goat to be slaughtered to purify the children. And if she becomes pregnant by another man, that particular man will be taken to court and fined two cows and a goat to be slaughtered to purify the children. Yet a child born in this way belongs to the husband and not to the biological father.

Divorce

To Päri, when divorce happens between a husband and wife, a woman returns to the care of her parents. If she has produced some kids, she takes them as her offsprings. The husband has no right to claim them. What he can do is to demand payment of his cattle back to him which is always given. According to the custom, not all cattle are returned to the husband. The father retains one cow for what is known as *karcurbeth* that is, a cow paid for having broken the virginity of the girl. When the woman is remarried to another man, that new husband takes the children as his own. The children too regard the new husband as their legal father. In the case where a woman decides alone to divorce the husband without the consent of her parents, the husband takes the children as his own. But no cattle will be returned to him.

Widow

To the Päri, if a husband dies, parents advised the widow to produce children with the brother or any other close relative to the deceased; in many cases, a brother or a son of the brother of the father, or a son by another wife. Anthropologists' call this practice *levirate.* The levirate serves as insurance that an alliance created by one marriage will not be dissolved by the death of one person. The parents of the late husband always want the children to follow the bloodline. But sometimes the widow refuse to cohabit any of the relatives or a brother proposed by the parents of the late husband and chooses to live with a non- relative. This sometimes creates misunderstanding between the widow and the parents of the deceased. Nevertheless, if the woman is so determined to cohabit with a non-relative, she can be allowed to do so provided that the man chosen must be of good character. If not, they can disapprove such a union. Once a widow is given the liberty to choose a man to produce children with, several men come forward to show their interests. Whoever is selected should immediately report to the parents of the late husband to get approval. If the man accepted is the right one in the opinion of the parents, they will allow him to live with the widow. However, before they start to stay together, the man is asked to bring a goat to be slaughtered so that God blesses the new family to live well. After this ritual, the widow can now live with the new husband without worry. In fact, this kind of a union is not a new marriage, but a continuation of the old one. The new husband is in fact a bull who will just produce children on behalf of the dead husband. This is what Middleton calls "the institution of widow inheritance and not a true levirate" Middleton, J. (1965, 72).

Actually, not all widows are willing to remain as wives of the dead husbands. In many cases, young widows choose to divorce the dead husbands and be remarried to other men. Here, the parents of the late will do nothing other than to demand payment of their cattle and goats back. These cattle will then be used to marry another wife to produce children for the dead son. In the case of old widows who have produced children, some perhaps old enough to help their mother with work, the widow refuses to be inherited and chooses to remain alone

Purification rite for married couple (Awuɔr)

Päri parents are anxious to know the fertility of their children. Usually.after marriage has been completed parents expect the married couple to bring in a newborn. If a woman spends six months or a year without getting pregnant, parents become agitated. Consequently, a diviner advice is sought to find a solution to the problem. If a diviner finds that the former boyfriend maliciously caused this disability by applying certain magics, the parents of the girl summon that man to come to the house to undergo purification rite. At the same time the husband is asked to quit his house to allow his wife and the former boyfriend try their luck to produce a child. He will have to go and stay in a distant area and will remain there until the period of purification expires which is always determined by the coming of the menstruation period. So, the wife and her former boyfriend will be locked in the room to make sexual intercourse in an attempt to produce a child. This is what the Päri called Awuɔr.

In the compound, clanwomen stay guiding the outside gate to prevent people from coming into the house. They also make sure the two are well fed. Whenever they become hungry food is served to them. They eat the best diet; meat, milk, fish and other delicious food. If any of them wants to go to the toilet, he/she will be accompanied by the old women. After defecation, the women escort her/

him back to the house to continue the struggle. After one month, the woman is asked to know whether or not she has conceived a baby in her womb. Whatever the case may be, the man is released after one month has elapsed. The real husband is then called to resume their lives with his wife. A child born in this way belongs to the husband and not to the boyfriend.

Adultery

If a woman or girl is caught red handed playing sex with a man, that man would be held responsible for the crime and often told to bring a goat to be slaughtered to purify the woman/girl concern. The goat given for this ritual is called 'rwodhi'. Customarily, the slaughter of the goat takes place at afternoon hours. The people who are eligible for conducting this ritual are members of mojomiji and elders of the clan. Usually, after the goat has been slaughtered, the content of the guts (weenyi) and some blood is collected and mixed. Thereafter, each one attending the occasion prays while smearing the mixture of chyme and blood and smears it on the woman wishing her good life. After this action, the goat is roasted and eaten whole by the elders. The women have no share in this meal. The children can only eat intestines which are always given to the wife to cook for them. Finally, a fine of one cow will be charged on the man to pay.

Impotent Man (Löör)

Men and women who do not produce children suffer scorn in Päri society. Customarily, if a man is known to be impotent, that is, his sperms are too weak to fertilize an egg in a woman, his father and other close relatives meet in secret and discuss the matter. They then advise the woman to try to produce children with another brother of the husband. If she chooses one, that individual will then be advised by elders not to make physical intercourse with the woman in the house of the husband. A similar advice will be given to the wife to observe the same. Further, the two are told to respect the husband and to make sure the affair is kept secret. To guarantee against any leakage of secret, the man and the woman must swear that they would not expose the secret at all. When the woman becomes pregnant, the man will distant himself leaving the woman to continue with the real husband. The children born in this way belong to the husband who is impotent and not to the biological father. If however suspicion decends on the wife as being baren, relatives, friends and sympathizers come openly and advise the man to marry another wife in order to produce children who would continue the family name. Some wives do suggest to their husbands to marry another wife to have children.

Naming of Child

Generally, a Päri child is named after the umbilical cord has fallen. On the naming day, relatives who have been invited come to attend the ceremony. Foremost, a child who has been kept inside the room since birth is finally brought out in the compound. Then the mother lays the child on her thighs. The attendants assemble near the mother who sits facing the door of the hut. Soon the oil for blessing the child is brought and poured in the calabash. From here, the person who is to give a name to the child comes forwards, takes the child from the mother and anoints him with oil. Then he or she lift up the child and calls him with this new name. *Nyipondo ki Pääro.* While playing with the child he or she utters words of prayers to God wishing the child to stay well and live longer. Then she or he hands back the child to the mother and returns to his or her seat. Before taking his/her seat, he/she anoints the mother with oil as well. This act will be repeated by all the participants in the ceremony.

To the Päri, personal names are important. Traditionally, parents give names to their children according to turns: the first turn is always for the mother of the child. She will name the child after her mother or father depending on whether the child is a male or female. The second turn is for the father; he will name the child after his mother or father depending on the sex of the child. A child may also take the name of a close relative such as, uncle, aunt, grandmother and grandfather.

Sometimes, the Päri give names to children according to the circumstances in which the child has come to birth. A child born during rain takes the name *Ukoth* for male and *Nyikoth* for female; the one born at the time of hunger or starvation will be called *Ukec* for male and *Nyikec* for female. Similarly, a child born on the road is named *Uyoo* for male and *Ayoo* for female. The one born during war is named *Uto*ng for male and *Nyito*ng for female child.

Dictated by some condition, a child may also be given a non-family name. For example, when a child is born while at the same time a great leader or a friend dies that child will be named after such a person... That is why it is difficult to trace some Päri boys from the father's name. The father may be called Ujwok Ubur while the son, who uses non family name, may be called Ukoth Ucala. Besides the given name, the first-born child will always be named Kayo. The second born is named Julu and third born will take the name Bongo. However, the fourth born child up to the one born before the last is named Ayaago. The last born is called Angudo. Concerning twins, the first one is called Upieu for male and Apieu for female; the second one is called Ucään for male and Acään for female. A child born after twins takes the name Acii or Akeelo for female and ucii or ukeelo. A boy born after girls is called Ukeeny.

After the child has been named, people are served with beer (koongo) and food. They will enjoy themselves till evening when they will finally disperse. In the mean time, visitors who come to the house do also anoint the child with oil in the same manner as was done by the participants. Anyone who fails to do this is suspected to have evil intention against the child. A few weeks later a goat is slaughtered and its skin removed to be used for carrying the child and known to Päri as bɛɛnhdho. Three months later, beads are worn on the child's wrists, neck, and waist and above the ankles '*nyipondo ki ngondo ki tii*'.

It is to be noted that the naming ceremony is always conducted by old women. However, if the child is to be named by a man, that individual will join the women in the naming ceremony. Some time later, the person who named the child offers some gifts to the child. The most common gifts are beads (to female) and spears (to male) children.

Chapter Nine

Beliefs and Customs

The word *Jwɔk* in Päri language refers to the Almighty God known as" *Jwɔk Atäng*" and to the evil spirits known as "*Jwɔk mar piny* "meaning, the god who lives on the ground. The Jwɔk Atäng lives up in the sky, *Jwɔk mar maalɔ*. However, the people do not pray to Him very frequently but only under certain circumstances. The Päri fear the god that brings diseases and misfortunes. Consequently, they worship several gods in various sacred places. Moreover, the people still practice traditional medicines and witches are still being respected as having supernatural powers to cure diseases or even to weaken the powers of the devil.

Deaths and illnesses are events associated with the actions of certain spirits, a curse from another person, witchcraft, sorcery and the like. When a young person dies, such a death will not be considered natural, someone must have caused such a death or else, a certain sacred place might have been defiled by the victim. To know the cause of misfortune, parents consult a diviner for his expert knowledge in providing the possible answers and their solutions. John Beattie rightly describes it this way;

> People usually seek magical help in situations of misfortune; if everything were for the best of possible worlds, there would be no need for magic. The commonest kind of misfortune is, of course, illness, either one's own or that of a person for whom one is responsible, such as a child or another member of the family.

Beliefs and Customs

The first thing to be done is to discover the cause of the illness and to do this it is necessary to consult a diviner' Beattie, J, (1960:71)

Diviners are also consulted to foretell what will happen in the future. For example, a man may want to construct a hut in a given place, the first thing to do is to consult a diviner to advice whether the site chosen is a good place for settlement or that a misfortune may happen to the family after settlement. Before going to war, the ruling age set consult a diviner to know whether the Päri people will win the war or lose it with or without casualties. Similarly, before a group goes hunting, a diviner is always consulted to discover if the group will kill the targeted animals or not. To identify the client's problems the diviner use cowries' shells called gaa or little fine stones called *ugwii*. These things *are* kept in a bag and just waiting to be used when a new customer comes in for the purpose.

People who seek diviners' services pay some quantity of dura in return. When the diviner receives this item, he starts the work. First, he spreads the shells on the ground and later asks the client to narrate his troubles. After hearing, he gets the shells in his hands, spits on them and while praying to the spirit which empowers him to work divination, he throws the shells up into the air. But without letting the shells fall on the ground, he immediately catches them from the air. Then he picks a number of them and begins counting these things on the ground: four pieces form a group. Should there be any remainder, which must be either one or two or three, that or those shells are put on the ground. The diviner will do this act many times until the final round is done. At each round the remaining shells are lined up on the ground, forming a chain, one group following the other. Based on this, the diviner interprets the meaning and says whether he or she can do something to help the situation

There are other techniques besides throwing of stones (ugwii). Some diviners use water put in a calabash or gourd to treat patients suffering from cases like stomach trouble or chest pain. In their treatment a patient is made to lie on his/her back and then a diviner places the calabash containing water on the affected area. Then he utters words of prayers to the spirit while at the same time shaking the water with his hand. Finally, he takes out the calabash now containing some visible objects claimed to have come out of the body and shows it to the patient. Then he tells the patient to go back home but to keep on coming for further treatment. Later, when the patient has recovered from the illness, a diviner makes some charges, the commonest ones being a goat/ram or a cock to be offered to god so that similar misfortune may not come again.

Sorcery (*Luok*)

To the Päri illness or death and any serious injury are sometimes connected to sorcery. Sorcerers carry out their activities against other persons in the hope of hurting or killing them by the use of secret harmful medicines or technique. It occurs more commonly among relatives, who are bound by such relations to share things in common.

Sorcerers consult diviners to advice on how best they can destroy or injure their opponents. The most common advice they get is to kill a lizard, wrap it like a dead human being and bury it in the compound of the opponent. This act implies that the enemy will die and be buried in the same manner. Other sorcerers throw human feaces in the compound of their enemies, a sign that the concerned family will suffer misfortune and death and thus, the remaining members will hate the compound like the smell of human feaces. Some sorcerers kidnap children, whiten their bodies with ashes and let them go unhurt. The ashes on the body symbolize sorrow, which will be experienced by the parents of the child. There are many more techniques used by sorcerers against their rivals. In fact, sorcery is one of the evil activities usually practiced by jealous persons against innocence. In the Päri society, people who produce a lot of grain, posses many cattle; goats/sheep become a target of sorcery. A fight between one village and another one causes sorcery.

Kuuk (Blessing)

Kuuk is a blessing in which a good thing is wished for a person. Elders usually apply it to a sick person or to someone who has killed an elephant, eland, leopard or any animal of great value to the society. To a sick person this blessing is made as the last resort after many attempts, such as seeking diviners' solution and the use of medicines have failed. In carrying out this blessing, parents must invite members of the ruling age sets and elders to come to bless the sick person. The blessing takes place in the morning. The general rule is that, people who participate in this blessing should not drink or eat anything. Not only that, they should not even brush their teeth before giving such a blessing. The Päri believe that the first spittle is holy and should be used for blessing.

In the house, after the people have gathered, the sick person is brought out and placed in front of the people facing the west where the sun sets. Soon a calabash containing water is brought and each man spits into it three times and four for women. Then people start giving their blessings one by one. The elders start first and concluded by members of the ruling age sets. What happens is that each person that gets up takes the spittoon, offers prayers and finally sprinkles the blessed water on the sick wishing him to recover from the illness. If there are children in the family, they too receive similar blessing. The people pray God asking Him to bless the family to live a happy life. After blessing beer is served and the people drink and disperse after completing it

In the case of someone who has killed any of the following animals; eland, Giraffe, leopard etc, elders themselves invite him to come to the camp to receive their blessings. The elders give this blessing to enable the man continues to kill more of such animals so that the elders continue eating meat.

Lam (invocation)

Lam is an ambiguous word. It can be an act in which people appeal to God asking him to bring good luck. For example, when there is shortage of rain in the village, the Päri pray God to send them rain. It can also mean blessing when a good thing is wished for a person or a thing. An elder person may give this blessing to a young person who has done him good. He will bless him and wishes him to live a longer life or marry a good woman. Cattle or goats/sheep may be blessed to stay well and multiply. When an elder person gives this blessing, he spits on the head or hands of the recipient. At times, he raises up the hands of the recipient.

Lam can also mean a curse, when a bad thing is wished for a person or animal. For example, if an unknown person kills somebody's cow, the owner of the cow may ask the ruling group together with the elders to curse the person who has done him wrong. So, he offers a bull to be killed. The people then kill the bull and take out the liver so that everybody spit on it as they curse the wrong doer to die. After cursing, the liver is roasted and distributed to each one to eat. The rest of the meat will also be shared and consumed as well. From there the people disperse

Sometimes a curse by means of *Lam* can be revoked through *Kuuk,* provided that the person cursed comes early before it is too late to rescue the situation. If a person cursed realizes his own deeds and confesses in the last moments when he is very ill and about to die, any blessing made to reverse the curse may not be possible. In the case of a person who confesses before a curse was conducted, no lam will be made upon him. Instead, he will be sued to court and punished to pay a cow or two cows to the owner of the cow.

Gwieth (blessing)

Gwieth is a sort of blessing usually given to a living person by someone who is about to die. It is a disembodied spirit of a dead person. These spirits are associated with the underground world. This is widely believed to be one of the most effective immaterial weapons useful for personal and group defense. For that reason, most Päri elders give it to their children wishing them to produce many children, get many cattle, goats and sheep. A society can also receive this blessing to live a prosperous life. The technique varies from one person to another. The giver may spit in the hands or on head of the recipient. Other givers spit on certain objects like a stone (symbol of long life), cattle noose (to get more cattle), head of grain (to have a good yearly harvest).

To the Päri, if an outstanding man dies without giving this blessing wishing the society good life, that individual will be suspected of having died with a grudge against the society. Prior to his death, the ruling age group secretly consults a diviner to tell whether the deceased has an evil intention agains the community as for example, wishing them to suffer serious famine, defeats from their enemies or anything that can obstruct societal progress. If a diviner discovers that the deceased had cursed the community, the ruling age set quickly mobilize and rush to the house of the deceased. There they seize the wife of the deceased and force her to expose all the evil wishes uttered against the people. If there is a witness (nyidhɔk), that person will also be seized and ordered to tell the last words of the deceased. When they get the necessary information, including objects used as symbols to destroy the community, the ruling age sets exhume the body, make the wife or witness carry the corpse to designated location and throw it into the river or burn it outright. The Päri believe that once the corpse and any object used as symbol for cursing the community are thrown into the water, any evil wished to befall the community will be washed and made harmless by water. In the past some witnesses were beaten with sticks for having conspired against the community. But during the Madan administration some witnesses were killed on the spot. A man called *Udier* was executed accused of having conspired against the community of Wiatuo by cooperating with the man who cursed the society.

Usually after this action, members of the ruling age set kill a bull taken from among the cattle of the deceased and purify themselves against any evil. Thus, the chyme (wɛɛnyi) of the animal will be painted on the fore faces, shoulders, chests, knees, and feet of all the members of the ruling age sets. This is done to prevent the people who participated in the exhumation not to contract leprosy (dhɔɔbɔ) disease. After performing this, the meat is roasted and eaten all right there in the bush. Nothing will be brought home for the children.

Cien (curse)

To the Päri a misfortune may be due to the action of Cien. Cien is a curse made by a dying person. What happens is, before a person dies, he utters words of curse wishing his enemy to die, become mad, poor or anything like that. However, for Cien to become effective, the dying person must call a witness *nyidhɔk* and say the words of curse in his presence so that after death, the witness can conduct invocation calling the spirit of the dead to kill the opponent.

In fact, most cien come from the deceased's relatives who have been neglected or angered in one way or another. An abuse or neglect of an elderly person creates grounds for cien; a quarrel between an elder person and a young one may result in cien. In many cases, when a young person angers the elder person, the old person may utter such expression ***ani uyuuti,*** meaning: you will find me. Such words may be taken as a threat of cien and may even be used as such.

Cien can be applied internally or externally. External cien is that which is applied against foreigners. A certain tribe may be cursed to suffer defeats from the Päri warriors. Others are cursed so that their crops fail consequently; they bring their cattle, goats, sheep and other trading goods to the Päri country for sale. Internal cien is that which is applied to Päri people in various forms.

Cien can be treated by a diviner. Usually when a sick person is brought, a diviner works his magic to discover the cause of the illness. If it is found that the sickness was caused by the action of cien, the agent is most likely to be the spirit of someone who has been neglected or angered either by the victim himself or by another member of the family. So then the diviner applies the magic to heal the disease. Cien can also be revoked by the use of gwieth. That is, a dying person can destroy the curses made upon his relative through gwieth blessing.

Wizardry (Jwɔk)

The Päri name for a wizard is cijwɔk. According to them witchcraft are caused by the wizard's greed for meat, milk, fish, or anything that can arouse desires. The Päri think that an invisible snake exists in the stomach of its possessor. Once this snake desires something, say meat, the wizard immediately asks for it. But if the owner refuses to give, the wizard bewitches him. Of course, this is done without the knowledge of the victim. But if the wizard is found, he/she will be forced to cure the person bewitched or else, he/she faces death.

Aliga

Some families in the Päri society such as Geri, Pukwari, Laali, practice the custom called Aliga. According to this custom, after the child is born, the mother stays inside the room and will not come out into open with the child until the umbilical cord pɛɛlo, falls. During this period, the mother eats hot food. Always, before taking any meal, she is served hot gruel (athuuru). When she is taking this food, old women stay near by watching. They tell the mother to keep taking the gruel without putting it down to take some rest. However, if the mother stops taking (even though she is not satisfied), the gruel is quickly taken away from her and will not be allowed to take it any more. This is done to prevent the child from becoming abnormal (Nyiboyo) or be deformed. The leftover gruel will then be put aside to be consumed later by the old women. In case the mother of the child asks for more gruel, fresh gruel is prepared again and served to her. But all the time these women keep watching her to prevent the mother not to make another mistake. In the meantime, visitors who happen to come to the house with things like, axe, hoe, calabash, pot, shoes, etc., in hands have their properties confiscated (Jammi *amak alige*). They will not be returned to them until the umbilical cord has fallen. This is done to avoid any misfortune coming to the life of the child.

When the umbilical cord falls, thick porridge *kwän* will be cooked and distributed to the children who have been invited to attend this occasion. After distribution, the children sing the song *Ajwanna walo walo. Ajwanna Ajwanna walo walo*. They sing this song repeatedly while eating the food and running out of the house. As soon as they are out of the house, old women give the new child a name. After the naming ceremony, whatever had been confiscated will then be returned to their owners.

Muna disease

Social customs vary from one society to the next. Like many, the Päri custom strictly prohibits a wife from having sexual intercourse with another man in the husband's homestead. They believe that if a wife commits adultery in the husband's homestead, and especially when the very act of adultery was done on the bed the woman shares with her husband, the husband will automatically contract a fatal disease known as Muna. This disease gradually drains blood and after a period of time, it kills. However, not all Päri married men are liable to catch muna disease in consequence of adultery. Men from the clan of *Libaalu* are not affected. For them, muna affects the adulterous wife instead.

Bii

Bii is a spirit believed to be residing in a man. This spirit is realized after the wife has given birth to a new born child. According to Pari, Bii spirit causes ill luck to the father of the baby. For example, when people go to hunt animals, a man in whom resides this spirit never kill an animal for meat. And during fishing, he catches no fish. For that matter, people avoid making contacts with the victims of bii spirit for fear that a similar misfortune might affect one's life. Hence, people avoid greeting or touching the victim's spears. The time Bii lives in a person is short. Its existence is assiciated to the fall of the umbilical cord. Once it falls, the spirit disappears and the man's life returns to normal.

Calamity during birth

During birth, when a child does not come out very quickly as expected, the delay is often linked to the actions of spirits. To help the situation, some families use sand 'ngɔɔm' collected from the sacred place and gives it to the woman to chew to appease the spirit in order to allow a normal birth. Other families used sand collected from the pathway (*ngɔmbi yoo*) to be chewed by the woman in the belief that she can give birth to a child immediately after chewing it. However, if the mother or a child dies after all these attempts, the god of a particular sacred place is blamed for being the cause of the mishap. At times, the blame is thrown on someone who has just died and had been at enmity with the family of the victim. They say, "*Man naa acieni*" meaning this is a curse obviously caused by the spirit of a dead person.

Winyo

Like Bii, winyo spirit brings misfortune to the father of the child. But the two vary as to the time of occurrence and duration. Bii happens after the child is born and ends when the umbilical cord falls. But winyo enters into the life of the father just as the wife becomes pregnant for the second time. It lives in a man throughout the period of pregnancy and disappears after birth. In both cases, the man affected by winyo or Bii is often prevented from doing certain activities. During hunting, he can not be allowed to go in front of the hunters lest he should bring ill luck; His presence among the fishermen too brings mishap. For these reasons, people always keep them isolated. In the place of fishing such as Keek, the victim of winyo or Bii is not allowed to come close to the fishing area. If he wants fish, he stops at a reasonable distance and calls the fishermen from there without coming close. The fishermen usually understand the situation then offer him the fish he needs. Nevertheless, the person giving the fish is warned not to touch the beggar for the fear of acquiring a misfortune. All he can do is simply to wave his hand when greeting and then puts down the fish and returns to the group. The beggar then collects fish and takes it home.

Women Annual Gathering

At the beginning of the rainy season known as *laci koth* (literally meaning the urine of rain), Päri women led by the wives of ruling age group make contribution of grain seeds. And on a fixed day these women assemble at Akobo in Pugäri village for a meeting. Traditionally wives of the ruling age sets must put on decorated skirts (duupe) made of goats' skins or cow hides and aprons from calf or goats' skins. They come to Akobo[39] carrying contributed seeds to be offered to the god of Lipul or that of the Liguthuuru respectively.

In Akobo the wife of a prince of the ruling age set in Pugäri village opens the ceremony and invites wives of retired ruling ageset start the prayers. One woman will address the audience by the following words:

> Jwɔk Lipul. 'god of Lipul',
> Wan a -oo. 'We have come'
> Wa kwanyo ki iini tin naa bɛɛgiwa ii ciekke.
> We have come here toady to pray to you to bless us with good harvest'

Then she concludes by uttering such words of prayers: *kwän u-oee.* Let there be food. And the group responds,' *u-oee.* Let it come. *Kɔth*

---

39 Note: Akoobo is a name of a place in Lafon. Do not confuse it with the one in Anywaa land currently homed to Nuer community.

u-oee. Let there be rain. And the people answer' *u-oee.* Let it come. *Bɛɛl u-ciekke.* Let there be enough grain (literally: let the grain ripe) and the people respond *uciɛkkɛ* let it ripe. *Jwɔk uloobe ki* cäng; let diseases disappear with the setting of the sun. And the people respond; *uloobe.* Let it go.

After the prayer leader has ended the prayers, other women come forward in turns and give speeches which will be closed by wives of the ruling age set. The people pray wishing the society prosperous life. At the end of the prayers, wives of the ruling age sets and those of the elders take off running. They race towards the east to know the fastest runner. Among those runners is a woman holding a defective head of grain called *Adwaak*. The moment the runners reached a predetermined destination, they stop and assemble together. Soon the defective head of grain is thrown out in the direction of the Lopit (their neighbor in the east) cursing them to have poor harvest but the Päri to get a good harvest. After this, the group returns to Akobo in a procession singing songs of praise.

Just as the group arrives at Akobo, the women of Kɔɔr village branch away from the main group. They move to their village taking with them their seeds to be blessed by the god of Liguthuuru. Meanwhile, the women of the five villages: Bura, Pucwaa, Wiatuo and Angulumeere move in procession to the dance court yard of Pugäri people where the group dances. There some women are made to climb up the mountain carrying the seeds to be offered to the god of Lipul. Upon arrival, the high priest welcomes them and receives the the seeds. The high priest then takes seeds from each basket and offers them to god as a sacrifice. He does this by scattering some seeds in the Lipul cave and in other places around. He prays, wishing god to bless the seeds so that they germinate and produce enough grain. After sacrifice, the blessed seed (*koodhi mu jwɔk) a*re stored in *odi jwɔk* god's hut, built close to Lipul cave. The seeds will remain there until the day people start planting when they will be distributed to every head of family.

In the meantime, women who help carry the seeds climb down to join their group dancing in the courtyard. A few minutes later, elders interrupt the dancers to give them blessings. They throw sand (*ngom*) on these women blessing them to live a happy life and produce many children. After this, the group starts moving in procession to Pucwaa, Bura, Wiatuo and Angulumeere villages. In each of these villages, they dance briefly and receive blessing from elders. At the end of the ceremony, each group returns to their village to continue their celebrations and enjoyment

Equally the same, the women of Kɔɔr celebrate the feast in their village. They take the seeds to the house where the Liguthuuru spear is kept. There, the keeper of the spear offers sacrifice to god by throwing the seeds on the spear asking god to bless the seeds so that people produce a lot of dura. After that the blessed seeds will be stored in the hut of god where the Liguthuuru spear is kept. They will remain there until the day of planting when they will be distributed to all the people who would then mix it with their own seeds and sow them in the fields with confidence. After the women who took gran seeds to the house where Liguthuru is kept have returned and joined the group, people dance to the tune of three songs. After a brief dance, the elders stop wonen from dancing to make blessings. So, elders throw on them sand as blessing wishing them a happy life. Later, the group moves to the house where the group beer has been prepared and enjoy themselves. It is to be noted that Liguthuuru is a spear, which is kept in a small hut in Kɔɔr village. It has a keeper who performs religious rites. Crazzolara wrote,

> The Jwok of Kor is to some extent personified in a famous spear called Laguturu, which in former times accompanied the people in war Crazzolara, J.P. (1951:166).

This assertion by Crazzolara seems not to agree with the findings so far made with regard to the role of the Liguthuuru in war. Crazzolara seem to have confused the spear of the king of Kɔɔr that was used to bless the village warriors' spears with the Liguthuuru. The Liguthuuru is purely used in the blessing of seeds and has no role or function in warfare.

There is a special corn known as *beendi Kɔɔr* (the grain of Kɔɔr people). According to Jacob Umol, the head of this corn contains various seeds of different colours. This head of corn appears mysteriously in the field without someone planting it. Once it appears in somebody's field, the owner of the field must report the case to the keeper of the liguthuuuru spear. Otherwise the family concerned would suffer series of misfortunes. The moment the information reaches him, the keeper of the spear together with some elders immediately goes to the field carrying a black goat offered by the owner of the field. There, the stalk is pulled out from the ground, then the ear of the goat is cut and the blood sprinkled in the field. From there the keeper of the Liguthuuru prays to the god asking him to divert any misfortune that would have happened upon the family and wishes them to stay in peace. After that, they return home carrying the stalk with its head and the goat. When they arrive, this corn will be fastened on the tamarind tree situated up there by the side of the mountain. A branch of grain taken from the head will be tied to the spear. Later, the goat is slaughtered and the content of the gut (*Weenyi*) will be smeared on the spear and the spear is then kept in the hut. The elders will later eat the rest of the meat

Sometimes later after the grains have been threshed, the owner of the field brews enough beer to be offered to god and invites the keeper of the Liguthuuru and elders to come to the family house to offer his blessings. There, the unsqueezed beer known as *Limuyangga* is brought and the keeper of the spear then sprinkles the beer on the spear while praying wishing the family prosperous life. After this, people drink beer and disperse when it finishes.

Cultivation period

Päri people start cleaning their fields before the first rains begin. When the appropriate time comes for sowing seeds (*piidho*) the ruling age sets announces to the entire people to start planting their seeds in their fields. Before this announcement, no body plant seeds lest he will face serious sanction from the ruling age set. The announcement usually made in the evening. And in the morning of the following day, the blessed seeds (*koodhi* mu *Jwɔk*) will be brought to the dance court yard (thwɔrɔ) and distributed to each family so that one mixes these seeds with his own and starts planting them with confidence. In 2016, however, the current rulers, Daaru have relaxed the restriction. They allowed the general public to plant seeds whenever a sufficient rain was available.

The role of the Bird controller

Normally after seeds have been planted, they are left to grow. Later, the fields are weeded. Note; the Päri weed their fields several times before their crops ripen. By the time the new grains start to ripen, the bird controller announces through the Wegipac that he wants to cleanse the land (*piny ki kweero*) from destructive birds. So shouting, quarreling or fighting in the whole country is strictly forbidden. This order is put into force by the members of the ruling age set. They force people to observe the general silence. He who disobeys the rule is punished by paying a goat to the bird controller. The bird controller then slaughters the goat and sprinkles blood to purify the land. Elders will eat the meat of this sacrificed goat. But sometimes he only cuts the ear of the goat, sprinkles the blood and keeps the goat for himself.

During this period, the bird controller himself is prohibited from eating fresh vegetables and porridge prepared from new grains. If he eats this food, the Päri say, swarms of birds will come and destroy the crops. To avoid that, the ruling age set provide him with; milk, meat, and fish. He eats this with porridge prepared from old grains. He will continue to eat this food until the grain is ripe. However, if he wants to be bribed, he works his magic and the birds come and eat up the crops. Foremost, he sends a servant to the bush to catch and bring alive a type of a weaverbird known as iruw. He instructs the servant to bring the male iruw called lidiit and the female one called ubɔw. This work is done in absolute secrecy to avoid punishment from the ruling age group. When these birds are brought, the bird controller ties their legs upon a piece of wood inside his operational room. Then he puts some grains in the mouth /beak of each bird and finally closes their mouths with mud. This act implies that the bird pest will destroy the crops. If by coincidence birds come and cause problems to the scarers, the ruling age set rush to the bird controller and offer him a number of gifts. The most common gifts are goats, cows, and bundles of smoked fish and recently money has come to use. When he receives these gifts from every village, he works his magic to drive away destructive birds. This time, instead of putting some grains in the mouths of the birds, he puts grass. Which means birds will only eat grass and not grains. At times he succeeds in controlling the bird pests. Other times, he fails.

When the bird controller fails to control the birds from eating the crops, the wegipac take drastic measures against him. He can be beaten badly by the rulers which may result in his death. In 1967 the son of the bird controller named Agirarii was put to death for allegedly causing birds to eat up the crops. In 1979, the corpse of his father was thrown into the river suspected of having died with a grudge against the community.

The making of Fire

Customarily, when the grains are about to ripen (bɛɛl *mar*) literally meaning green grain, elders from all over Päri villages assemble on a fixed day in Pucwaa village to make new fire. Before this day, all domestic fire must be put off so that people use newly made fire. The king of Pucwaa village starts fire-making process and then other kings and elders follow. Rubbing two sticks together makes the fire. When the fire kindles, senior headmen take it to their respective camps/clubs where it will be light so that each family comes and receives the new fire. The new fire symbolizes the hope for a better future. After new fire is produced, people can start eating fresh grains roasted (*twiinyo*) but not to eat porridge prepared from new fresh grains known as *adup*

Fresh grains not yet harvested. Bɛɛl tar (white grains)

Workers' building sorghum's comb after cutting them off from the stalk gi cudo ki bɛɛl

A Sorghum shelter built to protect it from rain and wind destructions

Sacred Places

In Päri, most families have divinities in which they believe. Often when grains begin to ripen each family offers the first grains to god so that a misfortune or death may be avoided. Normally when a believer wants to offer a sacrifice, he/she takes four heads of grain with stalks uprooted from the ground and presents them to the priest. When the priest gets these heads of grains with stalks tied together, he offers them to god. After this, he knocks the head of the believer with this head of grain wishing him to stay well. And then, he gives back two heads of the grain with their stalks *Nyieng* to be taken and fixed by the side of the hut just facing the door. The believers also receive sand taken from the sacred place to be mixed with water and drank. The places of worships have become holy. Moreover, priests of these sacred places wish people to become sick so that they continue to receive sacrificial presents: goats, sheep cocks and beer from their customers

Blessing of Food (Libangga)

Unless food made from new grain (adup) is first offered to the god of Lipul for his blessings, nobody shall dare to eat new food. People fear that a misfortune may happen to the family, if one eats the food before it is offered to god. This ritual is performed a few days after new fire has been produced and when the grains are not yet fully ripened (bɛɛl tar). Before the ritual is performed, the priest informs the ruling age sets of the day in which the ceremony will take place. Immediately after this, the servants of the priest begin gathering some grains from each field (except the fields belonging to members of Libaalu clan). They pull out two stalks of grains with their heads and bring them home to god's hut *(odi jwɔk)*. This is a tiresome work

High crop yields

Women threshing sorghum

that takes days. When the work is over, the grains are dried in the sun and later pounded into flour using wood mortar (*Pany*) and pestle (*Alɛɛk*). It is to be noted that the Päri nowadays use millstone (*pääm*) to grind grain into flour.

On the day of sacrifice, members of weegipaac in each village milk all cows in the morning (except the ones of the Libaalu clan). This milk will be given to the servant of the god of Lipul who will carry it in big gourds to the shrine to be offered to god. There, the milk is boiled in big pots. Some of this milk will be mingled with flour to form a type of food called *Nyatili*. The priest then throws some of this food in Lipul's cave and throws some in other parts. While throwing this food he prays asking God to favour man and the domestic animals who will share in the new food, which he has graciously given them. After sacrifice, elders enjoy the food and drink milk. From this day people are allowed to eat food made from new grains. While people eat grain, animals (goats/sheep and cattle) eat grain stalks. In this way both human beings and animals have shared the food.

Beer Blessing

Before the feast of harvest, the wife of the priest of Lipul supported by other women from the clan of Naam prepares beer made from new grains. The preparation begins with the gathering of grains from the fields, cleaning the grains and then soaks it into water. After two days they are taken out of the water by filtration and allowed to germinate. When it has germinated, it is dried in the sun and then pounded into flour. The flour will then be mixed with water and fried *Ki puo* to become what is called *moo*. From there, it is mixed with water in the pot and becomes beer known as *päri*. It is this beer which the priest offers to god for his blessing. After sacrifice, the priest and the attendance drink the new beer. On this same day, the priest announces to the public that they are free to make and drink beer made from new grains. The expression, *Pu ya karεε*. Meaning, it is as nice as it used to be will be announced by the priest for the public to know.

Feast of harvest (Nyalam)

Yearly after the beer ceremony has been performed, the Päri celebrate one of the most important feasts called Nyalam. Nyalam has a special meaning for the Päri people. It refers to a community holiday celebrated at the end of the harvest season. On a fixed day, elders gather under a tree call *ulaam* in Pucwaa village to review community past lives and offer prayers to God. The word Nyalam derives from the word *lam*, which means invocation. This occasion takes place in the middle of November after the harvest of crops and a particular star called *ceci nyalam* has appeared in the sky. The priest of the god of Lipul is the master of ceremony. Before this day, he sends his messenger to Wiatuo village to tell the people about the appearance of this star. In the Assembly house of Wiatuo, his messenger meets a man from the clan of Pukwari and informs him of the need to help organize the occasion. After deliverying the information, he comes to Adimac in Bura village and delivers the same message. From there, he returns to Pugäri village and informs the priest accordingly. The headman of Pukwari clan in Wiatuo then takes the responsibility of passing the message to the entire Päri people.

In this regard, members of wegipaac belonging to Pukwari clan organize and immediately consult a diviner to know whether the community will get many fortunes in the New Year. All in all, the success in the New Year can be determined by the killing of any of the following animals; hare, duiker, waterbuck buffalo or any other black animal. The god of Lipul accepts black animals only to be offered as sacrifices. Once a diviner ensures that such animals could be found and killed, the organizers decide the day to go for hunting.

Usually before the occasion, one of the organizers cuts an acacia tree called *Ajiga* and with the directives from a diviner, he pulls it around the villages in the morning hours. In the evening, an announcement is made inviting all elders and members of the ruling age sets to come for *Koor*. Koor is a general assembly meeting of the Päri community always done once in a year in which the people review their past lives, conduct invocation and set plans for the future.

On the day of Koor, the Päri elders and members of the ruling age sets assemble in the morning under a big tree situated between Pucwaa and Pugäri villages. There, they discuss various social and political issues of the country. Each person talking concludes his speech by uttering words of prayer to god to bless the society to live in prosperity. They too curse their enemies to suffer defeats from the Päri warriors and also curse carnivores (cwieny) to die or move far away from their animals. They pray wishing their weapons not to turn upon their fellow member but to hit a non-Päri man and wild animals. After invocation, the acacia tree, which was pulled round the villages, is put in an open area. Then elders and the youth touch it with their spears to receive blessing. Very soon the youth start running towards the bush. After a short distance, they stop, and return back to Pucwaa village in procession (ipuura) singing war songs and some songs of praise. In the mean time, the elders here begin to disperse each group going to their village. However, some elders from Pucwaa and Pugäri join the youth and altogether move in procession to the village. When they come close to the villages, they stop and disperse each one going to their home to hide his spears. Everyone waits for the morning to come to carry out the first hunting known as Dwan kidi (literally means the hunt for the mountain).

Kurimoto: Muthokori the high priest and elders of Pugeri blessing the spears of the youth

On this very day, while men are preparing to go for hunting, women too are busy preparing beer for the occasion. Meanwhile, one of the priests takes an oath not eat or drink anything until the hunters kill and bring home the animal that would be offered to god as sacrifice. And before sun rise, the hunters go to the bush and camped at Boole situated a short distant outside their homes. The priest waits there until the hunters come back home. When the hunters managed to killed any of the following animals; duiker, hare, or bushbuck the group returns home in a procession. The youth carry the animal(s) and walking in front the processession. Upon their arrival at the dance courtyard of the Pugäri, elders and members of wegipaac pick up dance while the youth climb up carrying the sacrificial animal to the Lipul shrine. There, they will be received by the high priest and elders from the clan of Naam. The priest gives some beer to the youth to drink. After drinking, they climb down and join the dancers at the dance court yard. In the meantime, the servants of the high priest cut a small piece of pancreas, liver, lung, heart, kidneys, intestines (which the Päri called *Läämbi)*, and cook it in one pot. The rest of meat is cooked in other pots. When *Läämbi* is readily cooked, the high priest offers it to god by throwing some pieces of meat to the cave of mount Lipul and scatters some to other places. Then he sprinkles the soup in the same way the meat was performed. While doing this, he prays wishing people to kill many wild animals so as to enjoy good meat.

After sacrifice ritual these gifts of meat will be left there in *Gudo* (a hole in a rock which they used as a plate) to be eaten by children of god **Nyitti Jwɔk**. The priest and the elders attending the ritual will then eat the rest of the meat and take home the left over. After the service, they climb down to join the people dancing in the dance courtyard. For three days, the Päri dance with drumming in Pugäri village. During these days, the people enjoy good food and heavy drinks.

The feast of nyalam is very important for the youth. It brings together various age groups to the village of Pugäri to celebrate the occasion. The ocassion gives them the opportunity to discuss their common interest and share their drinks as they move from one village to the next. They too eat rams and goats offered by princess and councilors for this occasion. As for teenagers, their princess offer cocks to be consumed by the group while their councilors offer spears to be distributed to some members of the age group.

Amoyo Blessing

Amoyo is a wild plant which produces fruits. The fruits of this plant are bitter and poisonous. Unless it is soaked in water and left there for a number of days, any one who eats it dies at once. Often when this fruit is ripe, the priest who lives in Pucwaa village sends some women to gather some of it to be offered as a sacrifice to god. When the fruits are brought, they are soaked in water and kept in it for a number of days until they become harmless. When the plant has become harmless, it is taken out and cooked. After cooking, the priest offers it to god wishing those who eat it no harm. He performs the ritual by biting a piece of charcoal three times, each time spitting it out. After this, he eats the fruit. From this day, every one is allowed to cook and enjoy the fruit.

Blessing of domestic animals (Libanga)

Towards the end of every autumn *aria*, when water and grazing lands is becoming scarce in close vicinity to the villages, Päri people move their cattle, goats and sheep to new sites where water and grazing

Cattle at thwɔrɔ of Wiatuo village

lands are available. These places are situated far away from homes. Often, before animals are moved there, the ruling age set and elders in each village perform the Libangga rite. Like food blessing, the milking of the cows is carried out by members of the ruling age set in the morning. Those milking the cows are to make sure they do not taste the milk before it is offered to God. After milking, the milk is boiled in big pots. Some quantity will be left in a container called *aweeri*, so that elders spit into it to bless domestic animals. So, elders and members of the ruling age set are made to spit into this container. When all have spat, they pray asking God to bless their cattle, goats and sheep to multiply and stay well. In conclusion, the blessed milk is sprinkled on the animals and the ceremony ends. The next day; all domestic animals are taken to the kraal (Kaalo*)*. Upon arrival, the sheperds performe another Libangga ritual as was done at the village. The people too pray wishing their animals to multiply and stay well. As it is always the case, carnivores are cursed to die.

Chapter Ten

Traditional Burial Customs

Death is that event which ends forever the relationships between the victim and the living kin. Customarily, when a Pari person dies, close relatives especially the deceased father's brothers come immediately and cover the head. Soon the dead body is wrapped in a cowhide. This is done inside the room. While doing this, the father, mother, sisters and brothers and relatives of the deceased cry and wail outside the room. When the body is well covered, the very clansmen wait inside the room near the corpse until the moment of burial when the corpse is brought out. Meanwhile outside the room, parents, and family members are kept under guard for fear that they may harm themselves with some harmful weapons.

The grave of about five feet deep is dug in the compound. The first man to start digging is a clan member of the deceased. Actually, two men come forward with hoes in their hands and position themselves accordingly: one man stands on the head side and another one on the leg side. Then the two men are told to dig simultaneously for three times to bless the grave. After that, the mourners' come in to help them finish the digging. They dig the grave until the required level is reached. When the grave is ready, the corpse is lowered into the grave. There, the dead body is made to lay on the right side with legs straight facing the direction of the east where the sun rises and the head facing the direction of the west where the sun sets. The Päri compare death with sunset. For

Traditional Burial Customs

they know that once a person dies, he will not come back again and so is the same with the day.

Before the grave is covered with earth, the children of the deceased (if any) throw some earth into the grave right on the corpse. The male child throws three times and the female child throws four times. The throwing of the earth is performed to avoid dreams and serious thoughts for the dead person. The difference in the number of times the earth is being thrown is associated with the fall of the umbilical cord. The umbilical cord of a baby boy falls the third day after birth. That of a female child falls after four days.

After the grave is covered with earth, a stone is fixed on the head and another one on the leg side. Then, the people who participated in digging start washing out dust from their legs and hands with water in a calabash. This is done right on the grave. After washing, the calabash is put on the head side and left there. The cleaning of the dust from the body proves that the person has really died and will not be seen any more. With this in mind, parents, brothers, sisters, relatives and neighbours burst out crying. After a few minutes, the mourners are ordered to be quiet. Members of the ruling age sets ask the parents of the victim to tell the public the deceased's last words. Anything left behind by the deceased such as cattle, goats, sheep and properties must be disclosed. If he is indebted to other persons, the witnesses must come out and say it. More importantly the ruling age sets are eager to know if the dead man has blessed the community to live prosperous life. The purpose for announcing this in public is to let everyone know all facts about debts or credits (if any) and also to ensure safety of the community. However, the deceased is given the liberty to deal in any way he pleases with anyone who may have caused his death. As soon as the witness has ended his speech, crying resumes. The victim's mother, mother's sisters, father's sisters, father, widow relatives and neighbours cry loudly and cover their heads and bodies with ashes. If the deceased is a young unmarried person, women throw themselves carelessly on the grave. The ashes on the body symbolize sadness caused by the death of a victim.

In the meantime, elders who buried the dead walk out of the house to slaughter the bull. (Note: the bull killed for the funeral is called *Bäk*). During the killing by spears, the first man to spear the animal must be a clansman. Others follow after him. When the bull is dead, its meat is divided accordingly: one of the hind legs is given to the king who will share it with his clansmen. Another one is given to the maternal uncles to share among themselves. The right front leg is given to distant clansmen *Tɛɛng* of the late. The organs are taken to the funeral place to be cooked for the mourners to eat. Non-relatives who went there to mourn for the dead person divide the rest of the meat. The content of the gut called **wɛɛnyi** will be painted on the foreface, chest, knees, shoulders and feet of each person present in the funeral place beginning from the deceased's mother or widow. But today, the system has changed. The whole meat is now cooked and eaten by the mourners in the funeral place *wi-läbo*.

It is to be noted that the Päri people do not bury the dead at mid-day or nighttime. Burial of a dead person is allowed to take place before midday or at the afternoon hours or before midnight. This is because, in the past, the Päri experience several attacks from their enemies during middays or mid-nights. The people abolished this system to enable them keep guard against enemy attacks. Another name for mid-day is *Liloonggi uduuce* meaning the hour of crying. So mid-day is the moment in which misfortune can likely occur to the people.

Generally, when a young unmarried person dies, people mourn for him/her seriously. The age group assembles and moves to the funeral place to mourn for their dead age mate. There, joined by deceased's brothers, sisters, relatives and neighbours, the whole group weeps over the dead fellow. After some times, the group goes around Lipul hill to demonstrate the death of their age mate. In their walk round the hill, the deceased's brothers, sisters, relatives and members of the senior age group join them. The mother, the widow and sisters put on dance ornaments on their bodies. The ornaments previously used by the deceased are won by the mother or the widow (incase the deceased has a wife). These things are worn to show that a particular individual has really died. In addition, the age group carries flags one of which is to be fixed on the grave.

During this movement round Lipul, whenever the group reach a particular village, they rotate the dance courtyard three times. Later, they move ahead. Throughout their movements, men sing songs while women keep crying. When the group arrives at the funeral place, the flag is fixed on the grave just on the head side. The people then mourn for the dead age mate. After some time, fellow age mates are accompanied to the camp/club belonging to the senior age group. They will stay there throughout the period of mourning which may take a month. During this period, shouting, quarreling or fighting is strictly forbidden in the village by the wegipaac. All people must observe silence. This is to respect the dead person and his family. He who yells is condemned by the whole society and especially by the deceased's parents. The people will consider him as a sorcerer.

Three days after death (in case of a male person) clansmen cut ebony wood *aredo* to shelter the grave. But if the dead person is female, clanswomen cut a type of tree called *känyo (pl. kääc)* to shelter the grave. This is done four days after death occurred.[40] Usually after sheltering the grave, people are served food and drinks. Later in the evening, the parents and relatives of the deceased are consoled for the loss of their dear son or daughter. They will be advised to resume their normal activities and that they should not continue to grieve for the dead. After a few words of consolation,

---

40 Note: the Päri consider a male person to be stronger compared to a woman and so is the same with ebony tree. A woman is considered weak and breaks very easily just like a type of tree called Känyo.

the people attending the funeral rite disperse leaving the deceased's family and close relatives in the funeral place.

Mourning of the dead is of three kinds: that of a child, young unmarried person and the old person. The mourning for a child is very short. For instance a child of seven days old or one month old is mourned briefly. The moment he/she dies, old women bury him/her by the door side on the right. After burial, no crying is encouraged. The wife and the husband are advised to keep calm. The Päri believe that if the parents grieve over the child's death (especially the first born) God will get angry with them and may not give them children anymore. For that reason, too much crying is always discouraged. Many people are not allowed to stay in the funeral place as well. People may come to offer condolence and return to their homes. In addition, no bull will be slaughtered for such a death. The period spent in the funeral place varies. For male child women spend three days only and disperse. But for female child, it takes four days after that the mourners disperse leaving the wife and the husband to resume their normal lives.

In the case of a young unmarried person (a girl or a boy), the mourning period is long. It may take a year for the age mates and the parents of the victim to mourn for the dead. Immediately after death, the age mates temporarily evacuate their camp (the center of which they use to discuss their common interest) and move to the camp belonging to the senior age group. Thus, the group activities are suspended. They neither go for hunting nor organize dances.

The Päri feel extremely sad for the death of a young unmarried person. In their cries one hears a mother or father blaming God for having taken away the life of the dear son or daughter. The Päri wish God to take away the life of an old person and leave the youngsters to live so that they too produce children. Thus, in many of their songs, they express words of anger and disappointment. They blame *Jwɔk* that causes death to young men. They wish to fight Jwɔk (God or god) had Jwɔk made himself visible. All these words indicate their hate for the death of a young person.

Living in the funeral place (wi-läbo) depends on the availability of constant supply of food and beer to the mourners. The period spent in the funeral place may exceed its limit if food and drinks are always supplied. This is possible for well to do persons. But for poor persons, the mourners stay very briefly and disperse. Similarly, the period the mourners spent in the funeral place for an old person varies from one family to the next. The mourners spend a longer time in the funeral place if food is available or otherwise, they will cut short their stay. The mourners are happier if the deceased has left behind a good number of children, grand children and wealth. Instead of being sorry for the dead, the mourners rejoice as they continue to eat and drink beer. In the funeral place, the expression *"athɔw ya mubɛɛr* meaning, he/she died a good death is commonly heard. The people consider such a death good because the deceased has left behind children who will continue the family's name.

Generally, when death occurs to a family, parents of the victim stay without doing any activity. They don't cultivate or participate in a communal works. When the period of mourning ends, the clansmen and other relatives join the parents of the dead and cultivate the field. Close relatives come to do the dead man homage. After work, they come home where they will be served food and drinks. At the end, the parents are advised to resume their normal lives. This ends the mourning.

As for the age group of the deceased, they too organize to go for a hunt of wild animals to pay homage to the dead age mate. When the group kills some animals, they contribute a certain quantity of meat and offer it to the parents of their lost member. A few days later, the deceased's age group consults a diviner to work out his magic to purify the camp/club which was abandoned when their age member died. After being assured by a diviner that no misfortune would happen again, the members return to their camp and resume their normal activities. Similarly, if a dead person is a girl, the age mates go to collect firewood and offer it to the mother of the victim.

Cala

In the Päri society, when the husband dies, a ritual known as Cala is performed. This ritual is performed to cleanse evil spirits believed to be residing in living partner. On the last day of mourning, a goat is brought, the widow is made to sit on it and very soon the goat is strangled. The people who are eligible for performing this ritual are old clanswomen who can no longer produce children. After the animal has been killed, its skin is removed and all the meat is cooked. In the meantime, the hair on the head of the living partner is shaved. The hair cut must all be collected without letting any of it be lost lest it would bring mishap. When the meat is cooked, it is served and eaten up by the old women. After the meal, the bones are all collected and altogether with the widow's hair are buried in the ground. So, the ceremony ends and the participants go back to their homes.

If the widow is still productive, she can be inherited by another brother. However, before such a union is approved, the new husband must bring a goat to be offered to God as sacrificed so that God blesses and grants them many children. This sacrificial goat is termed ***diendi rwoodhi.*** On the day of sacrifice, the husband and the mediator take the goat to the widow's homestead where the clansmen of the deceased are already waiting. There, the goat's ear is cut and its blood painted on the chest, breasts, forehead, knees, and shoulders of both the widow and the new husband. The painting of the human body with blood or chyme is known as ***rwoodho.*** The people who perform this blessing pray to God wishing the couple a happy life with many children. After the ceremony, the goat is returned to the kraal. More importantly the couple is advised to live a peaceful life. They should avoid quarreling or fighting each other. If the new husband has another wife, he is warned not to have sexual intercourse with her until the widow becomes pregnant. The custom further prohibits the couple from sharing their bed and stools with others during this period. Any negligence with respect to this custom makes God angry and automatically spoils the couple's chance of producing children.

When the woman gets pregnant, the husband is asked to give another goat to conduct the final Cala ritual. When the goat is provided, the widow and the husband sit on it and the old women strangle the goat. After taking out its skin, the meat is cooked at the same time the hair on the heads of the couples is being shaved. When the meat is ready, the women eat it and bury the bones together with the cut hair in the ground. This concludes the ceremony. The child that will be born after this ritual will be named Ucala for a male child and Acala for a female one.

Funeral Dances

Culture permits dances with drumming on the funeral place of a member of a ruling age set or of an old person only. A dance with drumming in the funeral place of a child remains uncultural. Usually, the Päri do not dance with drumming immediately after a person dies. With the exception of the death of a king, a funeral dance known, as **Twari** (a word borrowed from the Lotuko) is played after a period not less than a year from the time death occurred. Normally; it is the parents of the deceased who invite the community (through the ruling age set) to dance on the funeral place of their love one. This necessitates offering of a bull to be slaughtered by the ruling age set on that day. After receiving pledges from the bereaved families that they would offer bulls for the occasion, the ruling age sets then organize a funeral dance. On a fix day, all members of the ruling age sets collect the bulls and drive them to the bush in the morning. In the bush, after discussing their common interests, the bulls are slaughtered and the meat divided among themselves and the elders. After this, they come to dance courtyard and together with the elders and the youth they dance. The people dance with drumming up to mid-night. Then they take the drums to dance on the tombs of those whose parents have offered bulls to the mojomiji. The people dance briefly and then move the drums to another tomb and dance there. The mourners will rotate the drums until the last tomb. In each house, the mourners dance briefly singing to the tune of three songs (in case of a male person) and four songs (for a female). After that, they return to the dance courtyard to continue dancing. This will last for three days only and stops.

Death rites of a King

When a king of Wiatuo dies, the message is passed immediately to the members of the ruling age sets and elders residing in the Assembly house (*Kaboore*). There, the drums are brought out from the hut (*duol)* and placed on the king's ancestral common tomb. There, while wailing and crying is going on, the people beat drums to let everybody know about the death of the King. When the information has reached every village, people all come to Wiatuo to mourn for the King. People of each village come with flags to be fixed on the grave. Since the king is always buried in same ancestral grave, the bones of his father and ancestors have to be exhumed. The people of Bura village who belong to the king's clan group start the exhumation. Customarily, two men come forward. One man stands on the head side and another one stands on the leg side. Then, they dig simultaneously three times to bless the grave. After that, many people join in and very soon the bones are exhumed.

In the meantime, the corpse is being wrapped with the skin of a black bull freshly killed for the purpose. When everything is ready, the dead body is laid in the grave, the old bones put on top and finally, the grave is covered with earth. After burial, several flags are fixed on the tomb. And the mourners start dancing. The people dance for many days. During these times, several bulls are killed and the mourners enjoy good food and drink sufficient beer.

Generally, the Päri consider death to be something dirty. This is because when a person dies, parents and other family members stay dirty. They neither wash dust from their bodies nor shave their hair until the last day of mourning. On the last day, the king's wives, his children and other close relatives shave their heads, sweep the compound clean and wash their bodies clean to start a new life. This ends the mourning period.

Changing attitudes towards death

Communities that respect life pay greater respect to the dead relatives. They properly burry their dead relatives and conduct the ritual in a customery way. Earlier, the Pari honor their dead by keeping silent during grave digging and burial. No jokes or laughing is entertained during these activities. In a funeral place, one has a social obligation to appear crying in tears. In many cases women throw themselves over the tomb crying and at times fainting while, elderly people express their sorrow by singing personal songs popularly known as' acira'. After crying, every individual has to meet the bereaved family members and offer his/her condolences. Their presences reduce excessive grief and force a family to demonstrate sorrow for a certain period of time and resume their normal lives. In short, death was a public concern. It is public in the sense that the people recognize that death of the individual diminished the entire community. Nowadays, signs of cultural breakdown began to appear. People converse, laugh and sometimes make jokes while digging the grave. This was unusual thing thirty years ago. It seems people have lost the sense of fear of death itself and are not moved by death senses. Moreover, the social conventions regarding mourning are not observed these days by many. What used to happen was that, the mourners, once they arrive in the funeral place, express their sadness by bursting into tears. In other words, each one has a social obligation to appear crying in tears. Today you can see women do that but men rarely observe such norms.

Traditionally after death occurs, the ruling age set used to impose total silence in the village where death happens. The number of days imposed ranges from three days to one week. During this period, no one is allowed to shout or fight anybody. Anyone who disobeyed the rule was publicly condemned. At times, a disobedient person receives corporal punishment by members of the ruling age set. This is done to let the people honor the dead and the deceased's family. But these days, most young men refuse to observe these customs, considering them old traditions which they argue must be abandoned.

Death has become so common that many people find it less fearful. Thirty years ago (before SPLA war of liberation 1983), death was a real concern. People fear it and respect the berieved family. However, during and after the war of 1983, things began to change. Many people (including children) have become accustomed to seeing dead bodies at homes or in the bushes of South Sudan. Children familiarity of death led to change of attitudes as children consider death normal. The root cause of the morale anarchy of our time is linked to the long time of war in the country during which many lives were lost.

An interesting thing happened after the death of the rainmaker, King Peter Upwoyo who died on 6.6.2016 in Lafon. In my watch, the traditional way of burial and mourning for the king was not followed. Instead of laying his body in the common ancestral grave, the people buried him in a newly dug ground at *wi- Täär* outside the ancestral common tomb. Besides, the funeral was not well attended by all the Päri people as it used to be. The funeral was attended by the people of Wiatuo only. Relatives and friends from other villages couldn't even attend. This represents a complete break with what was common practice for several years. But so far, many blamed the general security situation in the country to be the cause for this poor participation of the people in the funeral. A dispute between Bura, Pucwaa and Wiatuo villagers that occurred in 2015 in which people fought (with guns) and lives were lost contributed to this factor. Also, long distances between villages made it difficult for the mourners to come together (as usual) and conduct the funeral.

Women mourning King Upwoyo

The tomb of King Peter Upwoyo Fidele buried at Witäär settlement on June 6th, 2016

The mourners of King Peter Upwoyo

Totem

Totem is related in the same general way to social groups. Totems could be animals or plants. Members of each totemic group believe themselves to be descendants of their totem. They neither kill nor eat it. Totem-like symbols may also represent other groups. Lɔlɔ is one of the clans in Päri that believes in a snake as their group totem. Members of this clan do not kill a snake. Whenever a member finds it, he/she spits salava on the snake to tame it and eventually drive it away from the people. At times, courageous members play with the viper but without being bitten. If a snake bites a member of this clan, the misfortune is often construed to be (guääd) a warning of serious danger to come in the family of the victim. The Geri clan on the other hand believes in a new calabash as their group totem. Customarily, members of this clan do not use a new calabash to drink water, beer, or eat food put in it. They use old calabash to take these things. Another group that believes in tokenism is the Adimac clan. Their group totem is a duiker called *Muur*. The Adimac clan members believe that the skull of a duiker can cure diseases. For that reason, each clan member keeps at least one skull of this animal in the house waiting to be used when a family member becomes sick. For example, if a child gets sick suffering from an eye infection, the father usually uses the duiker's skull to heal the sickness. He does this by touching the skull on the forehead of the patient, three times in the case of male and four times for a female child. While touching, he prays to the spirit of his ancestor to heal the disease. After this, the child is expected to recover from the sickness. But if the situation does not improve, the parents of the child consult a diviner to identify the problem and to find an alternative solution.

A similar belief is held by the Nywaagi clangroup. Their totem is a goat. To them, when a clan daughter is married, clan elders demand a goat from the parents of the husband. When it is brought, clan elders gather at the homestead of the bride's father to conduct the ritual. Here, the daughter is seated in front of the elders. Then the mediator leads the goat round the bride four times (*dhaago ki thɔɔkɔ ki diɛl*). After the mediator, follows the father of the bride and all the attendance repeat the same act. The people pray God to let their daughter stay well and produce many children. After prayers, the goat is slaughtered, roasted and eaten by the elders. The spear, which was used for the slaughter of the animal, is given to the mediator to take as his property.

Epilogue

The Päri deserted their villages when the SPLA (John Garang and William Nyuon) forces clashed in Lafon in February 1993 during which the villages were burned down. In 2005 when the Comprehensive Peace Agreement was signed, refugees from Kakuma (Kenya) Uganda and internally displaced people from Lobone came and settled at Lafon. Although a considerable number of the displaced people have returned and resetlled around Jebel Lafon, the majority still consider new settlements home and have no idea to rebuild in the old villages. For example, the people of Bura, Pucwaa and a small number of Pugäri villagers are still settled in a place called *Arɔmɔ* about four miles north-east of the mountain. The majority of Pugäri villagers live in Pacidi about fifteen miles south of Lafon Mountain. The Angulumeere villagers live in Adeeba area, approximately five miles west of the mountain. The people of Kɔɔr are scattered: a small group live in Ligirɛɛgɛ and Ungiɛbɛ about sixteen miles south of Lafon Mountain; another section of Kɔɔr live in Upuuyo, approximately sixteen miles south-west of the mountain; the largest group of Kɔɔr people live in Ruubo, about four miles west of the mountain. Similarly, the villagers of Wiatuo are split into a half: the main group live in Witäär, about four miles north of Lafon Mountain and the other section called Mɔlnyang group are settled in a place called Kuruji, about five miles west of the mountain.

Life in Päri society is not as it used to be. From the time the people settlements were destroyed in 1993 up to the period of the Comprehensive Peace Agreement (CPA) in 2005, the Päri society has experienced so many changes. These changes have affected the entire Päri population in many ways. A change of power which used to be conducted by way of negotiation between the prospective ruling age sets and the King, is taking on new direction in Päri society. An alarming tendency is evident. The generation known as *Akeem* went out of step with moods prevailing in Päri society. They took over power from *Kwodidhieng* on 22/7/2010 by way of physical fight with guns during which seven men were killed. Among the dead were; two from Wiatuo, four from Bura and one from Pucwaa. This drastic change of attitudes of the youth has been condemned strongly by elders who considered it a failure of the youth to follow the societal moral standards. Most elders I spoke to feel very worried about the future given the horrific behaviours of the present youth who are violent and do not respect nor listen to elders' advice. Besides, the present youth have taken up the habit of heavy drinking. When elders advise them to limit or stop the consumption of alcoholic drinks, they cause tension. In many cases, a single quarrel between a son and the sister sometimes result into death. That is a slight favouratism to the sister by the father makes the son feels abandoned and hence he will decide to commit suicide or alternatively kills the father for that matter. This behaviour has made many parents fear correcting their children.

Before 1980, suicide was commited by young girls who were forced to marry wealthy husbands they did not love. Yet it occurred less frequently compared to the present generation. Today, suicide is taking on new direction in Päri society. The rate of suicide has increased tremendously among the youth. From 1988 up to the present time, so many youngters have commited suicide. Five to ten yongsters died every year. This is a big number for a small community like the Päri. At times, these youth, because of frustrations caused by economic hardships, killed their own fathers or mothers. This situation made many elderly persons to conclude that the present generation have diverted from ethical and moral codes that are shared within the society. They too blame the series of wars in the country as being the major cause of all these changes in attitudes and norms.

Art form such as dancing can be a source of great prestige and pride not only within the indigenous community but also among the society at large. Therefore, it is a duty of every member of the society to protect and promote the custom. However, instead of preserving dance activity, and hence maintain a sense of identity, the Päri continue losing some of the long-established traditional dances. Previously, the Päri have four types of dances: *Käruma, Aliila, Nyikiro and Buul.* In the late 1950s, the Kilang age group borrowed and adopted a Lotuko type of dance known as *Kathar*. In the same period, the society dropped aliila type of dance and substituted it with kathar. After the Sudan Peoples' Liberation Army (SPLA/SPLM) war of liberation ended in 2005 and peace returned to the country, both karuma and kathar types of dances were dropped leaving buul and nyikiro dances at practice. Moreover, in 1973, chief

Käruma dance

Albano Urua, in collaboration with King Fidele Ungang, abolished a youth dance known as 'nyibundi' on the pretext that the youth do fight during such occasions.

For quite a time, the king of Wiatuo has been in charged of rain administraton in Päri society. No any other king besides him was allowed to perform or own rain medicine. But in 2015, after the villagers of Wiatuo fought with those of Bura and Pucwaa villages respectively, the situation changed. The power to control rain administration enjoyed by the king of Wiatuo has become invalid. Today, each village king has acquired rain medicine and performs it independently. What remains in the hands of the king of Wiatuo is the power to approve the change of authority, giving it to the new rullers *cippi paac bang jɔɔ nyään*. I am afraid, if these and other important cultural traits not revitalized and sustained, this society will experience a major swift in its culture.

About the Author

UKAL KAWANG JULU MUTHO was born in 1964 at Lafon, Torit district, in the then southern Sudan. I attended primary school at Lafon in 1971. Initially, I did not like schooling but to follow cattle. My father, Celestino Uyo, had to force me walk to school situated two miles away. But many times, instead of going to school, I branched away to follow cattle, or go fishing. When my father learnt about that, he ordered my mother not to serve me food. Finding no alternative, I accepted the new way of life- that of western education and became a regular class attendant. When my age mates noticed my interest in schooling, they became jealous and organized to block my education. One day, as I was walking to school, the group ambushed me. One elder boy tried to block the way, but I resisted. Other gangs that stood by also jeered at me. Even my best friend questioned me as to why I had to go to school when my father had many cows. I replied that I wanted school to understand life better. After exchanging words of insults, they left and I proceeded to school. For a number of days, they kept attacking trying to discourage me from going to school. It was after I reported the issue to my father that the boys were warned not to repeat such a provocation. Hence, the aggression temporarily halted.

Attempts to block my education did not end up just there. The same group created another obstacle. They organized to do communal work at the garden of the bird controller during school working days to prevent me from attending lessons or otherwise, punish me if I fail to participate. And indeed, I did not participate but went to school instead. Consequently, I was fined a tin- full of dura. This trick was done repeatedly until the paramount chief intervened and stopped it.

MIGRATORY ROUTES OF THE LUO IN THE SUDAN

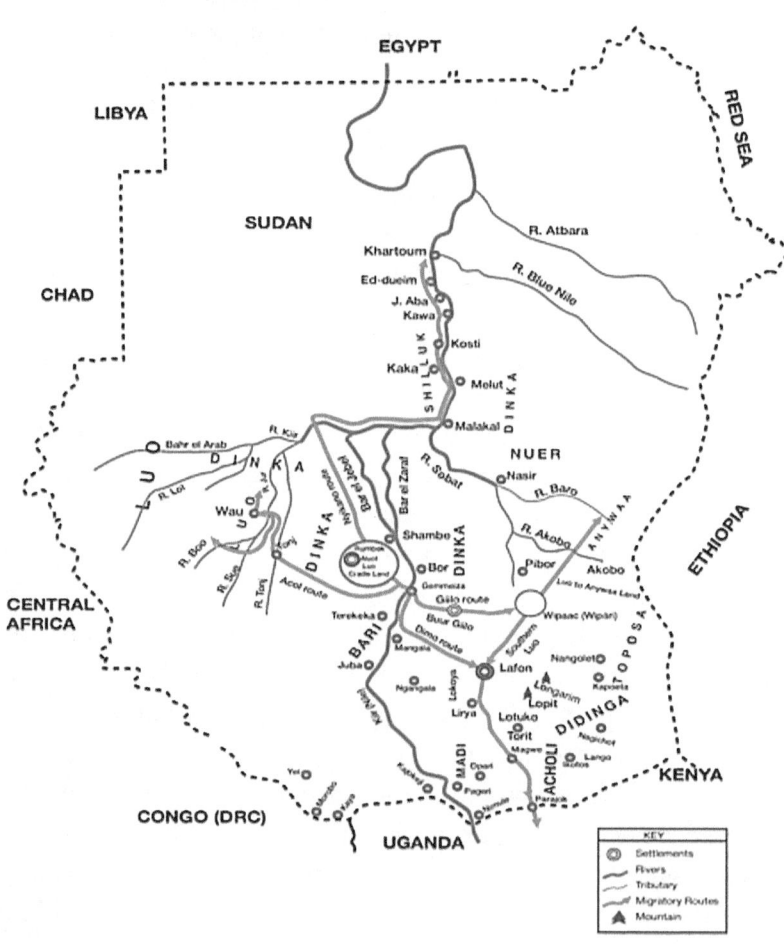

About the Author

In 1976, I joined St. Mary minor Seminary Torit. My aunts however protested angrily as to why I, the only son in the family, should join the seminary. Their concern was to let me marry and have children. The issue created a rift in the family. In 1978, my father gave in due to pressure and threats of curses against me, hence, he advised me to shift to Torit one intermediate, a government school; then joined Juba commercial secondary school in 1979. Before the year ended (1979), the government closed most schools in Southern Sudan due to the tribal fighting among students. So, I left and continued with my studies at Comboni El-Obeid Secondary school. In 1985-86, I sat for school leaving examination at Khartoum Commercial Secondary School, joined University of Juba in 1987 and obtained Bachelor degree in Accounting. In total, my father sold nine cows to finance my education.

After graduation, I served as a teacher at El Gedarif Commercial Secondary School and at St Mary Minor Seminary Khartoum. In 2003, I studied for the Post Graduate Diploma in Sudanese and African languages from the Institute of African and Asian Studies University of Khartoum and completed it in 2004. I also studied for Masters in the same Institute. However, my thesis was not passed because I failed to pay the university fees. From 2006-9, I worked as senior accountant with the Nile Commercial bank: served as chief administrator for Lafon Area in 2010; worked with South Sudan Investment Authority as a Director of investor services in 2011; served as the Acting Director General with the Ministry of Commerce, Industry and Investment (GOSS) in 2011-2016; I became the first commissioner of Lafon County in the year 2016.

I have published two books: *Päri Alphabet Book* and *The Päri Story book*.

I am married and have children.

Bibliography

Bashir Mohammed Omer., The Southern Sudan Background to conflict, London: C. Hurst and Co: 1968

Beattie. J.Hm. Bunyoro an African kingdom. New York: 1960

Beattie, J. The Nyoro state, Oxford: 1971

Bender, Samuel. (ed) 1989. The Niger Congo Languages, Lanham: University Press of America

Comboni Missionary, History of Lafon Mission., Khartoum: St. Paul Major Seminary, 1997

Crazzolara, J.P. The Lwoo, part I Verona 1950

Crazzolara, J.P. The Lwoo part II – Verona 1951

Crystal, David. Language Death: Cambidge University Press, 2000

Daly. M.W., Modernization in the Sudan, New York 1985

Dellagiacoma, V., Missionaries in Southern Sudan 1900-1964, Khartoum: St. Paul Seminary, 1986 (rev 1998)

Dellagiacoma, V., History of the Catholic Church in Southern Sudan, 1900-1995, Khartoum: St. Paul Seminary, 1998

Evans Pritchard. E.E., Witchcraft, Oracles and Magic among the Azande, New York 1937

Greenburg, Joseph H, The Languages of Africa. The Hague: Mouton & Co, 1966

Holt, P.M., -Daly, M.W., History of the Sudan, London 1979

Kurimoto, E. & S. Simonse, Conflict, Age & Power in North East Africa: Age system in Transition, PP (38-39) Oxford: James Currey, 1998

Lloyd Wanner, W., A black civilization: a social study of an Australian tribe, New York 1937

Lowie, R, Social Organizarion, New York: Holt, Rinehart and Winston 1948
Mair, Lucy. African Societies, London 1974
Middleton, J.D. Tait (eds), Tribes without rulers, London 1958
Middleton, J, The Lugbara of Uganda, New York 1965
Middleton, J. Lugbara Religion: Rituals and authority among East African people, London, 1960
Nalder, L.F., A tribal survey of Mongala Province, London 1937
Nyombe, Bureng. G.V. Some Aspects of Bari History: A Comparative Lingistic and Oral Tradition Reconstruction. Kenya: University of Nairobi Press 2007
Sanderson, L.P. – Sanderson, G.N., Education, Religion and Politics in Southern Sudan., 1899-1964, London 1979
Santandrea, S., A Tribal History of the Westen Bahr el Ghazal, Italy; Bologna: 1964
Shillington, K., History of Africa, London 1989
Simeoni, A., Päri, a Luo language of Southern Sudan, Bologna 1978
Tucker, A.N. and Bryan, M.A. The Non-Bantu Languages of North-Eastern Africa, London: Oxford University Press, 1956.
Tucker, A.N. and Bryan, M.A. Linguistic Analysis: the Non-Bantu Languages of North-Eastern Africa. London: Oxford University Press, 1966.
Warburg, G., The Sudan under Wingate Administration in the Anglo-Egyptian era, 1899-1916, New York 1937

www.ingramcontent.com/pod-product-compliance
Lightning Source LLC
Chambersburg PA
CBHW020856020526
44107CB00076B/1882